W9-ARQ-527

THE **PRINCETON** REVIEW

STUDENT ADVANTAGE
GUIDE TO

PAYING

FOR

COLLEGE

1997 Edition

Books in The Princeton Review Series

Cracking the ACT
Cracking the ACT with Sample Tests on CD-ROM
Cracking the CLEP (College-Level Examination Program)
Cracking the GED
Cracking the GMAT
Cracking the GMAT with Sample Tests on Computer Disk
Cracking the GRE
Cracking the GRE with Sample Tests on Computer Disk
Cracking the GRE Biology Subject Test
Cracking the GRE Literature in English Subject Test
Cracking the GRE Psychology Subject Test
Cracking the LSAT
Cracking the LSAT with Sample Tests on Computer Disk
Cracking the LSAT with Sample Tests on CD-ROM
Cracking the MAT (Miller Analogies Test)
Cracking the NTE with Audio CD-ROM
Cracking the SAT and PSAT
Cracking the SAT and PSAT with Sample Tests on Computer Disk
Cracking the SAT and PSAT with Sample Tests on CD-ROM
Cracking the SAT II: Biology Subject Test
Cracking the SAT II: Chemistry Subject Test
Cracking the SAT II: English Subject Tests
Cracking the SAT II: French Subject Test
Cracking the SAT II: History Subject Tests
Cracking the SAT II: Math Subject Tests
Cracking the SAT II: Physics Subject Test
Cracking the SAT II: Spanish Subject Test
Cracking the TOEFL with Audiocassette
Flowers & Silver MCAT
Flowers Annotated MCAT
Flowers Annotated MCATs with Sample Tests on Computer Disk
Flowers Annotated MCATs with Sample Tests on CD-ROM

Culturescope Grade School Edition
Culturescope High School Edition
Culturescope College Edition

LSAT/GRE Analytic Workout
SAT Math Workout
SAT Verbal Workout

All U Can Eat
Don't Be a Chump!
How to Survive Without Your Parents' Money
Speak Now!
Trashproof Resumes

Biology Smart
Grammar Smart
Math Smart
Reading Smart
Study Smart
Word Smart: Building an Educated Vocabulary
Word Smart II: How to Build a More Educated Vocabulary
Word Smart Executive
Word Smart Genius
Writing Smart

American History Smart Junior
Astronomy Smart Junior
Geography Smart Junior
Grammar Smart Junior
Math Smart Junior
Word Smart Junior
Writing Smart Junior

Business School Companion
College Companion
Law School Companion
Medical School Companion

Student Advantage Guide to College Admissions
Student Advantage Guide to the Best 310 Colleges
Student Advantage Guide to America's Top Internships
Student Advantage Guide to Business Schools
Student Advantage Guide to Law Schools
Student Advantage Guide to Medical Schools
Student Advantage Guide to Paying for College
Student Advantage Guide to Summer
Student Advantage Guide to Visiting College Campuses
Student Advantage Guide: Help Yourself
Student Advantage Guide: The Complete Book of Colleges
Student Advantage Guide: The Internship Bible
Hillel Guide to Jewish Life on Campus
International Students' Guide to the United States
The Princeton Review Guide to Your Career

Also available on cassette from Living Language

Grammar Smart
Word Smart
Word Smart II

THE **PRINCETON** REVIEW

STUDENT ADVANTAGE
GUIDE TO

PAYING

FOR

COLLEGE

Random House, Inc. New York 1996
http://www.randomhouse.com

1997 Edition

ISBN: 0-679-77363-0
ISSN: 1076-5344

Manufactured in the United States of America

9   8   7   6   5   4   3   2

First 1997 Edition

ACKNOWLEDGMENTS

I'd like to thank The Princeton Review and particularly John Katzman, president of The Princeton Review, who has always been so supportive of the concept of financial aid planning; Isidore Matalon, my longtime friend and a constant source of new ideas; Jay Schulman from the accounting firm of J. T. Schulman & Co. in Carle Place, New York, and Steven Levine of the accounting firm of Lederer & Levine in Secaucus, New Jersey, for their helpful suggestions regarding tax law; Catherine Gelfand, my associate at Campus Consultants without whom I could never have managed; my friends Stuart Foisy and John Brubaker for their assistance with the worksheets at the back of this book; the high school counselors and independent college consultants who have entrusted students and their parents to me over the years; my own parents, who somehow managed to pay for my college education without the benefit of having read a book like this.

Last but not least, I would like to thank our clients who have allowed us the opportunity to prove that financial aid planning really works.

—K.C.

Thanks, also, to the editors at Random House and the production staff at The Princeton Review for all their help.

—G.M.

CONTENTS

INTRODUCTION

The college application process has been described as the closest thing America has to a "savage puberty rite." In fact, entire books have been written about the traumatic effect the application process has on students. Much less attention has been paid to another group of unsung heroes who are going through a similar ordeal all their own: the parents who are supposed to pay for all this.

If This Is So Good for Me, Why Does It Feel So Bad?

The cost of a four-year private college education has passed the $100,000 mark at many schools, which is enough to cause even the most affluent parent to want to sit down and cry. The public Ivies—state schools with excellent reputations—have been raising their tuition as fast as the privates. This year, an out-of-state student will have to pay almost $23,000 to attend the University of Michigan.

Meanwhile, falling enrollment at the colleges along with cuts in the education budgets of both the federal and state governments have combined to create a crisis in higher education. Many colleges have had to slash their budgets, lay off professors, even eliminate whole departments. And of course, the financial aid available per student has shrunk as rising tuition has forced more and more parents to apply for assistance.

The Joy of Aid

If there is a bright side to all this it is that in spite of all the cuts, there is still a great deal of financial aid available—and we are talking *billions* of dollars. At these prices, almost every family now qualifies for some form of assistance. Many parents don't believe that a family that makes over $75,000 a year, owns their own home, and holds substantial assets could possibly receive financial aid. These days, that family—provided it is presented in the right light—almost certainly does. Many parents who make $20,000, rent their home, and have no assets, don't believe they can afford to send their child to any type of college at all. They almost certainly can—in fact, they may find to their surprise that with the financial aid package some schools can put together for them, it may cost less to attend an "expensive" private school than it would to go to a "cheap" state school.

Who Gets the Most Financial Aid?

You might think that the families who receive the most financial aid would be the families with the most need. In fact, this is not necessarily true. The people who receive the most aid are the people who best understand the aid process.

A few years ago, we had a client who owned a $1 million apartment in New York City and a stock portfolio with a value in excess of $2 million. Her daughter attended college—with a $4,000-a-year financial aid package.

Is This Fair?

No. But lots of things in life aren't fair. In that particular case, we were able to take advantage of a financial aid loophole involving the way state aid is computed in New York. There are lots of financial aid loopholes.

Is This Legal?

You bet. All of the strategies we are going to discuss in this book follow the law to the letter.

Is This Ethical?

Let us put a hypothetical question to you: If your accountant showed you a legal way to save $4,000 on your income tax this year, would you take it?

The parallels between taxes and financial aid are interesting. Both have loopholes that regularly get exploited by the people who know about them. But more important, both also involve adversarial relationships. In the case of your taxes, the IRS wants as much money from you as it can get. You, in turn, want to give the IRS as little as possible. This pas de deux is a time-honored tradition, a system of checks and balances that everyone understands and accepts. And as long as both sides stick to the rules, the system works as well as anyone can expect.

In the case of college, it is the job of the financial aid officer (known in college circles as the FAO) to get as much money from you as he can. In the pursuit of this task, he will be much more invasive than the IRS ever is, demanding not just your financial data but intimate details of your personal life such as medical problems and marital status. He wants to protect the college's assets and give away as little money as possible. Let the financial aid officer do *his* job—believe us, he's very good at it. But meantime, you have to do *your* job—and your job is to use the rules of financial aid to make your contribution to college as small as possible.

Parents who understand these rules get the maximum amount of financial aid they are entitled to under the law. No more, and no less.

Besides, You've Already Paid for Financial Aid

Whether you know it or not, you've been contributing to financial aid funds for years. Each April 15, you pay federal taxes, a piece of which goes straight to the federal student aid programs. You pay state taxes, part of which goes directly to state schools and to provide grant programs for residents attending college in-state. You probably even make contributions to the alumni fund-raising campaign at your own college.

Your son or daughter may not go to your alma mater, may not attend a school in your state, may not even go to college, but you have paid all these years so that *someone's* son or daughter can get a college education.

You may now have need of these funds, and you should not be embarrassed to ask for them.

Is This Only for Rich People?

Many people think that tax loopholes and financial strategy are only for millionaires. In some ways, they have a point: certainly it is the rich who can reap the greatest benefits.

But financial aid strategy is for everyone. Whether you are just getting by or are reasonably well off, you still want to maximize your aid eligibility.

A College Is a Business

Despite the ivy-covered walls, the slick promotional videos, and a name that may intimidate you, a college is a business like any other. It provides a service and must find customers willing to buy that service.

You may have heard of an education scam that's been cropping up in different parts of the country in which bogus "trade schools" provide valueless educational courses to unwary consumers. These "beauty academies," "computer programming schools," and "truck driver schools" talk students into paying for their courses by taking out government-guaranteed student loans. The schools pocket the money, the student receives very little in the way of education, and then must spend the next ten years paying off the loan. Or not paying off the loan, in which case the taxpayer must pick up the tab.

Higher education sometimes seems like a slightly more genteel version of the trade school scam. As enrollments decline, the colleges need warm bodies to fill their classrooms. Many of these warm bodies qualify for federal aid (including guaranteed student loans), which helps keep the colleges afloat. Meanwhile, the financial aid officers do their bit by trying to get as much money from the student and her family as possible.

The Ivy-Covered Bottom Line

Of course there is a great deal more to college than merely a business selling a service—there is the value of tradition, the exploration of new ideas, the opportunity to think about important issues, the chance to develop friendships that will last for the rest of a student's life—but do not lose sight of the bottom line. Colleges stand accused by many experts of wasting a good part of their endowment through sloppy management, misguided expansion, and wasteful expenditures. A college tuition would cost much less today if the colleges had been run in a businesslike manner over the past twenty years.

If colleges are in trouble right now, there are many who would say it is their own doing, and that they will be better off once they have lost some of the excess fat they allowed themselves to gain during the baby boom. Certainly it is not your responsibility to pay for their mistakes if you don't have to.

But the FAOs have their own bottom line to consider.

An Uneducated Consumer Is Their Best Customer

It is not in the FAO's best interest for you to understand the aid process. The more you know about it, the more aid they will have to give you from the school's own coffers. You can almost *feel* the FAO's reluctance to let the consumer know what's going on when you look at the standardized financial aid applications (known as *need analysis forms*), which are constructed in consultation with the colleges. These forms (unlike the federal tax forms that allow you to calculate your own taxes) require you to list your information but do not allow you to calculate the amount of money you will be required to pay to the college. This calculation is done by the need analysis company. Mere parents are not allowed to know how the formula is constructed.

We are going to show you that formula and much more.

Understanding and Taking Control of the Process

In this book we will first give you an overview of the process of applying for aid, and then show you how to begin to take control of that process. We will discuss long-term investment strategies for families that have time to plan, and short-term financial aid strategies for families that are about to begin the process. We have devoted an entire chapter to a step-by-step guide to filling out the standardized need analysis forms, because the decisions the colleges will make on the basis of these forms are crucial to your ability to pay for college. Once you have received your aid packages from the schools, you will want to compare them. Part four of this book, "The Offer," shows you how to do that, as well as discussing how to negotiate with the colleges for an improved package.

A Word of Caution

Some of the aid strategies we will discuss in this book are complicated, and because we do not know the specifics of your financial situation, it is impossible for us to give anything but general advice. Nor can we cover every eventuality. We recommend that you consult with a competent professional about your specific situation before proceeding with a particular strategy. In chapter 7, we discuss how to find a good financial aid consulting service.

Unfortunately, because of the volume of correspondence, we can't answer individual letters or give specific advice over the telephone. If we did, we'd have no time for our private clients—or for the daunting task of preparing next year's edition of *Paying for College*.

Keeping You Up-to-Date

One reason we resisted writing this book for so long was our reluctance to put out a book that might be bought after it was out of date. In the world of financial aid, things change rapidly. We agreed to do this book only after getting a commitment from our publisher that there would be a new edition every year.

However, even within the space of a year, things can change: tax laws can be amended, financial aid rules can be repealed. By filling out and returning the postcard that is bound into this book, you will automatically be put on our update mailing list. If any important changes occur before the next edition of this book is released, you will receive a packet from us outlining those changes.

A Final Thought

One bizarre consequence of falling enrollments has been that the application process itself has actually become less "savage" on the student. Depending on which survey you read, between 70% and 80% of all college-bound high school students were accepted by their first-choice college last year. Except for a handful of schools, selectivity is going by the board. Nowadays, the problem is not so much how to get into college, but how to pay for it once you are there.

In the following pages we will show you how to pay for college. This is not about ripping off the system, or lying to get aid you don't deserve. We merely wish to make available to you some information that the FAOs are not in a hurry to tell you on their own, so that you can get the maximum amount of aid you are entitled to receive under the law.

PART ONE

Understanding the Process

CHAPTER ONE

Overview

How the Aid Process Works:
Paying for College in a Nutshell

Ideally, you began this process many years ago when your children were quite small. You started saving, at first in small increments, gradually increasing the amounts as your children got older and your earning power grew. You put the money into a mixture of growth investments like stock funds, and conservative investments like treasury bonds, so that now as the college years are approaching you are sitting pretty, with a nice fat college fund, a cool drink in your hand, and enough left over to buy a vacation home in Monte Carlo.

However, if you are like most of us, you probably began thinking seriously about college only a few years ago. You have not been able to put away large amounts of money. Important things kept coming up. An opportunity to buy a home. Taxes. Braces. Private school tuition. Taxes.

If you are foresighted enough to have bought this book while your children are still young, you will be especially interested in our section on long-term planning. If your child is already a senior in high school just about to apply for college, don't despair. There is a lot you can do to take control of the process.

Most people cannot afford to pay the full cost of four years of college. Financial aid is designed to bridge the gap between what you can afford to pay for school and what the school actually costs. Parents who understand the process come out way ahead. Let's look at the aid process in a nutshell and see how it works—or at least how it's supposed to work. Later on, we will take you through each step of this process in greater detail.

The Standardized Need Analysis Form

While students start work on their admissions applications, parents should be gathering together their records in order to begin applying for financial aid.

To apply for financial aid you fill out a standardized need analysis form. These forms, available from high school guidance offices, can be filled out only after January 1 of the student's senior year in high school.

Different organizations process need analysis forms, and different colleges require different forms. To find out which form is accepted by a particular school, consult the individual school's general information bulletin.

At a minimum, the Free Application for Federal Student Aid (FAFSA) will be required of all undergraduate applicants for aid. Many private colleges and some state supported institutions may also require you to fill out the Financial Aid PROFILE form as well. This form is developed and processed by a division of the same company that brings you the SAT—the College Board's College Scholarship Service (CSS). A few schools will require other forms as well—for example, the selective private colleges often have their *own* financial aid forms. Graduate and professional school students might have to complete a graduate/professional school student supplement to the PROFILE form and/or a Need Access Application Diskette, which is a computer program developed by The Access Group in Wilmington, Delaware. All of the forms ask the same types of questions.

These questions are invasive and prying. How much did you earn last year? How much money do you have in the bank? What is your marital status? A hundred or so questions later, the need analysis company will have a very clear picture of four things:

1. *the parents' available income*
2. *the parents' available assets*
3. *the student's available income*
4. *the student's available assets*

The processor of the FAFSA form uses a federal formula (called the *federal methodology*) to decide what portion of your income and assets you get to keep and what portion you can afford to give toward college tuition this year. This amount is called the Expected Family Contribution (EFC), and it will most likely be more than you think you can afford.

However, some schools do not feel that the EFC generated by the FAFSA gives an accurate enough picture of what the family can contribute to college costs. Using the supplemental information on the PROFILE, or their own individual forms, they perform a separate need analysis (using a formula called the *institutional methodology*) to determine eligibility for aid that those schools control directly.

A Family's "Need"

Meanwhile, the admissions offices of the different colleges have been deciding which students to admit and which to reject. Once they've made their decision, the financial aid officers (known as FAOs) get to work. Their job is to put together a package of grants, work-study, and loans that will make up the difference between what they feel you can afford to pay and what the school actually costs. The total cost of a year at college includes:

tuition and fees
room and board
personal expenses
books and supplies
travel

The difference between what you can afford to pay and the total cost of college is called your "need."

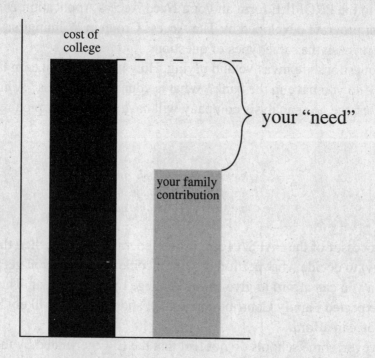

In theory, your Expected Family Contribution will be approximately the same no matter what schools your child applies to. If your EFC is calculated to be $8,300 and your child is accepted at a state school that costs $10,300, you will pay about $8,300, and the school will make up the difference—in this case $2,000—with an aid package. If you apply to a prestigious Ivy League school that costs $31,000, you will still pay about $8,300 and the school will make up the difference with an aid package of approximately $22,700.

In theory, the only difference between an expensive school and a cheaper school (putting aside subjective matters like the quality of education) is the amount of your need. In some cases, depending on how badly the college wants the student, parents won't pay a penny more for an exclusive private college than they would for a state school.

This is why families should not initially rule out any school as being too expensive. The "sticker price" doesn't necessarily matter; it's the portion of the sticker price that you have to pay that counts. Parents are often under the impression that no matter what type of school their child attends—be it a very expensive private college, an expensive out-of-state college, or their local state university—they will receive the same amount of aid. In fact, as you saw from the previous example, the amount of aid you get is in part determined by the cost of the school you choose.

Theory vs. Reality

Of course, the reality is slightly more complicated. Because some schools are using supplemental data (such as home equity) to determine eligibility for their private aid, your expected contribution at a more selective university will most likely be different, and in many cases higher. In later chapters we'll be talking about what factors can cause the schools to adjust the EFC calculated under the federal methodology, and more important, we'll be showing you how to minimize the impact of these adjustments.

The Aid Package

About the time your child receives an offer of admission from a particular college, you will receive an award letter. This letter will tell you what combination of aid the FAO has put together for you in order to meet your need. The package will consist of three different types of aid:

> **Grants and Scholarships**—These are the best kinds of aid, because they don't have to be paid back. Essentially a grant is free money. Some grant money comes from the federal government, some comes from the state, and some comes from the coffers of the college itself. Best of all, grant money is almost always tax-free. If you are in the 40% tax bracket, a $2,000 grant is the equivalent of receiving a raise of $3,334.

> Scholarships are also free money, although there may be some conditions attached (academic excellence, for example). Contrary to popular wisdom, scholarships are usually awarded by the schools themselves. The amount of money available from outside scholarships is actually quite small.

> **Federal Work-Study (FWS)**—The federal government subsidizes this program, which provides part-time jobs to students. The money earned is put toward either tuition or living expenses.

> **Student Loans**—These loans, usually taken out by the student rather than the parents, are often subsidized (and guaranteed) by state or federal governments. The rates are usually much lower than regular unsecured loans. In most cases, no interest is charged while the student is in school, and no repayment is required until the student has graduated or left college.

Preferential Packaging

The FAOs at the individual colleges have a lot of latitude to make decisions. After looking at your financial information, for example, they might decide your EFC should be lower or higher than the need analysis processor computed it originally.

More important, the package the FAOs put together for a student will reflect how badly the admissions office wants that student.

If a school is anxious to have your child in its freshman class, the package you will be offered will have a larger percentage of grant money, with a much smaller percentage coming from student loans and work study. If a college is less interested, the award will not be as attractive.

Your award will also reflect the general financial health of the college you are applying to. Some schools have large endowments and can afford to be generous. Other schools are financially strapped, and may be able to offer only the bare minimum.

If the school is truly anxious to get a particular student, it may also sweeten the deal by giving a grant or scholarship that isn't based on need. A non-need scholarship may actually reduce your family contribution.

Unmet Need

In some cases, you may find that the college tells you that you have "unmet need." In other words, they were unable to supply the full difference between the cost of their school and the amount they feel you can afford to pay. This is bad news. What the college is telling you is that if your child really wants to attend this college, you will have to come up with even more money than the college's need analysis decided that you could pay.

Usually what this means is that you will have to take on additional debt. Sometimes the colleges themselves will be willing to lend you the money. Sometimes you will be able to take advantage of other loan programs such as the Federal Parent Loans for Under-graduate Students (PLUS), which is a subsidized loan to parents of college students. The terms are less attractive than the subsidized student loans but still better than unsecured loans you would get from banks if you walked in off the street.

Sifting the Offers

The week the acceptances and award letters arrive can be very tough, as you deal with the economic realities of the different schools' offers. The school your child really wants to attend may have given you an aid package you cannot accept. The week will be immeasurably easier if you have taken the financial aid process into account when you were selecting schools to apply to in the first place.

Just as it is important to select a safety school where your child is likely to be accepted, it is also important to select what we call a *financial* safety school" that is cheap enough to afford out of your own pocket in the event that the more expensive schools you applied to do not meet your full need. In some cases, the admissions safety school and financial safety school may be the same. If a student is a desirable candidate from an academic standpoint, she is likely to get a good financial aid package as well. However, you should also consider the economic health of the schools you are applying to as well as the past history of financial aid at those schools. This information can be gleaned from many of the college guides (including The Princeton Review's *Student Advantage Guide to the Best 310 Colleges*) available at bookstores.

It is also vital to make sure that there is a reasonable expectation that the package will be available for the next three years as well. How high do the student's grades have to be in order to keep the package intact? Are any of the grants or scholarships they gave you one-time-only grants? Once you've received an offer, these are questions to ask the FAO.

Negotiating with the FAOs

Even if a school's award letter has left you with a package you cannot accept—perhaps the percentage of student loan money in your package is too high; or perhaps your need was not fully met—you may still be able to negotiate a better deal.

Over the past few years we have noticed that the initial offer of aid, especially at some of the more selective schools, seems to have become subject to negotiation. In many cases, if you just accept the first offer, you will have accepted an offer that was not as high as the FAO was willing to go.

The key in these negotiations is to be friendly, firm, and in control. Know what you want when you talk to the FAO and be able to provide documentation. In some cases, the FAO will alter the aid package enough to make it possible for you to afford to send your child to the school.

There is an entire chapter of this book devoted to the award letter—how to compare award letters, how to negotiate with FAOs, and how to apply for next year.

Same Time Next Year

The financial aid package you accept will last only one year. You will have to go through the financial aid process four separate times, filling out a new need analysis form each year until your child reaches the senior year of college. If your financial situation were to stay *exactly* the same, then next year's aid package would probably be very similar to this year's. We find, however, that most parents' situations do change from year to year. In fact, after you finish reading this book, there may be some specific changes you'll *want* to make.

How the Aid Process Really Works

Parents who understand how to apply for financial aid get more. It's that simple. We aren't talking about lying, cheating, or beating the system. We're talking about understanding the system and taking advantage of the rules to get the best deal.

In part two, you will learn how to take control of the process. For those parents who are starting early we have a chapter on long-term investment strategies that minimize taxes and maximize aid eligibility; for those parents who have children in the sophomore, junior, or senior year of high school, we have five chapters that completely explain how to use the financial aid formulas to save money.

In addition, we discuss how to pick colleges that will give the best aid packages, how to apply for state aid, and—very important—what the *student* can do.

In part three, we provide line-by-line instructions for the most commonly used standardized financial aid forms.

In part four, we discuss the offer. What does an award letter look like? What are the different types of aid you may receive, in detail? How do you compare award letters? How do you negotiate with the FAOs to get an improved package?

In chapter 8 we talk about innovative payment options and in chapter 9 we cover in more detail some special topics such as divorced and separated parents, graduate students, independent students, and other topics that may be of interest to some of our readers. In chapter 10, we'll talk about managing student loans during and after school. In chapter 11, we'll discuss future trends in financial aid.

In part five you will find worksheets that will enable you to compute your expected family contribution as well as sample copies of the FAFSA and the Financial Aid PROFILE form.

PART TWO

How to Take Control of the Process

Now that you know how the financial aid process works, it's time to start figuring out how to take control of that process—and prevent the process from taking control of you.

If you have read part one of this book, then you have already taken the first step toward this goal:

Understanding What's Going On

The college FAOs don't really want you to understand all the intricacies of the financial aid process. If parents don't know what's going on, they can't ask embarrassing questions, and they will accept whatever the FAOs tell them.

We know of one case in which a financial aid officer from a private college told a parent who had called asking for an increase in aid, that "our hands are tied. Federal regulations prevent us from giving you any more money." The parent, not knowing any better, accepted this as the truth. In fact, it was a bald-faced lie. Almost all colleges (and this one was no exception) hand out their own grants, funded by private funds, which are not regulated by federal law at all.

Another thing parents are often too willing to accept at face value is the initial financial aid offer by the college. In a recent trend, many schools (particularly the most competitive) have begun to build some bargaining room into their initial offers. They expect you to ask for more. In many cases, accepting that first offer means taking a lower number than the FAO was willing to give. These are just two examples of the facts you will learn in the next few chapters—facts that will enable you to understand and begin to take control of the financial aid process.

Parents whose children are years away from college will find the next chapter on long-term planning particularly useful. In it, we will show you how to begin building a fund for college that will take advantage of both tax law and financial aid law. Families who are already getting ready to apply to college should skip long-term planning and go directly to chapter 3 on short-term strategies. Here we will begin to show you how linking your income tax strategies and your financial aid strategies can save you big bucks. We will show you how the colleges assess your income, your expenses, your assets, your liabilities, and how to influence these assessments to your advantage.

A word of caution, before we begin.

Don't Let the Terminology Intimidate You

In the course of counseling thousands of families, we've seen how confusing financial aid jargon can be to the nonprofessional. Just remember, the FAOs don't mind if you are a little confused. In fact, they would prefer it. And since they have a large influence on the instructions that come with the aid forms you will have to fill out, it shouldn't surprise you to learn that the instructions to the forms are confusing and full of unfamiliar terminology as well. The introduction to one particularly confusing financial aid form states that some questions are "self-explanatory, and therefore no instructions are given."

Don't worry. By the time you finish reading this book, the jargon will be second nature. At the back of this book is a comprehensive glossary; feel free to refer to it at any time.

To avoid confusion, we have taken care to use the same terminology used by the need analysis companies and the IRS. Even though it seems a little ridiculous to refer to certain deductions as "unreimbursed employee expenses," we did so anyway, just so that you will know what the terms mean once you start completing the forms and negotiating with the FAOs.

CHAPTER TWO

Long-Term Strategies for Paying for College

Congratulations! If you are reading this section you've had the foresight to begin planning early for the expense of paying for college. What do we mean by early? We will be presenting strategies for parents with children who are two years away, five years away, ten years away, and 15 years away from their first year of college.

The point of this chapter is not to make specific investment recommendations or tout individual stocks or investment instruments, but rather to show you the ways and means to begin a long-term college fund for your children. Our purpose is not to be your financial planner, for no financial planner could responsibly set up a ten-year plan without being around to administer it (and obviously, we can't do that). Things change. Investment opportunities come up suddenly. Interest rates go up or they go down. Tax laws are amended; financial aid laws are revised. We are going to outline some general strategies, but we advise you to invest cautiously, perhaps with the aid of a financial planner whom you can consult day to day.

If your child is applying for college next month, we recommend that you skip this section. It will only depress you. Instead, skip to the next chapter (which begins on page 35), where we begin talking about short-term strategies. We think you will be pleased.

How Much Should We Save Every Month?

Any realistic long-term plan is more of an educated guess than an exact prediction. There are so many unknown factors—how much will college cost in ten years? or 15 years? What will the inflation rate average over the next decade? Will stocks continue to be the best long-term investment as they have for the past 40 years, or will some unforeseen trend make real estate or bonds a better investment?

Any financial planner who says you have to save exactly $562 per month to reach your goal is being unrealistic—in part because you don't even know with certainty what that goal will be. An article in *Newsweek* recently stated with great authority that if you are five years away from the beginning of a private college education you should be saving $1,347 every month. We think the main thing such pronouncements do is scare parents into paralysis. "We don't *have* that kind of money," clients wail to us on the phone after they read these articles. "What are we supposed to do?"

The Important Thing Is to Start

It is easy to get so paralyzed by the projection of the total cost of a four-year college education that you do nothing. The important thing is to begin saving *something* as early as possible as regularly as possible. It doesn't matter if you can't contribute large amounts. The earlier you start, the longer you give your investments to work for you.

If you have not saved the total cost of four years' tuition at a private college (and very few parents ever have), all is not lost. That is why there is financial aid.

So Why Bother to Save at All? If We Don't Have Any Money, We'll Just Get More Financial Aid

This is partly true, but only partly. A poor family without the means to pay for college will find concerned FAOs ready to look in every corner of their coffers to come up with the aid necessary to send that family's child to college. An affluent family that has lived beyond their means for years and is now looking for the college to support this lifestyle with financial aid will find the FAOs to be very unsympathetic and tightfisted.

An honest attempt to save money, and a willingness to make sacrifices can make a large impression on the FAOs. These men and women have broad powers to increase or decrease your family contribution; to allocate grants; to meet your family's *entire* need—or just part of it.

Trust us, you will be much happier if you have saved for college. Who can say whether in five years there will be many colleges left that can afford to continue "need-blind" admissions policies? Perhaps by the year 2005 virtually *no* colleges will be able to meet a family's full remaining need—meaning that if you are without resources, your child will simply not be able to attend college at all. If you still aren't convinced, think about this: A significant proportion of financial aid packages comes in the form of loans. You have the choice of saving now and *earning* interest, or borrowing later and *paying* interest. Earning interest is more fun.

Finally, under the aid formulas, colleges will assess parents' assets at a top rate of only 5.65%. In other words, if you have managed to build up a college fund of say, $40,000, as long as it is in the parents' name, the colleges will assess up to approximately five and a half cents of each dollar of that fund each year. We'll be discussing the pros and cons of putting money in your child's name later. You can certainly spend more if you like, but it is important to understand that having money in the bank does not mean the colleges get to take it all.

Money in the Bank Gives You Options

A college fund, even a small one, gives you control over your own destiny. What if the college your child really wants to attend doesn't fully meet your need? What if you lose your job just as the college years are approaching? By planning a little for the future now, you can ensure that you'll have options when the college years are upon you.

How Much Will a College Education Cost in *X* Years?

Every year, the price of a college education goes up. In the past couple of years the rate of increase at private colleges has actually slowed, the result in part of market forces: Families have been turning to state schools in greater numbers, forcing the private colleges to cut their prices, or at least to slow the increase of their prices. Partly in response to increased demand and partly because state budgets have been slashed, the rate of tuition increase at state schools has risen dramatically—especially for out-of-state students who must pay extra. Will these trends continue? The best we can do is make broad predictions based on current trends. Let's look at some numbers.

The Cost of a Private College

The average cost of a year's tuition, room and board, and fees at a private college this year was $17,631 (according to the College Board). Many experts predict that the cost of private college will increase at a rate of about 6% per year. Here is a chart of what the average cost of a year of private college would be over the next 15 years, based on 6% yearly growth:

Average Annual Cost of a Private College in	
1996: $17,631 (today)	2004: $28,101
1997: $18,689	2005: $29,787
1998: $19,810 (2 years)	2006: $31,574 (10 years)
1999: $20,999	2007: $33,469
2000: $22,259	2008: $35,477
2001: $23,594 (5 years)	2009: $37,606
2002: $25,009	2010: $39,862
2003: $26,510	2011: $42,254 (15 years)

Of course, if your child decides on one of the most prestigious private schools, the cost will be even more. This year, most of the top colleges have crossed the $27,000-a-year barrier. In five years, at 6% growth per year, that will be more than $36,000.

The Cost of a Public University

The average cost of a year's tuition, room and board, and fees at a public university this year was $6,823 (according to the College Board). Many experts predict that the cost of public university will increase at a rate of about 6% per year over the next decade. Here is a chart of what the average cost of a year of public university could cost over the next 15 years, if the experts are right:

Average Annual Cost of a Public University in

1996:	$6,823 (today)	2004:	$10,875
1997:	$7,232	2005:	$11,527
1998:	$7,666 (2 years)	2006:	$12,219 (10 years)
1999:	$8,126	2007:	$12,952
2000:	$8,614	2008:	$13,729
2001:	$9,131 (5 years)	2009:	$14,553
2002:	$9,679	2010:	$15,426
2003:	$10,259	2011:	$16,352 (15 years)

Of course, if you are attending one of the "public Ivies" such as the University of Michigan as an out-of-state resident, the cost right now is already over $22,000. In five years, at a 6% growth rate per year, that would be nearly $30,000.

How Much Money Will You Need?

If your child is 15, 10, or even five years away from college, she has probably not even begun to think about what kind of school she would like to attend. Since you can't ask your child, ask yourself: What kind of college could you picture your son or daughter attending?

If you have picked a private college of average cost, and your child is ten years away from college, look up the price on the first chart we gave you above. Rather than concentrating on the cost of freshman year, look at the cost of junior year, two years further on. Whatever this number is, multiply it by four. This is a rough approximation of an average college education at that time.

If you picked an average public university, and your child is five years away from college, look up the price on the second chart above. Count two years more and multiply that number by four. This is a rough approximation of a college education at an average public university at that time. Of course, if costs increase faster than the experts are projecting, the tuition could be more.

Get the Smelling Salts

If you wish to be even more precise, find a guide to colleges and look up the current price of a particular school you are interested in. Let's choose Spelman College, which has a current price of about $14,300, and let's say your daughter is going to be ready to go to college in five years. Multiply the current price by our assumed rate of increase:

$$\$14,300 \times 1.06 = \$15,158$$

The new number is the price of that school next year. To find out the projected price of Spelman in five years, just repeat this operation four more times ($15,158 × 1.06 = $16,067; $16,067 × 1.06 = $17,031; etc.). For ten years, repeat the operation nine more times.

Of course, these will only be rough estimates since no one has a crystal ball. If your daughter were to start Spelman five years from now, the first year would cost roughly $19,135. By the time she is a junior, the projected cost would be $21,500. To figure out the grand total, multiply the cost of junior year by four. This is a rough projection of the cost of a four-year education. At Spelman five years from now, a college education will cost about $86,000. At Stanford or Yale, the bill will certainly exceed $150,000.

Now don't faint just yet. This is a great deal of money, but first of all, there's a lot of financial aid out there—and the majority of this book will be devoted to showing you how to get that financial aid. Second of all, you still have time to plan, save, and invest—and because of the joys of compounding, your investments can grow much faster than you might believe possible. Third, your earning power will most likely increase over time.

In the rest of this chapter you will find investment strategies for saving money for college. Try not to obsess about the total projected cost. The important thing is to begin.

When Do You Begin Saving?

Right now. The more time you give your investments to multiply, the better. Even if you can manage only a small amount each month, you will be surprised at how much you have put away by the end of the year, and even more surprised at how quickly that money multiplies.

The Joys of Compound Interest

Let's say that you had a pretty good year this year and were able to save $5,000. Sound like too much? Okay, let's say $4,000. You invest this money in a high-yield mutual fund or a high-yield bond fund. Some of these funds have been consistently earning over 15% a year, but let's be more conservative and say you get a 10% rate of return, which you plow back into the fund. Don't like mutual funds? That's fine. If you are uncomfortable with this level of risk, we'll be discussing other investment vehicles a little later. This is just an example to show you how investments grow.

The calculation is actually the same one we used to figure out what college would cost in the future. To find out how much $4,000 would earn in one year at 10%, multiply $4,000 times 1.10.

$$\$4,000 \times 1.10 = \$4,400$$

To find the value of the investment over five years, repeat this calculation four more times ($4,400 × 1.10 = 4,840; $4,840 × 1.10 = $5,324; etc.) In five years, your original $4,000 will be worth $6,442. In ten years, it will have grown to $10,374. Not bad, especially when you consider that this comes from only one year of saving.

Of course, this example is a little simplified. One or two of those years might be bad years and the fund might not pay 10%. Other years might be extremely good years and the yield could be much higher. There are tax implications to consider as well. However, $10,374 is a reasonable forecast of what one $4,000 investment could be worth in ten years.

And if you continued to invest another $4,000 each year for the next ten years, with the same rate of return—well, now we're talking real money. At the end of ten years, you would have a college fund in excess of $70,000.

Too Much Risk?

Let's say you are too uncomfortable with the risk of high-yield instruments. You decide to invest your $4,000 per year in safe, dependable government bonds (or in a fund that buys government bonds), and you get an average yield of 6 to 7%. If you reinvest the yield, in ten years you will have built a college fund of over $55,000.

A Young Couple Just Starting Out

Let's take the fictional couple David and Lisa, who have a daughter who is now seven years old. David and Lisa are pretty young, and they can't afford to save much, but they decide they can manage $1,000 a year. They invest the $1,000 in an aggressive mutual fund with an average return of 10%, which they reinvest in the fund. By the time their daughter is ready to go to college in ten years, that first $1,000 has become $2,593. Each year, they invest another $1,000. The money they invest the second year has only nine years to grow, but it is still worth $2,357 by the time their child is ready for college. The money they invest the third year has only eight years to grow, but is still worth $2,144.

If Lisa and David invest $1,000 a year in this manner for ten years, they will have built a college fund of $17,525. Of course this is not enough to pay the entire cost of college, but there are several factors we haven't taken into account yet:

- No one is asking them to pay the entire amount. If David and Lisa aren't earning big money by the time the college years arrive, they may qualify for significant amounts of financial aid.

- David and Lisa might begin earning more money over the next ten years. Promotions and/or raises could allow them to save more than $1,000 per year as time goes on.

- The couple may have been able to make other investments as well (such as buying a house), against which they can borrow when their daughter is in college.

- During the college years, David and Lisa may be able (in fact are expected) to pay some of the cost of college from their current income.

Timing

Because of the way compounding works it would be better, in theory, to make your largest contributions to a college investment fund in the early years when the investment has the most time to grow. Unfortunately the reality of the situation is that a couple just getting started often doesn't have that kind of money.

If you get a windfall—an inheritance, a large bonus, a year with a lot of overtime—by all means put that money to work for you. However, for most parents, it will be a matter of finding the money to invest here and there.

Many financial advisers recommend an automatic deduction plan, in which a certain amount of money is automatically deducted from your paycheck or your bank account each month. Parents often find that if the money simply disappears before they have time to spend it, the process of saving is less painful.

Should Money Be Put in the Child's Name?

One of the most important decisions you will have to make is whether to put the college fund in your own name or in your child's name.

There are some wonderful tax advantages to putting the money in your child's name, but there can also be some terrible financial aid disadvantages. Let's look at the tax advantages first.

Each year a parent is allowed to make a "custodial gift to minors" of up to $10,000 per parent per child. Thus if you live in a two-parent household, you can give up to $20,000 per year to your child, without gift-tax consequences. This is not a $20,000 tax deduction for you, but neither is it $20,000 in taxable income to the child. You have merely shifted money from you to your child. From now on, some of the interest that money earns will be taxed not at the parents' rate, but at the child's rate, which is almost always much lower. Here are the rules:

For a child under the age of 14—as long as the custodial account generates less than $650 per year in interest or dividend income and there is no other income—there will be no income tax due at all. As long as the custodial account generates less than $1,300 in income and there is no other income, the excess over $650 will be taxed at the child's rate

(15% federal). Once the child's unearned taxable income exceeds the $1,300 cap, the excess will be taxed at the parents' higher rate, which can go up as high as 39.6% federal. State and local taxes will push this even higher.

For a child 14 and older: all the money in the custodial account will be taxed at the child's rate.

The child is not allowed to have control over the account until the age of 18 (21 in some states). By the same token you are not allowed to take that money back either. The money can be spent only on behalf of the child. You could use the money to pay for an SAT prep course, or braces, say, but not on the rent or a vacation to Hawaii—even if you took the child along.

Of course, if this gift is being made as part of a fund for college, this should be no problem. You don't plan to touch it until your son or daughter is ready to enroll anyway. You can shift the money between different investments, or even give it to a financial planner to invest.

The restrictions on custodial accounts for children under the age of 14 have only been in effect for a few years. One way to avoid this "kiddie tax" is to invest custodial account money in growth stocks, which generally appreciate in value but pay small dividends. Then, after the student turns 14, you can sell the stock and take the capital gain, which will then be taxed solely at the child's rate. Ideally, you would want to have some investments generate a little less than $1,300 in income per year, and the remainder allocated to investment instruments that generated little or no income.

If your very young child's college fund was paying 4% interest, the fund could contain $32,500, and the interest the money earned would still be taxed at the child's rate. As the fund gets larger than $32,500, some of the interest would begin to be taxed at your rate. However, when the child hits 14, the entire amount in the fund would get taxed at the child's presumably lower rate.

Thus the tax savings from putting money in the child's name are considerable. Unfortunately, because of the rules under which financial aid is dispensed, putting money in the kid's name can be a very expensive mistake.

If You Have Any Hope of Financial Aid, *Never* Put Money in the Child's Name

When you apply for financial aid, you will complete a need analysis form, which tells the colleges your current income, your child's income, your assets, and your child's assets. The colleges will assess these amounts to decide how much you can afford to pay for college. Your income will be assessed up to 47%. Your assets will be assessed up to 5.65%.

However, your *child's* income will be assessed at up to 50% and your *child's* assets will be assessed at a whopping 35%. A college fund of $40,000 under *your* name would be assessed (as an asset) for up to $2,260 the first year of college. That is to say, the college would expect you to put as much as $2,260 of that money toward the first year of school.

The same fund under your child's name would be assessed for $14,000.

That's a big difference. You might say, "Well that money was supposed to be for college anyway," and you would be right—but remember, the colleges aren't just assessing *that* money. They will assess 35% of *all* of the child's assets, 5.65% of *all* the parents' assets, up to 50% of *all* the child's income, and up to 47% of *all* the parents' income. By putting that money in the child's name, you just gave them a lot more money than you had to.

We've already noted the similarities between a college financial aid office and the IRS. Both see it as their duty to use the rules to get as much money as possible from you. It is up to you to use those same rules to keep as much money as possible away from them. It is an adversarial relationship, but as long as both sides stick to the rules, a fair one.

If you are going to qualify for financial aid, you should never, ever put money in the child's name. It is like throwing the money away. You've worked too hard to save that money to watch it get swallowed up in four giant gulps. By putting the money in the parents' name, you keep control over it. If you choose to, you can use it all, or not use it all, on your timetable.

What If You're Pretty Sure You Won't Qualify for Aid?

If you are certain you won't qualify for aid, then you're free to employ every tax-reducing strategy your accountant can devise, including putting assets in the kid's name. But be very certain. People are often amazed at how much money you have to make in order NOT to qualify for aid.

In the introduction we told you about a family who received financial aid despite huge assets. Parents always want to know exactly what the cutoff is. Unfortunately, it is not as simple as that. Each family is a separate case. Don't assume that just because your friend didn't qualify for aid that you won't either. There are so many variables it is impossible to say the cutoff is precisely X dollars. It just doesn't work that way.

If you are close to the beginning of the college years and you want to figure out if you qualify for aid, read the rest of this book and then use the worksheets in the back to compute your Expected Family Contribution. There is really no shortcut. We have seen books that give you a simple chart on which you can look up your EFC. These charts are much too simplistic to be of any real use.

And as you'll soon discover, there are strategies you can employ to increase your chances of receiving aid.

What If You Aren't Sure Whether You'll Qualify for Aid?

If your child is a number of years away from the freshman year of college, your dilemma is much more difficult. How can you predict how much you'll have in five years or 15 years? For safety, it would be better to avoid putting large sums of money in the child's name until you are sure you won't be eligible for aid.

Once the money is put into the child's name it is extremely difficult to put it back in the parents' name. If you set up a custodial account sometime in the past and have come to regret it, consult a very good financial consultant or tax lawyer.

Now that you've decided whose name to put the money under, let's talk about what kind of investments you can make.

What Types of Investments to Choose for a College Fund

The key to any investment portfolio is diversity. You will want to spread your assets among several different types of investments, with varying degrees of risk. When your child is young, you will probably want to keep a large percentage of your money in higher-risk investments in order to build the value of the portfolio. As you get closer to the college years, it is a good idea to shift gradually into less volatile and more liquid investments. By the time the first year of college arrives, you should have a high percentage of cash invested in short-term treasuries, CDs, or money market funds.

To stay ahead of inflation over the long term, there is no choice but to choose more aggressive investments. At the moment almost all the experts agree that the stock market is your best bet for long-term high yields. Of course, if the market crashes next year the experts will all be saying something else. However, it is worth noting that over the past 40 years, in spite of various bear markets, recessions, crashes, and acts of God, stocks have on average outperformed every other type of investment.

Stock Mutual Funds

Rather than buying individual stocks, you can spread your risk by buying shares in a mutual fund that manages a portfolio of many different stocks. Over the past five years, many stock mutual funds have increased in value by over 80%, and a few by over 100%. Most newspapers and financial magazines give periodic rundowns of the performance of different mutual funds. In general, we recommend no-load or low-load funds that charge a sales commission of 4.5% or less. The minimum investment in mutual funds varies widely, but often you can start with as little as $1,000. Many of the large mutual fund companies control a few different funds and allow you to switch from one type of fund to another or even to a regular money market fund without charge. In this way, you can move in and out of investments as events change, just by making a phone call.

You can spread your risk even further by purchasing stock mutual funds that specialize in several different areas. By putting some of your money into a blue-chip fund and some into whatever you think will soon be hot, you can hedge your bets.

It should be noted that over the past several years, individuals who never invested in the stock market before have been pouring money into mutual funds in an effort to earn a higher return than the current rates offered on CDs and savings accounts. We would just like to add our cautionary voice to the chorus of experts who have been warning the public that investing in mutual funds is not the same thing as having money in the bank.

High-Yield Bonds

Another aggressive investment to consider is high-yield bonds. For high yield, read "junk." Junk bonds, which pay a high rate of interest because they carry a high level of risk, helped to bring the boom-boom decade of the 1980s to its knees. However, if purchased with care, these bonds can get you a very high rate of return for moderate risk. The best way to participate in this market is to buy shares in a high-yield bond fund. The bonds are bought by professionals who presumably know what they are doing, and again, because the fund owns many different types of bonds, the risk is spread around.

Normal-Yield Bonds

If you want less risk, you might think about buying investment-grade bonds (such as Treasury securities), which can be bought so that they mature just as your child is ready to begin college. If you sell bonds before they mature, the price may vary quite a bit, but at maturity, bonds pay their full face value and provide the expected yield, thus guaranteeing you a fixed return. At present, the total annual return on this type of bond if interest is reinvested can top 6% according to Ken and Daria Dolan, editors of the monthly newsletter *Straight Talk on Your Money*.

One way of avoiding having to reinvest interest income is to buy zero-coupon bonds. You purchase a zero-coupon at far below its face value. On maturity, it pays you the full face value of the bond. You receive no interest income from the bond along the way; instead the interest you would have received is effectively reinvested at a guaranteed rate of return. You still have to pay tax every year on the "imputed interest," but the rate of return on zero-coupons can be substantial.

EE Savings Bonds

If you don't earn too much money, Series EE Savings Bonds offer an interesting option for college funds as well. The government a few years ago decided that if an individual over 24 years of age with low to moderate income purchases EE Savings Bonds after 1989 with the intention of using them to pay for college, the interest received at the time of redemption of the bonds will be tax-free. The interest earned is completely tax-free for a single parent with income up to $43,500 or a married couple filing jointly with income up to $65,250. Once you hit those income levels, the benefits are slowly phased out. A single parent with income above $58,500 or a married couple with income above $95,250 is not eligible for any tax break. All of these numbers are based on 1996 tax rates and are subject to an annual adjustment for inflation. EE Savings Bonds are issued by the federal government, and are as safe as any investment can be. They can also be purchased in small denominations without paying any sales commission.

However, EE Savings Bonds have several drawbacks. One is their low rate of return. You might do better with a taxable investment that pays a higher rate, even after taxes. It is also hard to predict in advance what your income level will be when you cash in the bonds. If your income has risen past the cutoff level for the tax break, your effective rate of return on the bonds just plunged into the low single digits. To make it worse, the IRS adds the interest from the bonds to your income *before* they determine whether you qualify for the tax break. Finally, whether the interest from these bonds is taxed or untaxed, it will still be considered income by the colleges and will be assessed just like your other income.

Tax-Free Municipal Bonds

Those families that are in the 28% income tax bracket (or higher) may be tempted to invest in tax-free municipal bonds. If you factor in the tax savings, the rate of return can approach 8 or 9%. As usual, you can reduce your risk by buying what is called a tax-free muni fund. These come in different varieties, with different degrees of risk.

One thing to be aware of is that while the IRS does not tax the income from these investments, the colleges effectively do. Colleges call tax-exempt interest income "untaxable income" and assess it just the way they assess taxable income. If you're eligible for aid, the real effective yield of munis will be pushed down by these assessments.

Trusts

Establishing a trust for your child's education is another way to shift assets and income to the child. Trusts have all the tax advantages of putting assets in the child's name—and then some; they allow more aggressive investment than do custodial accounts; they also give you much more control over when and how your child gets the money.

The drawbacks of trusts are that they are initially expensive to set up, costly to maintain, and very difficult to change—more important, they also jeopardize your chances of qualifying for financial aid.

If you have no chance of receiving aid, a trust fund can be an excellent way to provide money for college. There are many different kinds of trusts, but all involve you (called the grantor) transferring assets to another party (called the trustee) to manage and invest on behalf of your child (called the beneficiary). Typically, the trustee is a bank, financial adviser, or a professional organization chosen by you. You can design the trust so that your child will receive the money in a lump sum just as she enters college, or so that it is paid out in installments during college, or so that the child receives only the interest income from the trust until she reaches an age selected by you. Trusts must be set up with care to envision all eventualities because once they are in place, they are almost impossible to change. When you create the trust, you essentially give up the right to control it.

The tax advantage of a trust over a simple custodial account is that the trust pays its own separate income tax, at its own tax bracket. Not the child's bracket. Not yours. This is especially useful when the child is under the age of 14: A regular custodial account of any size would mostly be taxed at the parents' higher rate.

The investment advantage of a trust is that there is no limit on the type of investment instrument that may be used. Unlike custodial accounts, which are not allowed to invest in certain types of instruments, a trust can dabble in real estate, junk bonds, or any new-fangled scheme the investment bankers can invent.

Obviously, trusts must be set up with care, and you have to find a suitable trustee; someone you can, well, trust. Parents should never try to set up a trust on their own. If you are considering this strategy, consult a good tax attorney.

Financial Aid and Trusts

For various reasons, financial aid and trusts do not mix. It is partly the "rich kid" image that trust funds engender in the FAOs, and partly certain intricacies of the financial aid formulas, which we will describe in more detail in chapter 3 of this book. A trust of any size may very well nix any chance your family has of receiving aid.

Prepayment Plans

In the past few years, colleges, states, banks, and brokerage houses have begun to offer plans under which you can prepay your child's tuition. These come in two varieties. In the first variety, you pay the college four years of tuition in a lump sum just before your child starts college. This does not involve any long-term planning, so we will discuss it in the chapter "Innovative Payment Options."

The second variety lets you prepay the costs of tuition (though usually not room and board) years before your child is ready to enter college, either in a lump sum or in installments. Again, you get to lock in the price of tuition, but there are some problems associated with this type of plan.

Most of these problems can be summed up by asking yourself a question:

Would you put a down payment on a 2005 Ford Taurus right now?

Of course not. First of all, Ford might not even be around by then. The '05 Taurus might be a lousy car, and even if it weren't, you still might prefer a Chevy. When you put down money toward a particular college, or even toward an education in a particular state, you are making a commitment that you may not want, or even be able, to keep. The college might be out of business; you might have moved to another state (thus losing the advantages of in-state rates); your child might not be able to get in; your child might want to go somewhere else.

In many cases, if your child does not attend the school, you get back just the principal and perhaps a small amount of the interest that has accrued. The question of whether the IRS will tax this interest is still up in the air. Before you choose this option, consider these questions, and check out what kind of interest rate the plan offers. It might be that you can do well enough investing on your own to exceed the difference between the cost of tuition now and the cost of tuition then.

A Supplementary Form of College Fund: Owning Your Own Home

If you can swing it, owning your own home is a top priority in any plan for paying for college. Equally important, building equity in your home provides you with collateral you can use to help pay for college.

In addition, owning your home provides you with an investment for your own future, which you should never lose sight of. The real estate market may still be somewhat depressed right now, but in five years or ten years many experts predict it will be doing quite nicely. Also, when the kids rush off to embark on their own lives, clutching their diplomas, will there be something left for you? What good is a college education for the child if it puts the parents in the poorhouse?

The Home as a Credit Line?

No matter how well prepared, almost every family ends up at some point having to borrow money to pay part of the family contribution. Unfortunately, the financial aid formula doesn't recognize most types of debt; that is to say they do not subtract these liabilities from your assets before they decide how much in assets you have available to pay for college.

We will be explaining this in great detail in the chapters on financial aid strategies, but here's a quick example. Suppose you had $25,000 in assets, but you also owed $6,000 on a consumer loan. If you asked any accountant in the world, she would say your total net assets were only $19,000; but as far as the colleges are concerned, you still have $25,000 available for them to assess. Many kinds of debt (such as consumer loans and outstanding credit card bills) don't make sense during the college years.

However, the more selective colleges that elect to use the institutional methodology (which looks at home equity) rather than the federal methodology (which does not) do recognize one kind of debt—mortgages, first and second, on your home. This means that your home can be a particularly valuable kind of college fund. Generally, the more equity you have in your home, the more you can borrow against it. And the best part is that if your child attends a school that assesses home equity, and you borrow against your home, you reduce your total assets in the eyes of the FAOs, which can reduce how much you have to pay for college.

Remember to Invest in Other Things Besides Your Child's College Education

Providing a college education for your child is probably not the only ambition you have in life. During the years you are saving for college you should not neglect your other goals, particularly in two important areas: owning your own home (which we have just spoken about) and planning for your retirement.

While the colleges assess your assets and income, they generally don't assess retirement provisions such as Individual Retirement Accounts (IRAs), 401(k) plans, Keoghs, etc. Any money you have managed to contribute to a retirement provision will be off-limits to the FAOs at most schools.

Thus contributions to retirement plans will not only help provide for your future but also will shelter assets (and the income from those assets) from the FAOs. In addition, many employers will match contributions to 401(k) plans, in effect doubling your stake. And let's not forget that, depending on your income level, part or all of these contributions may be tax-deferred.

Now that you have an overview of some long-term investment strategies, let's talk about some specific plans for investing based on how many years away your child is from college.

If You Have 15 Years . . .

Because there is so much time, you can afford to choose aggressive investments of the types we've outlined above. We recommend that you invest about 75% of your fund in these higher-risk investments, and the remaining 25% in investments that lock in a reliable rate of return. There is little point in keeping this money in a bank account because the rate of return will probably not even keep up with inflation. However, as college years get closer, start transferring out of stock funds into something less subject to temporary setbacks.

If possible, try to invest large amounts in the early years to take advantage of compounding. When you get closer to the first year of college, take a hard look at your college fund. You may find that you have already accumulated enough money to pay for school, in which case you can start investing your money in other directions. On the other hand, you may find that you need to increase the amounts you are saving in order to get closer to your goal.

In spite of what you may have heard, as long as you qualify for financial aid it is better to have two kids in school at the same time. If you are planning on having another child, but were putting it off to avoid staggering college bills, reconsider. Whether you have only one child in college, or two or three children in college at the same time, the parents' contribution (the amount colleges think you can afford to pay for college) stays the same. Having two kids in school at the same time is like a two-for-one sale.

With this much time to plan, you should consider long-term ways to increase your earning power. Perhaps you might go back to school to pick up an advanced degree. Perhaps if one parent is not working at present you could begin thinking about a long-term plan for setting up a career for that parent to increase your family's earning power.

As you get closer to the college years, you will need to consider other points. In order not to repeat ourselves too much, we will cover these points below. Please keep on reading.

If You Have Ten Years . . .

With ten years to go, you still have plenty of time to build a sizable college fund. To build your capital quickly, try to save as much as you can in the first several years when compounding will help you the most. Aggressive investments will also help to build your fund quickly. We recommend that with ten years to go, you keep 70% of your money in aggressive investments of the type outlined above. The other 30% can be put into fixed-return investments with limited risk. As you get closer to the first year of college, you should gradually shift your fund into investments with more liquidity and no risk.

Because your child's academic ability will have an important effect not only on which colleges he can apply to but also on what kind of aid package the college will offer you, it is vital that you find a good elementary school that challenges his abilities.

In spite of taxes, braces, and saving for college, do not neglect your own future. If you have not already bought a home, consider buying one (in a good school district) if at all possible. Contributions to retirement provisions should also be made regularly.

Now is also the first time you can realistically speculate about how much money you might be earning by the time your child is in college. If you believe you will be earning too much to qualify for aid, it becomes even more important to build your college fund. If you are not going to qualify for aid, you might want to put assets into the child's name.

As you get closer to the college years, you will need to consider other points. In order not to repeat ourselves too much, we will cover these points below. Please keep on reading.

If You Have Five Years . . .

There is still plenty of time to build up a large college fund. Even if it entails a sacrifice, a large contribution in the first year will help build your investment faster through the miracle of compounding. In the first year or so, you can still afford to invest aggressively, although we recommend that you keep only about 50% of your money in aggressive investments, with 30% in limited-risk fixed rate of return financial instruments, and 20% in liquid accounts that are completely insured.

With about three years to go, reconsider whether you are going to qualify for financial aid. You may have received promotions, raises, inheritances, or made investments that take you out of range of financial aid. In this case, start moving assets into the child's name. On the other hand, you may discover that you are doing less well than you anticipated, in which case you will want to start thinking about the strategies that are outlined in the rest of this book.

Find a great high school for your child and try to encourage good study habits. Good grades will increase your child's options tremendously. It's probably too early to tell, but try to get a sense of what type of school your child will be applying to, and how much that school will cost.

As you get to the last two years before college, you will need to consider other points. In order not to repeat ourselves too much, we will cover these points below. Please keep on reading.

If You Have Two Years . . .

Parents find that with the specter of college tuition looming imminently, they are able to save substantial amounts in only two years. After all, many parents are at the height of their earning power at this time. However, because you will need the money relatively soon, it is probably better to stay away from high-risk investments that may suffer a temporary (or permanent) setback just as you need to write a check.

These two academic years are the most important for your child. Sit down with him and explain (in as unpressured and nonjudgmental a tone as you can manage) that because colleges give preferential packaging to good students, every tenth of a point he adds to his grade point average may save him thousands of dollars in loans he won't have to pay back later.

If your child did not score well on the PSAT, consider finding a good test preparation course for the SAT. Several recent studies have shown that coaching can raise a student's score by over 100 points. Again, every ten points your child raises her score may save your family thousands of dollars—and of course allow her to apply to more selective colleges. We are partial to The Princeton Review SAT course. Over the past ten years, Princeton Review students have had an average improvement of about 150 points.

If you have any interest in running a business on the side, this may be the ideal moment to start setting it up. Most businesses show losses during their first few years of operation. What better time to have losses than during the tax years that affect your aid eligibility? There are also many tax benefits to this strategy, but the business cannot exist just on paper. For tax purposes it will almost certainly have to show a profit in three out of five years in order not to run afoul of the "hobby loss" provisions of the tax code. If this seems like it might be for you, please read our financial aid strategies section, and the section on running your own business in the chapter "Special Topics."

Maneuvering

The most important thing to realize is that at this point, you are one year away from the all-important base income year. Colleges use the tax year *before* college begins (from January 1 of the student's junior year of high school to December 31 of the student's senior year in high school) as their basis for deciding what you can afford to pay during freshman year.

Thus you have one year to maneuver before the base income year begins. Read the financial aid strategies that we outline in the rest of this book extremely carefully. After you have read these chapters and consulted your accountant or financial aid consultant, you may want to move some assets around, take capital gains, take bonuses before the base income year begins, and so on. During the base income year itself, you may want to make some major expenditures, pay down your credit card balances, establish a line of credit on your home, make the maximum contributions possible to retirement provisions.

Many times, parents come to consult us when their child is just about to fill out the need analysis forms in the senior year of high school. There is still a lot we can do to help them qualify for more aid, but we always feel bad for the family because if only they had come to us before the base income year started, there would have been so much more that we could have done.

You are in the fortunate position of having that extra year to maneuver. Read the rest of this book, and enjoy.

CHAPTER THREE

Short-Term Strategies for Receiving More Financial Aid

Financial Aid and Your Income Tax Return—
Joined at the Hip

When you sit down to take your first look at the financial aid form, it may occur to you to wonder why they didn't simply ask for your tax return. The need analysis form has evolved over the years from a subjective, difficult-to-verify set of questions compiled separately by each of the colleges, into a standardized set of questions that in many instances mimics the federal income tax return.

The companies that process the forms say this is "to make the [forms] easier to complete." Of course, it is also done so that the information you supply can be verified. Every figure on your financial aid forms must in the end agree exactly with the information you will supply to the IRS.

In fact, in recent years, it has become almost routine for colleges to request copies of your tax returns. A few schools (Washington University in St. Louis and St. Francis College in Brooklyn, New York spring to mind) go even further, and require you to authorize the IRS to send them a copy of the return you actually filed.

How to Stay in Control of the Process

The instructions for filling out need analysis forms make it seem as if there is a natural order to the financial aid process that must be adhered to: first you do your taxes, *then* you fill out the financial aid forms. However, you should realize that by filling out the forms separately, you have already missed the boat. Once you copy line 31 from your 1996 IRS 1040 federal income tax return (your adjusted gross income) onto the FAFSA, you have already given up much of the control you could have had over the financial aid process.

> By the way, if you use form 1040A, the adjusted gross income is found on line 16; if you use the 1040EZ form, it is on line 4. For simplicity's sake, from now on we will refer just to the 1040 long form and line 31.

Because the financial aid form and your federal taxes are so inextricably linked, your tax planning and your financial aid planning must also be linked.

A "Snapshot" of Your Financial Picture

Each year your son or daughter is in college, the school will ask you to fill out a form reporting the prior year's income and your current assets—in effect a snapshot of your overall financial picture at that moment. You've probably noticed that snapshots can be very misleading. In one picture, you may appear youthful and vibrant. In another, you may look terrible, with a double chin and 20 extra pounds. Perhaps neither photograph is exactly correct. Of course, when you are deciding which picture to put in the scrapbook, the choice is easy: throw away the one you don't like and keep the one you do.

In choosing which financial snapshot to send to the colleges, the object is a little bit different: send them the worst-looking picture you can find.

To be very blunt, the single most effective way to reduce the family contribution is to make line 31 on your 1040 federal income tax return look as small as possible.

Well, This Is Not Revolutionary Advice

After all, you've been trying to do this for years.

We're sure you and your accountant are generally doing a fine job of keeping your taxes to a minimum. However, certain long-term tax strategies that normally make all kinds of sense, can explode in your face during college years. Neither you nor your accountant may fully grasp how important it is to understand the ins and outs of the financial aid formulas.

How College Planning Affects Tax Planning

There are two reasons why tax planning has to change during college years.

First, the FAOs (unlike the IRS) are concerned about only *four years* of your financial life. Using strategies we will be showing you in the next few chapters, you may be able to shift income out of those four years, thus increasing your financial aid.

Second, financial aid formulas *differ* from the IRS formulas in several key ways. Certain long-term tax reduction strategies (shifting income to other family members, for example) can actually *increase* the amount of college tuition you will pay. However, astute parents who understand these differences will find that there are some wonderful, legal, logical alternatives they can explore to change the four snapshots the college will take of their income and assets.

Tax accountants who do not understand the financial aid process (and in our experience, this includes most of them) can actually hurt your chances for financial aid.

The First Base Year Income

Colleges base your ability to pay *this* year's tuition on what you made *last* year. This may seem a bit unfair, but colleges point out that they have no way to verify what you are going to make this year. Thus the first financial aid scrutiny you will undergo will not be directed at the calendar year during which your child will start her freshman year of college, *but the year before*. This year is called the first base income year and is the crucial one.

Aug	Sept	Oct	Nov	Dec	Jan	Feb	Mar	Apr	May	June	July
	High School Junior Year Begins										
Aug	Sept	Oct	Nov	Dec	Jan	Feb	Mar	Apr	May	June	July
	High School Senior Year Begins			Application Deadline	Financial Aid Deadlines						
Aug	Sept	Oct	Nov	Dec	Jan	Feb	Mar	Apr	May	June	July
	College Begins										

The base income year (shaded in the diagram above) extends from January 1 of your child's junior year in high school to December 31 of your child's senior year in high school. This is when first impressions are formed. The college will get an idea of how much you are likely to be able to afford, not just for the first year of school, but for the remaining years as well. First impressions are likely to endure and are often very difficult to change.

Thus it would be helpful to remove as much income as possible from this calendar year.

I'm About to Get a Raise. Should I Say No?

It's easy to get carried away with the concept of reducing income, and it may appear at first that you would be better off turning down a raise. However, the short answer to this question is,

"Are you crazy?"

More money is always good. Our discussion here is limited to minimizing the *appearance* of more money. Let's say you get a raise of $3,000 per year. This will certainly reduce your eligibility for college aid, but will it negate the entire effect of the raise? Not likely. Let's say you're in the 28% federal tax bracket, your raise is still subject to social security taxes of 7.65%, and your income is being assessed at the maximum rate possible under the aid formulas. Looking at the chart below, you'll see that even after taxes and reduced aid eligibility are taken into account, you will still be $1,136 ahead, though state and local taxes might reduce this somewhat.

raise of $3,000

minus

federal tax $840

FICA $230

reduced aid $794

what you keep: $1,136

My Wife Works. Should She Quit?

The same principle applies here. More money is good. Not only are you getting the advantage of extra income but also under the financial aid formula, for a two-parent family with both parents working, 35% of the first $7,714 the spouse with the lower income earns is deducted as an "employment allowance." Even if this increased income decreases your aid eligibility, you will still be ahead on the income. In addition, you will be creating the impression of a family with a work ethic, which can be very helpful in negotiating with FAOs later. FAOs work for their living, and probably earn less than you do. They are more likely to give additional aid to families who have demonstrated their willingness to make sacrifices.

Income vs. Assets

Some parents get confused by the differences between what is considered income and what are considered assets. Assets are the money, property, and other financial instruments you've been able to accumulate over time. Income, on the other hand, is the money you actually earned or otherwise received during the past year, including interest and dividends from your assets.

The IRS never asks you to report your assets on your 1040—only the income you received from these assets. Colleges, on the other hand, are very interested in your income *and* your assets. Later in this chapter, there will be an entire section devoted to strategies for reducing *the appearance* of your assets. For now, let's focus on income.

The colleges decided long ago that income should be assessed much more heavily than assets. The intention is that when a family is finished paying for college, there should be something left in the bank. (Don't start feeling grateful just yet. This works only as long as the colleges meet a family's need in full.)

INCOME

For financial aid purposes, the colleges will be looking at taxable income (including income earned from work, interest, dividends, alimony, unemployment benefits, etc.) and untaxable income (including child support, tax-free interest, deferred compensation such as a contribution to a 401(k) plan, etc.).

When considering their chances for financial aid, many families believe that the colleges are interested only in how much income you make from work. If this were the case, the colleges would just be able to look at your W-2 form to see if you qualified for aid. Unfortunately, life is not so simple. The college's complicated formulas make the IRS tax code look like child's play.

Before we begin discussing the components of taxable income, it is important to understand that even the decision as to which tax form to file (1040 long form vs. the 1040EZ or the 1040A) can have a significant impact on your eligibility for financial aid.

Form **1040**

Department of the Treasury—Internal Revenue Service

U.S. Individual Income Tax Return **1996**

IRS Use Only—Do not write or staple in this space.

For the year Jan. 1–Dec. 31, 1996, or other tax year beginning _____ 1996, ending _____ , 19 ___ | OMB No. 1545-0074

Label
(See instructions.)

Use the IRS label. Otherwise, please print or type.

L A B E L   H E R E

Your first name and initial | Last name | Your social security number

If a joint return, spouse's first name and initial | Last name | Spouse's social security number

Home address (number and street). If you have a P.O. box, see page 11. | Apt. no.

City, town or post office, state, and ZIP code. If you have a foreign address, see page 11.

For help finding line instructions, see pages 2 and 3 in the booklet.

Presidential Election Campaign (See page 11.)

Do you want $3 to go to this fund? . . . .
If a joint return, does your spouse want $3 to go to this fund? . . . .

Yes | No | **Note:** *Checking "Yes" will not change your tax or reduce your refund.*

Filing Status

Check only one box.

1 ☐ Single
2 ☐ Married filing joint return (even if only one had income)
3 ☐ Married filing separate return. Enter spouse's social security no. above and full name here. ▶
4 ☐ Head of household (with qualifying person). (See instructions.) If the qualifying person is a child but not your dependent, enter this child's name here. ▶ _____
5 ☐ Qualifying widow(er) with dependent child (year spouse died ▶ 19 ___). (See instructions.)

Exemptions

If more than six dependents, see the line 6c instructions.

6a ☐ **Yourself.** If your parent (or someone else) can claim you as a dependent on his or her tax return, **do not** check box 6a . . . .
b ☐ **Spouse** . . . .
c Dependents:

(1) First name Last name	(2) Dependent's social security number. If born in Dec. 1996, see inst.	(3) Dependent's relationship to you	(4) No. of months lived in your home in 1996

d Total number of exemptions claimed . . . .

No. of boxes checked on lines 6a and 6b ____
No. of your children on line 6c who:
• lived with you ____
• didn't live with you due to divorce or separation (see instructions) ____
Dependents on 6c not entered above ____
Add numbers entered on lines above ▶ ☐

Income

Attach Copy B of your Forms W-2, W-2G, and 1099-R here.

If you did not get a W-2, see the line 7 instructions.

Please send any payment separately with **Form 1040-V.** See the line 62a instructions.

7 Wages, salaries, tips, etc. Attach Form(s) W-2 . . . . | 7
8a **Taxable** interest. Attach Schedule B if over $400 . . . . . . | 8a
b **Tax-exempt** interest. DON'T include on line 8a . . . | 8b |
9 Dividend income. Attach Schedule B if over $400 . . . . . . | 9
10 Taxable refunds, credits, or offsets of state and local income taxes (see instructions) | 10
11 Alimony received . . . . | 11
12 Business income or (loss). Attach Schedule C or C-EZ . . . . | 12
13 Capital gain or (loss). If required, attach Schedule D . . . . | 13
14 Other gains or (losses). Attach Form 4797 . . . . | 14
15a Total IRA distributions . | 15a | b Taxable amount (see inst.) | 15b
16a Total pensions and annuities | 16a | b Taxable amount (see inst.) | 16b
17 Rental real estate, royalties, partnerships, S corporations, trusts, etc. Attach Schedule E | 17
18 Farm income or (loss). Attach Schedule F . . . . | 18
19 Unemployment compensation . . . . | 19
20a Social security benefits | 20a | b Taxable amount (see inst.) | 20b
21 Other income. List type and amount—see instructions _____ | 21
22 Add the amounts in the far right column for lines 7 through 21. This is your **total income** ▶ | 22

Adjusted Gross Income

If line 31 is under $28,495 (under $9,500 if a child didn't live with you), see the line 54 instructions.

23a Your IRA deduction (see instructions) . . . . . | 23a
b Spouse's IRA deduction (see instructions) . . . . | 23b
24 Moving expenses. Attach Form 3903 or 3903-F . . . | 24
25 One-half of self-employment tax. Attach Schedule SE | 25
26 Self-employed health insurance deduction (see inst.) . | 26
27 Keogh & self-employed SEP plans. If SEP, check ▶ ☐ | 27
28 Penalty on early withdrawal of savings . . . . . . | 28
29 Alimony paid. Recipient's SSN ▶ _____ | 29
30 Add lines 23a through 29 . . . . | 30
31 Subtract line 30 from line 22. This is your **adjusted gross income** . . . . ▶ | 31

The above form is a draft version of the 1996 IRS 1040. It is for information purposes only. Do not send in.

Not All Tax Returns Are Created Equal

By filing one of the short forms, and meeting certain other requirements, you may be able to have all of your assets excluded from the federal financial aid formulas, which could qualify you for increased federal aid. This is a brand-new middle class financial aid loophole known as the "Simplified Needs Test." Here's the way it works: If the parents have adjusted gross income below $50,000, and everyone in your family who must file a tax return uses the 1040EZ or the 1040A form (or doesn't file at all) then all your family's assets will be excluded from the federal financial aid formulas. This means that eligibility for the Pell Grant and the subsidized Stafford loans will be determined without regard to how much money you have in the bank or your brokerage accounts.

It can also be vital to parents with large assets, but little real earned income. You can have $49,999 of *interest* income, and still possibly meet the simplified needs test—in which case even assets of several million dollars will not be used in calculating your EFC.

This can be particularly vital to parents with income below $35,000 but who have significant assets because they now may be able to qualify for the Pell Grant, which is free money that does not have to be paid back.

Of course, many colleges use the institutional methodology (which does not utilize the simplified needs test) in awarding their *own* grant money. They may also insist that assets be used to determine eligibility for certain federally funded campus-based aid programs—such as the SEOG grant, Perkins loan, and work-study.

However, if you meet the simplified needs test, they cannot use the family assets in determining eligibility for the Pell Grant and subsidized Stafford loans. If you aren't sure if you can use the short tax forms, consult the IRS instructions to the forms, or your tax preparer. A few examples of people who can't use the short form: a self-employed individual, a partner in a partnership, a shareholder in an S corporation, a beneficiary of an estate or trust. In addition, if you had rental or royalty income and expenses, had farm income and expenses, took capital gains or losses, or itemized deductions, you will have to file the long form.

However, for some taxpayers who could itemize deductions, but won't save much money by doing so, it may still make sense to file the short form. You'll pay slightly higher taxes, but this may be more than offset by a larger aid package. Since this strategy requires a trade-off between tax benefits and aid benefits, we recommend you consult a competent advisor.

Unfortunately, even if you fit the simplified needs test, your accountant may unwittingly blow this lovely loophole for you by insisting on filing the wrong form.

Not All Accountants Are Created Equal

Many accountants are not aware of the new laws and will try to talk you into using the 1040—simply because that is the only form their computer programs will print out. If you meet the simplified needs test, be prepared to insist that your tax preparer use the 1040EZ or the 1040A forms. It might not even be a bad idea to take this book along with you when you go for your annual appointment with your tax preparer. We have heard of some accountants who tell their clients that if they file the 1040 without itemizing deductions, it is the same as using the short forms. Unfortunately, for financial aid purposes, this is not necessarily true. The federal rules state that you can qualify for the Simplified Needs Test even if you file a 1040, provided you were eligible to file a 1040A or 1040EZ and you meet the income guidelines. However, a representative at the U.S. Department of Education said that this is a "murky area" and that guidelines are still being developed to advise FAOs on how to determine if a family that filed a 1040 was eligible to file a 1040A or 1040EZ. Since you may have to do a lot of explaining and go through a lot of red tape to convince the FAO (who is not a CPA) that you could have done the short forms (and you may not be successful), we recommend that you use the 1040A or 1040EZ if you are eligible to do so. For your benefit, we have listed the headings of the different returns for 1996 so you can identify which are the short forms and which is the long form.

The long form (1040):

1040 Department of the Treasury—Internal Revenue Service
U.S. Individual Income Tax Return   **1996** | IRS Use Only—Do not write or staple in this space.

The short forms (1040A and 1040EZ):

Form
1040A   Department of the Treasury—Internal Revenue Service
U.S. Individual Income Tax Return   **1996**   IRS Use Only—Do not write or staple in this space.

Department of the Treasury—Internal Revenue Service
Form
1040EZ   **Income Tax Return for Single and Joint Filers With No Dependents**   **1996**

The Automatic Zero-EFC

The federal government has a great break for parents who
- have 1996 combined adjusted gross income of $12,000 or less
- and can file the 1040A or the 1040EZ tax form, or are not required to file a tax form at all

Even if your child has substantial assets or income, your family EFC will be judged to be zero if you meet these requirements.

Some accountants encourage retired, disabled, unemployed, or low-income parents to file the long form—which would prevent taking advantage of this break. Many of these parents could file the short form or may not be required to file at all.

> *Tip #1: There may be some financial aid advantages to filling out the short forms (the 1040A or the 1040EZ) or not filing at all, if the IRS permits you to do so.*

A Parents' Step-by-Step Guide to the Federal Income Tax Form

By reducing your total income (lines 7–21 on the 1040) you can increase your financial aid, which, you should remember, is largely funded by your tax dollars anyway. Let's examine how various items on your tax return can be adjusted to influence your aid eligibility. The IRS line numbers below refer to the 1996 IRS 1040.

LINE 7—WAGES, SALARIES, TIPS, ETC.
For most parents, there is not much to be done about line 7. Your employers will send you W-2 forms, and you simply report this income. However, there are a few points to be made.

Defer Your Bonus

If you are one of the thousands of Americans in the workplace who receive a bonus, you might discuss with your boss the possibility of moving your bonus into a non–base income year. For example:

If your child is in the beginning of her junior year of high school (in other words, if the first base income year has not yet begun) and you are due a year-end bonus, make sure that you collect and deposit the bonus *before* January 1 of the new year (when the base income year begins). As long as the bonus is included on your W-2 for the previous year, it will not be considered income on your aid application.

The money will still appear as part of your *assets* (provided you haven't already spent it). But by shifting the bonus into a non–base income year, you will avoid having the colleges count your bonus twice—as both asset and income.

If you are due a year-end bonus and your child is starting his senior year of high school, see if you can arrange to get the bonus held off until *after* January 1. Yes, it will show up on next year's financial aid form, but meantime you've had the benefit of financial aid for this year.

Just as important, FAOs make four-year projections based on your first base income year. Your FAO will have set aside money for you for the next three years based on the aid your child receives as a freshman in college. Who knows what might happen next year? You might need that money. If the FAO hasn't already set it aside for you, it might not be there when you need it.

> Tip #2: *Move your bonus into a non–base income year.*

If You've Had an Unusually Good Year

Maybe you won a retroactive pay increase. Or perhaps you just worked a lot of overtime. If you can arrange to receive payment during a non–base income year that would, of course, be better, but there are sometimes compelling reasons for taking the money when it is offered (for example, you are afraid you might not get it later).

However, unless you explain the details of this windfall to the colleges, they will be under the impression that this sort of thing happens to you all the time.

If this year's income is really not representative, write to the financial aid office of each of the colleges your child is applying to, and explain that this was a once-in-a-lifetime payment, never to be repeated. Include a copy of your tax return from the year *before* the base income year, which more closely reflects your true average income.

Don't bother sending documentation like this to the companies that process the standardized analysis forms. They are only interested in crunching the numbers on the form, and anyway have no power to make decisions about your aid at specific schools. Documentation should never be sent to the processing companies. Send it directly to the schools.

> Tip #3: *If you've had an unusually good year, explain to the colleges that your average salary is much lower.*

Become an Independent Contractor

If you are a full-time employee receiving a W-2 form at the end of the year and you have significant unreimbursed business expenses, you might discuss with your employer the viability of becoming an independent contractor. The advantage to this is that you can file your income under schedule C of the tax form ("profit or loss from business"), enabling you to deduct huge amounts of business-related expenses *before* line 31, where it will do you some good.

A regular salaried employee is allowed to take an itemized tax deduction for unreimbursed employee expenses (in excess of 2% of the AGI). Unfortunately, because this deduction comes *after* line 31, it will have no effect on reducing income under the financial aid formula.

An independent contractor, on the other hand, can deduct telephone bills, business use of the home, dues, business travel, and entertainment—basically anything that falls under the cost of doing business—and thus lower the adjusted gross income.

You would have to consult with your accountant to see if the disadvantages (increased likelihood of an IRS audit, difficulties in rearranging health insurance and pension plans, possible loss of unemployment benefits, increased social security tax, etc.) outweigh the advantages. In addition, the IRS has recently begun to crack down on employers who classify their workers as independent contractors when they are really salaried employees. Like all fuzzy areas of the tax law, this represents an opportunity to be exploited, but requires careful planning.

> *Tip #4a: If you have significant unreimbursed employee expenses, try to become an independent contractor so that you can deduct expenses on schedule C of the 1040.*

Even better, you might suggest to your boss that she cut your pay. No, we haven't gone insane. By convincing your employer to reduce your pay by the amount of your business expenses, and then having her reimburse you directly for those expenses, you should end up with the same amount of money in your pocket, but you'll show a lower AGI and therefore increase your aid eligibility.

> *Tip #4b: If you have significant unreimbursed employee expenses, try to get your employer to reimburse these business expenses directly to you—even if it means taking a corresponding cut in pay.*

If your employer won't let you pursue either of these options, you should be sure to explain your unreimbursed employee expenses in a separate letter to the FAOs.

LINES 8A AND 9—TAXABLE INTEREST AND DIVIDEND INCOME

If you have interest or dividend income, you have assets. Nothing prompts a "validation" (financial aid jargon for an audit) faster than listing interest and dividend income without listing the assets it came from.

For the most part, there is little you can do, or would want to do, to reduce this income, though we will have a lot to say in later chapters about reducing *the appearance* of your assets.

Some parents have suggested taking all their assets and hiding them in a mattress or dumping them into a checking account that doesn't earn interest. The first option is illegal and dumb. The second is just dumb. In both cases, this would be a bit like turning down a raise. More interest is *good*. The FAOs won't take all of it, and you will need it if you want to have any chance of staying even with inflation.

The one type of interest income you might want to control comes from Series E and EE U.S. Savings Bonds. When you buy a U.S. Savings Bond, you don't pay the face value of the bond; you buy it for much less. When the bond matures (in five years, ten years, or whatever) it is then worth the face value of the bond. The money you receive from the bond in excess of what you paid for it is called interest. With Series E and EE Savings Bonds, you have two tax options: you can report the interest on the bond as it is earned each year on that year's tax return, or you can report all the interest in one lump sum the year you cash in the bond.

By taking the second option, you can in effect hold savings bonds for years without paying any tax on the interest, because you haven't cashed them in yet. However, when you finally do cash them in, you suddenly have to report all the interest earned over the years to the IRS. If the year that you report that interest happens to be a base income year, all of the interest will have to be reported on the aid forms as well. This will almost certainly raise your EFC.

The only exception to this might be Series EE bonds bought after 1989. The U.S. government decided to give parents who pay for their children's college education a tax break: low- or middle-income parents who bought Series EE bonds after 1989 with the intention of using the bonds to help pay for college may not have to pay any tax on the interest income at all. The interest earned is completely tax free for a single parent making up to $43,500 or a married couple earning up to $65,250. Once you hit these income levels, the benefits are slowly phased out. A single parent earning above $58,500 or a married couple earning above $95,250 becomes ineligible for any tax break. All of these numbers are based on 1996 tax rates and are subject to an annual adjustment for inflation.

However, we still recommend that parents who bought these bonds with the intention of paying for college cash them in *after* the end of the last base income year (after January 1 of the student's junior year in college). Whether the interest from these bonds is taxed or untaxed, the FAOs still consider it income and assess it just as harshly as your wages.

Thus if at all possible, try to avoid cashing in any and all U.S. Savings Bonds during any base income year. With Series E or EE bonds, you may be able to roll over your money into Series H or HH bonds and defer reporting interest until the college years are over. There is also no law that says you have to cash in a savings bond when it matures. You can continue to hold the bond, and in some instances it will continue to earn interest *above* its face value.

> *Tip #5: If possible, avoid cashing in U.S. Savings Bonds during a base income year, unless you've been paying taxes on the interest each year, as it accrued.*

If You Have Put Assets in Your Other Children's Names

Parents are often told by accountants to transfer their assets into their children's name so that the assets will be taxed at the children's lower rate. While this is a good tax reduction strategy, it stinks as a financial aid strategy, as you will find out later in this chapter. However, if this is your situation and you have *already* put assets under the student's *younger siblings'* names, there is one small silver lining in this cloud: The tax laws give parents with children under 14 the option of reporting their child's interest income on a separate tax return or on the parents' own tax return.

Either way, the family enjoys the reduced tax benefits of the child's lower bracket. The principal advantage of reporting the child's income on the parents' return is to save the expense of paying an accountant to do a separate return.

However, if you are completing your tax returns for a base income year, we recommend that you do not report any of the student's siblings' interest on your tax return. By filing a separate return for those under-14 children, you remove that income from your AGI, and lower your Expected Family Contribution.

> *Tip #6: During base income years, do not report younger children's interest income on the parents' tax return. File a separate return for each child.*

Leveraged Investments

An important way in which the financial aid formulas differ from the tax code is in the handling of the income from leveraged investments. You leverage your investments by borrowing against them. The most common example of leverage is margin debt. Margin is a loan against the value of your investment portfolio usually made by a brokerage house so that you can buy more of whatever it is selling—for example, stock.

Let's say you had $5,000 in interest and dividend income, but you also had to pay $2,000 in tax-deductible investment interest on a margin loan. The IRS lets you deduct your investment interest expenses from your investment income on schedule A. For *tax* purposes, you have only $3,000 in net investment income.

Unfortunately, for *financial aid* purposes, interest expenses from schedule A are not taken into account. As far as the colleges are concerned, you had $5,000 in income.

Of course you will be able to subtract the value of your margin debt from the value of your *total assets*. However, under the aid formulas, you cannot deduct the *interest* on your margin debt from your investment *income*.

During base income years, you should avoid—or at least minimize—margin debt because it will inflate your income in the eyes of the FAOs. If there is no way to avoid leveraging your investments during the college years, you should at least call the FAO's attention to the tax-deductible investment interest you are paying. Be prepared to be surprised at how financially unsavvy your FAO may turn out to be. He may not understand the concept of margin debt at all, in which case you will have to educate him. In our experience, we have found that if the situation is explained, many FAOs will make some allowance for a tax-deductible investment interest expense.

> *Tip #7: During base income years, avoid large amounts of margin debt.*

LINE 10—TAXABLE REFUND OF STATE AND LOCAL INCOME TAXES

Many people see their tax refunds as a kind of Christmas club—a way to save some money that they would otherwise spend—so they arrange to have far too much deducted from their paychecks. Any accountant knows that this is actually incredibly dumb. In effect, you are giving the government the use of your money, interest-free. If you were to put this money aside during the year in an account that earned interest, you could make yourself a substantial piece of change.

So Why Does Your Accountant Encourage a Refund?

Even so, many accountants go along with the practice for a couple of reasons. First, they know that their clients are unlikely to go to the bother of setting up an automatic payroll savings plan at work. Second, they know that clients feel infinitely better when they walk out of their accountant's office with money in their pockets. It tends to offset the large fee the accountant has just charged for his or her services. Third, a large refund doesn't affect how much tax you ultimately pay. Whether you have your company withhold just the right amount, or way too much, over the years you still end up paying exactly the same amount in taxes.

So accountants have gotten used to the practice, and yours probably won't tell you (or maybe doesn't know) that a large refund is the very last thing you want during base income years. Unfortunately, a large refund can seriously undermine your efforts to get financial aid. Here's why:

If you itemize deductions and get a refund from state and local taxes, the following year you'll have to report the refund as part of your federal adjusted gross income. Over the years, of course, this will have little or no effect on how much you pay in taxes, but for aid purposes, you've just raised your line 31. This might not seem like it could make a big difference, but if you collect an average state and local refund of $1,600 each year over the four college years, you may have cost yourself as much as $3,000 in grant money.

During college years, it is very important to keep your withholding as close as possible to the amount you will actually owe in taxes at the end of the year.

> *Tip #8: If you itemize your deductions, avoid large state and local tax refunds.*

LINE 11—ALIMONY RECEIVED

Even though this may seem like an obvious point, we have found it important to remind people that the amount you enter on this line is not what you were *supposed* to receive in alimony, but the amount you actually got. Please don't list alimony payments your ex never made.

In fact, if your ex fell behind in alimony payments, it's important that you notify the college financial aid offices that you have received less income this year than a court of law thought you needed in order to make ends meet.

By the same token, if you received retroactive alimony payments, you would also want to contact the colleges to let them know that the amount you listed on this line is larger this year than the amount you normally receive. In a situation like this, you might be tempted to put down on the financial aid form only the amount of alimony you were supposed to receive. Please don't even think about it. Your need analysis information will be checked against your tax return. By the time they've finished their audit, and you've finished explaining that this was a retroactive payment, all the college's aid money might be gone.

LINE 12—BUSINESS INCOME

As we mentioned earlier, it can be to your advantage to become an independent contractor if you have large unreimbursed business expenses. A self-employed person is allowed to deduct business expenses from gross receipts on schedule C. This now much smaller number (called net profit or loss) is written down on line 12 of the 1040 form, thus reducing both taxable income and the family contribution to college tuition.

We will discuss running your own business in greater detail in the "Special Topics" chapter of this book; however, a few general points should be made now.

Many salaried people run their own businesses on the side, which enables them to earn extra money while deducting a good part of this income as business expenses. However, before you run out and decide that your stamp collecting hobby has suddenly become a business, you should be aware that the IRS auditors are old hands at spotting "dummy" businesses, and the colleges' FAOs aren't far behind.

On the other hand, if you have been planning to start a legitimate business, then by all means, the time to do it is NOW.

> *Tip #9: Setting up a legitimate business on the side will enable you to deduct legitimate business expenses, and may reduce your AGI.*

Just bear in mind that a business must make a profit three out of five years to avoid running afoul of the IRS "hobby loss" provision. Many private colleges do not recognize business losses, while many other schools add back business depreciation to your AGI.

LINES 13 AND 14—CAPITAL GAINS OR LOSSES, OTHER GAINS OR LOSSES

When you buy a stock, bond, or any other financial instrument at one price and then sell it for more than you paid in the first place, the difference between the two prices is considered a capital gain. If you sold it for less than you paid in the first place, the difference may be considered a capital loss. We say "may be" because while you are required to report *gains* on all transactions, the IRS does not necessarily recognize *losses* on all types of investments.

When you sell an asset, your net worth really stays the same; you are merely converting the asset into the cash it's worth at that particular instant. However, for tax and financial aid purposes, a capital gain on the asset is considered additional *income* in the year that you sold your asset.

During base income years, you want to avoid capital gains if you can because they inflate your income. When you sell a stock, not only does the FAO assess the cash value from the sale of the stock (which is considered an asset) but she also assesses the capital gain (which is considered income).

If you need cash it is usually better to borrow against your assets rather than to sell them. Using your stock, or the equity in your house as collateral, you can take out a loan. This helps you in three ways: you don't have to report any capital gains on the financial aid form; your net assets are reduced in the eyes of the FAO since you now have a debt against that asset; and in some cases, you get a tax deduction for part of the interest on the loan.

> *Tip #10: If possible, avoid large capital gains during base income years.*

However, there may be times when it is necessary to take capital gains. Below you will find some strategies to avoid losing aid because of capital gains. The following are somewhat aggressive strategies, and each would require you to consult your accountant and/or stockbroker:

- If you have to take capital gains, at least try to offset them with losses. Examine your portfolio. If you have been carrying a stock that's been a loser for several years, it might be time to admit that it is never going to be worth what you paid for it, and take the loss. This will help to cancel your gain.

- You can elect to spread your stock losses and gains over several years. One example: The IRS allows you to deduct capital losses directly from capital gains. If your losses exceed your gains, you can deduct up to $3,000 of the excess from other income—in the year the loss occurred. However, net losses over $3,000 *are carried over to future years.* It might be possible to show net losses during several of the base income years, and hold off on taking net gains until after your kids are done with college.

- Many private colleges do not recognize capital losses that exceed gains. However, certain kinds of government aid are awarded without reference to the schools—for example, the Pell grant and some state-funded aid programs. Because this aid is awarded strictly by the numbers, a capital loss can make a big difference. (Consult your state aid authorities, and the individual schools to see how capital losses will be treated.)

- If you are worried about falling stock prices but don't want to report a capital gain, you should consult your stockbroker. There may be ways to lock in a particular price *without* selling the stock.

- If you sell your primary residence, under current law you are allowed to defer your capital gains ad infinitum, so long as you buy another property of equal or greater value and occupy it within 24 months.

Sellers who aren't sure whether they're going to buy another house still get 24 months to make up their mind. Even if you have no intention of buying another house, you might try to time the sale of your current residence so that the capital gain is deferred into a non–base income year. If you don't buy another residence within the 24-month period, you will have to pay interest on the tax you owe. However, there are no penalties, and the interest *may* be more than offset by your increased aid eligibility. You would have to consult with a professional to see if this makes sense for you.

- If you sell your primary residence, and you are over age 55, you may qualify for a one-time exclusion of up to $125,000 in capital gains on the sale of the house.

- As always, if you are forced to take an atypically large capital gain in a base income year, you should write to the colleges explaining that your income is not normally so high. This is particularly true if the gain came from the sale of the primary residence (or your second home), because the FAOs understand that you won't be selling your house every year.

- Above all, try to avoid gains in the *first* base income year. Nothing can be more expensive than giving your FAO the erroneous first impression that you are some kind of Wall Street wizard.

Line 15—IRA Distributions

Early withdrawal of IRAs (called "distributions" by the IRS) should be avoided at all costs. In most cases, when you withdraw money from an IRA before you reach the age of $59\frac{1}{2}$, you pay taxes on the entire amount that you withdrew, *and* you pay a 10% penalty to the IRS, *and* (because your AGI is higher) you lose aid eligibility. After you subtract the penalties, increased taxes, and lost aid, a family in the 28% tax bracket who uses an IRA to pay for college will net about 32 cents on the dollar.

It would be better to borrow from any source, even at high rates. As soon as you are out of the base income years, *then* take the IRA distribution and pay off the loan. If you are still under $59\frac{1}{2}$, you'll have to pay the penalty for an early withdrawal; much better to do it after the college years, when the extra income won't affect your aid eligibility.

A legitimate rollover of an IRA (when you move your money from one type of IRA investment into another within 60 days) is not considered an early withdrawal. You do have to report a rollover to the IRS on the 1040 form, but it is not subject to penalties (so long as you stick to the IRS guidelines) nor is it considered income for financial aid purposes.

Tip #11: Try to avoid IRA distributions during base income years.

Parents sometimes ask whether it is possible to borrow against the money in their IRAs. You are not allowed to borrow against the assets you have in an IRA. The IRS calls this a "prohibited transaction."

If You've Just Retired

As people wait until later in life to have children, it is becoming more commonplace to see retirees with children still in college. If you have recently retired and are being forced to take IRA distributions, we suggest that you pull out the minimum amount possible. The government computes what this minimum amount should be based on your life expectancy (the longer you're expected to live, the longer they are willing to spread out the payments). Because it turns out that the average American's life expectancy is higher at 66 than it is at 65, it pays to get them to recalculate your minimum distribution for each year your child is in college. Obviously, if you need the money now, then you should take it, but try to withdraw as little as possible, since IRA distributions increase your AGI and thus reduce financial aid.

LINE 16—PENSION DISTRIBUTIONS
The same is true of pension distributions. Sometimes it is possible to postpone retirement pensions or roll them over into an IRA. If you can afford to wait until your child is through college, you will increase your aid eligibility. The money isn't going anywhere, and it's earning interest.

LINE 17—RENTS, ROYALTIES, ESTATES, PARTNERSHIPS, TRUSTS, AND LINE 18—FARM INCOME
Like schedule C income, items coming under these categories are computed by adding up your gross receipts and then subtracting expenses, repairs, and depreciation. Be especially thorough about listing all expenses during base income years.

If you have a summer house or other property, you may have been frustrated in the past, because costly as it is to operate a second home, you haven't been able to deduct any of these expenses. You could consider renting it out while your son or daughter is in college. The extra income might be offset (perhaps significantly) by the expenses that you'll now be legitimately able to subtract from it. By changing how interest expense and real estate taxes are reflected on your tax return (from an itemized deduction on schedule A to a reduction of rental income on line 17) you reduce the magical AGI. There are special tax considerations for "passive loss" activities and recapture of depreciation, so be sure to consult your adviser before proceeding with this strategy, and remember that many private colleges and a few state schools will not recognize losses of this type when awarding institutional funds.

LINE 19—UNEMPLOYMENT COMPENSATION

If you are unemployed, benefits paid during the base income year are considered taxable income under the aid formula. However, some special consideration may be granted to you. We will discuss this in more detail under the "Recently Unemployed Worker" heading in chapter 9.

LINES 20A AND B—SOCIAL SECURITY BENEFITS

Total social security benefits are listed on line 20a. The taxable portion of those benefits is listed on line 20b. Whether you have to pay tax on social security benefits depends on your circumstances. Consult the instructions that come with your tax return. For some parents who have other income, part of the social security benefits received may be taxable.

LINE 21—OTHER INCOME

Any miscellaneous income that did not fit into any of the other lines, goes here. Some examples: money received from jury duty or from proctoring SAT exams, extra insurance premiums paid by your employer, gambling winnings.

Gambling winnings present their own problem. The IRS allows you to deduct gambling losses against winnings. However the deduction can, once again, only be taken as part of your itemized deductions on schedule A. Since this happens *after* line 31, it is not a deduction as far as the need analysis computer is concerned.

Since gambling losses are not likely to provoke much sympathy in the FAOs, we don't think there would be any point to writing them a letter about this one. During the college years, you might just want to curtail gambling.

This is the last type of taxable income on the 1040, but don't start jumping for joy yet. The colleges are interested in more than just your taxable income.

Untaxed Income

We've just looked at all the types of income that the IRS taxes, and discussed how the financial aid process impacts on it. There are several other types of income that the IRS doesn't bother to tax. Unfortunately, the colleges do not feel so benevolent. While the IRS allows you to shelter certain types of income, the colleges will assess this income as well in deciding whether and how much financial aid you receive.

Here are the other types of income the need analysis forms will ask you to report, and some strategies.

Untaxed Social Security Benefits

Any social security benefits that are not taxable are considered untaxable income. The colleges will want their piece of this money as well. Be sure not to double-count when you fill out the need analysis forms. We'll discuss this in greater detail in part three, "Filling Out the Standardized Forms."

Benefits paid on behalf of a child end when the child graduates from high school or turns 18, whichever comes later. If you have been receiving social security benefits on behalf of your child, you should let colleges know that this income will end just as college bills begin, so they can make some allowance for this in their formulas.

Social security benefits paid to the parent on behalf of the child (whether the IRS considers them taxable or untaxable) are considered income to the parent under the financial aid formulas. The only silver lining to this is that parents' income is generally assessed less heavily than the child's. The colleges assess up to 50% of the child's income, but only up to 47% of the parents'.

Unfortunately, if you have other dependent children who still receive benefits, this money will also be assessed as part of your income.

Payments Made into IRAs, Keoghs, 401(k)s, 403(b)s, and TDAs

IRAs (Individual Retirement Accounts), Keoghs, 401(k)s, 403(b)s, and TDAs (short for Tax Deferred Annuities) are all retirement provisions designed to supplement or take the place of pensions and social security benefits. The tax benefit of these plans is that in most cases they allow you to defer paying income tax on contributions until you retire, when presumably your tax bracket will be lower. The interest on the funds is also allowed to accumulate tax-deferred until the time you start to withdraw the funds.

The 401(k) and 403(b) plans are supplemental retirement provisions set up by your employer in which part of your salary is deducted (at your request) from your paycheck and placed in a trust account for your benefit when you retire. Some companies choose to match part of your contributions to the plans. Keoghs are designed to take the place of an ordinary pension for self-employed individuals. TDAs fulfill much the same purpose for employees of tax-exempt religious, charitable, or educational organizations.

IRAs are supplemental retirement provisions for everyone. Contributions to these plans are tax-free up to certain limits. For example, if a person is not covered by a retirement plan at work or a self-employed retirement plan, she can make tax-deductible contributions to an IRA of up to $2,000 regardless of her income level. If a person is covered by a retirement plan, his contribution to an IRA may or may not be tax-deductible, depending on his income level.

Financial Aid Ramifications of Retirement Provisions

Retirement provisions are wonderful ways to reduce your current tax burden while building a large nest egg for your old age—but how do they affect financial aid?

The intent of current financial aid laws is to protect the money that you have built up in a retirement provision. *Assets* that have *already* been contributed to IRAs, Keoghs, 401(k)s, and so on by the date you fill out the standardized aid form do not have to appear on that form. In most cases, the FAOs will never know that this money exists. Thus loading up on contributions to retirement provisions before the college years begin makes enormous sense.

However, the *income* that you defer into these plans voluntarily during the base income years is treated just like regular income. The IRS may be willing to give you a tax deduction on this income, but the FAOs assess it just like all the rest of your income, up to a maximum rate of 47%. Contributions made to retirement provisions during base income years will not reduce your income under the aid formula. If you can still afford to make them, fine. Most parents find they need all their available cash just to pay their family contribution.

These plans remain an excellent way of protecting assets, provided you don't think you're going to need the money before you retire. Try to contribute as much as you can before the first base income year. Parents sometimes ask us how colleges will know about their contributions to 401(k) or 403(b) plans, or to tax-deferred annuities. These contributions show up on box 13 of your W-2 form. Don't even think about not listing them.

A possible exception to this scenario would come up if contributions to these plans would reduce your income below the $50,000 AGI cut-off for the simplified needs test. For example, let's say your total income from work is $45,000, your only other income is $7,000 in interest income (from $175,000 in assets you have parked in Certificates of Deposit) and you don't itemize your deductions. By deferring $2,500 for the year into a 401(k) plan, your adjusted gross income will now be $49,500, and your untaxed income will be $2,500—making you potentially eligible for the simplified needs test which will exclude your assets from the federal formula. Had you not made the deferral, your AGI would be $52,000 and your assets would be assessed at up to 5.6% per year.

Tax-Exempt Interest Income

Even though the government is not interested in a piece of your tax-free investments, the colleges are. Some parents question whether there is any need to tell the colleges about tax-free income if it does not appear on their federal income tax return.

In fact, tax-free interest income is supposed to be entered on line 8b of the 1040. This is not an item the IRS tends to flag, but there are excellent reasons why you should never hide these items. For one thing, tax law changes constantly. If your particular tax-free investment becomes taxable or reportable next year, how will you explain the sudden appearance of substantial taxable interest income? Or what if you need to sell your tax-free investment? You will then have to report a capital gain, and the FAO will want to know where all the money came from.

More Untaxed Income

Other untaxed income that is included in the financial aid formula includes the earned income credit, untaxed portions of pensions, welfare benefits, Aid to Families with Dependent Children (AFDC), child support, workers' compensation, veterans' benefits, living allowances paid to members of the military and clergy, and cash support provided by a relative. There is little to do about this kind of income except write it down. As with alimony, child support reported should include only the amount you actually received, not what you were supposed to receive.

Note: The federal methodology excludes contributions to, or payments from, flexible spending arrangements. However, the institutional methodology considers pre-tax contributions withheld from wages for dependent care and medical spending accounts to be part of your untaxed income.

EXPENSES

After adding up all your income, the need analysis forms allow you to deduct some types of expenses. A few of these expenses mirror the adjustment to income section of the 1040 income tax form. Many parents assume that *all* the adjustments to income from the IRS form can be counted on the standardized financial aid forms. Unfortunately this is not the case. Likewise, many parents assume that all of the itemized tax deductions they take on Schedule A will count on the financial aid forms as well. Almost none of these are included in the financial aid formula. Let's look at adjustments to income first.

Expenses According to the IRS:
Adjustments to Income

LINES 23 AND 27—IRA DEDUCTIONS AND KEOGH DEDUCTIONS

As we explained above, while these constitute legitimate tax deductions, contributions to IRAs and Keoghs will *not* reduce your income under the college financial aid formula.

However, some forms of state aid (which does not use the federal methodology employed by the colleges themselves) may be boosted by contributions to IRAs and Keoghs. These state programs are based solely on taxable income. We'll discuss this in detail in chapter 6, "State Aid." As we mentioned earlier, contributions to an IRA could lower your AGI below the $50,000 cap for the simplified needs test. Individuals who make KEOGH contributions are, by definition, self-employed and cannot meet the simplified needs test.

LINE 24—MOVING EXPENSES

Under the tax law, job-related moving expenses are now deductible as an adjustment to income. In the past, these expenses could be taken only as part of your itemized deductions, and did not affect your aid eligibility. Since this item will now both reduce your tax liability and potentially increase your aid eligibility, you should be sure to include all allowable moving expenses. There have been changes to the tax law regarding what constitutes a moving expense (for example, pre-move house hunting trips are no longer deductible) so be sure to read the IRS instructions or consult a competent advisor.

LINE 25—ONE HALF OF SELF-EMPLOYMENT TAX

Self-employed individuals can deduct one half of the self-employment taxes they pay. The financial aid formula also takes this deduction into account.

LINE 26—SELF-EMPLOYMENT HEALTH INSURANCE DEDUCTION

This is another adjustment to income recognized by the FAO. If you are self-employed or own more than 2% of the shares of an S corporation, there are two places on the 1996 IRS 1040 form where you may be able to take medical deductions. On line 26, you get to deduct 30% of your qualifying health insurance premiums. It is to your advantage to take the deduction here, rather than lump it with all your other medical expenses on Schedule A. First, because it will reduce your AGI, and second, because it is a sure deduction here. If your total medical expenses do not add up to a certain percentage of your total income, you won't get a deduction for medical expenses at all on your taxes.

In addition, starting with the 1993–94 year, high medical expenses (other than those included here on line 26) are no longer an automatic deduction in the federal aid formula as they were in prior years. We'll describe this in detail, under "Medical Deduction" on pages 62-65.

Note: At the time of publication, Congress had just passed legislation which provides for an increase in the self-employed health insurance deduction by the year 2006 to be phased in as follows: 40% for 1997; 45% for 1998 through 2002; 50% for 2003; 60% for 2004; 70% for 2005; 80% for 2006 and beyond. President Clinton is expected to sign this legislation.

LINE 28—PENALTY ON EARLY WITHDRAWAL OF SAVINGS, AND LINE 29—ALIMONY PAID

If you took an early withdrawal of savings before maturity, which incurred a penalty and/or you paid out alimony, write down the amounts here. The college aid formula grants you a deduction for these two adjustments to income as well.

Other Expenses According to the Financial Aid Formula

You've just seen all the adjustments to income that the IRS allows. The colleges allow you a deduction for several other types of expenses for financial aid purposes as well:

Federal Income Tax Paid

The advice we are about to offer may give your accountant a heart attack. Obviously, you want to pay the lowest taxes possible, but timing can come into play during the college years. The higher the taxes you pay during a base income year, the lower your family contribution will be. This is because the federal income taxes you pay count as an *expense* item in the aid formula. There are certain sets of circumstances when it is possible to save money by paying higher taxes.

The principle here is to end up having paid the same amount of taxes over the long run, but to *concentrate* the taxes into the years the colleges are scrutinizing, thus increasing your aid eligibility.

Let's look at a hypothetical example. Suppose that you make exactly the same amount of money in two separate years. You are in the 28% income tax bracket, and the tax tables don't change over these two years. Your federal tax turns out to be $6,120 the first year and $6,120 the second year, for a total tax bill of $12,240 for the two years.

Let's also suppose that you decide to make an IRA contribution during only one of the two years, but you aren't sure in which year to make the contribution. You're married, and neither of you is covered by a pension plan at work, so you are able to make a tax-deductible IRA contribution of $4,000. This turns out to reduce your federal taxes by $1,120 for the year in which you make the contribution. Since, in this case, your tax situation is precisely the same for both years, it doesn't make much difference in which year you take the deduction.

$12,240 total taxes over 2 years
(if no IRA contribution made)
− $ 1,120 tax savings for IRA contribution
$11,120 total taxes for the 2 years

Over the two years, either way, you end up paying a total of about $11,120 in federal taxes.

It's All a Matter of Timing

Here's where timing comes in. What if the second of the two years also happens to be your first base income year? In this case, you're much better off making the contribution during the previous year. By doing so, as we've already explained, you shelter the $4,000 from the need analysis formula, and get a $1,120 tax break in the first year.

But much more important, by making the contribution during the first year, you choose to pay the higher tax bill in the second year—the base income year—which in turn lowers your Expected Family Contribution. Over the two years, you're still paying close to the same amount in taxes, but you've *concentrated* the taxes into the base income year where it will do you some good.

> *Tip #12: Concentrate your federal income taxes into base income years to lower your Expected Family Contribution.*

Obviously, if you can afford to make IRA contributions every year, you should do so; building a retirement fund is a vital part of any family's long-term planning. However, if like many families, you find that you can't afford to contribute every year during college years, you can at least use timing to increase your expenses in the eyes of the FAOs. By loading up on retirement provision contributions during non–base income years, and avoiding retirement provision contributions and other tax-saving measures during base income years, you can substantially increase your aid eligibility.

Charitable Contributions

Large donations to charity are a wonderful thing, both from a moral standpoint and a tax standpoint—but not during a base income year. When you lower your taxes, you raise your family contribution significantly. We aren't saying you should stop giving to charity, but we do recommend holding off on large gifts until after the base income years.

Deduction for Social Security and Medicare Taxes

The financial aid formulas give you a deduction for the Medicare and social security taxes (otherwise known as FICA) that you pay. Parents often ask how the colleges do this since there doesn't seem to be a question about social security taxes on the financial aid forms. The deduction is actually made automatically by computer, but it is based on two questions on the financial aid form. These questions are in disguise.

On the FAFSA, the two questions are "father's income earned from work," and "mother's income earned from work." At first glance these questions appear to be about *income*. In fact, these are *expense* questions. If you minimize the amounts you put down here, you will cost yourself aid.

Therefore, you should be sure to include all sources of income from work on which you've paid FICA or Medicare taxes: wages (box 1 of your W-2), income from self-employment (line 12 of the 1040), income from partnerships (not including income from limited partnerships), and deferred compensation.

A Financial Aid Catch-22

Wages that you defer into a 401(k), 403(b), or other retirement plan are not subject to income tax by the IRS, but you still pay social security taxes and/or Medicare taxes on them. (Currently, income above $62,700 is exempt from FICA. However, there is no longer any income ceiling on Medicare taxes.)

The strange thing is that, while the purpose of the questions regarding income earned from work on the financial aid forms is to allow the need analysis companies to calculate the social security and Medicare taxes you paid, the instructions for the forms don't tell you to include deferred income. For example, if your income was $40,000 last year and you deferred $5,000 of it into a 401(k), the instructions tell you to put down $35,000 as your income from work.

Welcome to the Wacky World of Financial Aid

The instructions are wrong. It's just that simple. We have filed a motion at the Department of Education suggesting that they be changed. In the meantime, please ignore the instructions. If you deferred *any* income, include it as part of the question on income earned from work on the FAFSA.

Will this make a real difference to your aid package? It depends on how much you defer. Say you and your spouse defer $5,000 each, and you are in the 47th percentile in aid assessment. By including this money as part of income earned from work, you could increase your aid eligibility by about $380 per year.

This might seem petty, but these small amounts—$380 here, $200 there—can add up. Put another way, this is $380 a year ($1,520 over four years) that you won't have to borrow and pay interest on.

State and Local Tax Deduction

This is another calculation that is done automatically by the need assessment computer. The computer takes the sum of your taxable and untaxable income and multiplies it by a certain percentage based on the state you live in to determine your deduction. The formula for each state is slightly different, because of differing tax rates.

This works very well for people who live and work in the same state, but presents real problems for everyone else. If you live in one state but work in another where the taxes are higher, you may be paying more in taxes than the formula indicates. The financial need computer isn't programmed to deal with situations like this, and people who don't fit the program get penalized.

The only way to deal with this is to write to the individual colleges' aid offices to let them know about your special situation.

Employment Allowance

Under the federal methodology, if you are a single parent who works, or if you are part of a two-parent, two-income family, then you qualify for the employment allowance.

In the 1996 base income year, married couples will get a deduction of 35% of the lower wage earner's salary up to a maximum deduction of $2,700. Single parents (i.e., separated, divorced, widowed, or never married) will be able to deduct 35% of their own salary up to a maximum deduction of $2,700. The employment allowance is figured out for you automatically by the need analysis computer based on three questions you answered on the FAFSA—namely father's income earned from work, mother's income earned from work, and of course, the question about the parent's marital status.

As we've said before, while these questions look like income questions, they are actually expense questions. It is in your interest to make these figures as big as possible. Remember to include all your sources of income from work.

The Income Protection Allowance

Most parents find the income protection allowance (formerly known as the standard maintenance allowance) to be a bad joke. This is the federal financial aid formula's idea of how much money your family needs to house, feed, and clothe itself during one year. According to the formula:

> *a family of 5 (one in college) can live on $21,320*
> *a family of 4 (one in college) can live on $18,070*
> *a family of 3 (one in college) can live on $14,630*
> *a family of 2 (one in college) can live on $11,750*

The income protection allowance is based solely on the number of family members currently living in the household and the number of family members in college. It is determined by the U.S. government figures for the poverty line and does not take into account the cost of living in your part of the country.

Many parents assume that a portion of their monthly mortgage payments will be deducted from their income on the aid formulas in much the same way as it is on their taxes. Unfortunately, this is not the case. The income protection allowance is supposed to include all housing expenses.

We strongly recommend that you sit down and write out a budget of how much it actually takes to keep your family going, and send it to the individual college. Include everything. In many parts of the country, the income protection allowance is fairly ludicrous, but it is up to you to show the FAO just how ludicrous it is in your case.

We are told that the CSS institutional methodology is using current consumer expense survey data to determine this allowance on their form. Because the numbers haven't been released yet, we can't guarantee that the CSS protection allowance will be any more reasonable than the federal protection allowance.

Optional Expenses

Under the federal methodology, high unreimbursed medical and dental expenses as well as elementary/secondary school tuition for the student's siblings are no longer automatically deducted from income. However, you are probably going to have to answer questions about these categories anyway on both the CSS PROFILE form and the school's own aid forms—the reason being that under the institutional methodology or the schools' own aid policies, these items may be considered as deductions against income.

Even if you are only completing the FAFSA (which does not ask about these items) it still makes sense to let the FAOs know about *any* high expenses they would not otherwise find out about. As we have already mentioned, information like this should be sent directly to the schools under separate cover.

Here are some tips on how to answer questions about medical and tuition expenses.

Medical Deduction

To be able to deduct medical expenses on your federal tax return, you must have expenses in excess of 7.5% of your AGI. However college financial aid guidelines are not necessarily as strict. Some families who don't qualify under federal tax law just assume they won't qualify under the financial aid rules either, so they enter "0" for their medical expenses on the aid forms. This can be a costly mistake.

Here's a quick example. Let's say your family's adjusted gross income is $50,000, and you had medical expenses of $3,000. As far as the IRS is concerned, you won't get a medical deduction this year. Your $3,000 medical bills fall well short of 7.5% of $50,000 ($3,750). However, under the financial aid formulas, you may indeed receive a deduction against income. Under the federal methodology, the FAOs can use their discretion for this item. Under the institutional methodology, the rules for this expense category are more defined.

Therefore even if you don't have enough medical and dental expenses to qualify under the federal tax law, don't assume that it would be a waste of time to disclose these figures. Many colleges are using the CSS institutional methodology which will make an allowance for unreimbursed medical expenses in excess of 4% of your income. If you are filling out the PROFILE form, there is a place on the form to report this information. Many of the schools' separate financial aid forms ask for this information as well.

What Constitutes a Medical Expense?

There are more than 100 legitimate medical deductions. Here are just a few: doctors, dentists, prescription eyeglasses, therapists, health insurance premiums that were deducted from your paycheck or that you paid personally, medical transportation, and lodging.

Self-employed individuals are better off deducting 30 percent of their health insurance premiums back on line 26 of the 1040 form and including the other 70 percent as part of medical expenses on the PROFILE form, or in a separate letter to the FAO.

Whose Medical Expenses Can Be Included?

You should include medical expenses for every single member of your household, not just the student who is going to college. When families come in to see us, they inevitably start out by saying that they do not have much in the way of unreimbursed medical expenses.

However, when we get them to write it all down, it often turns out to be a hefty sum. Keep careful records and include EVERYTHING. Did you take a cab to and from the doctor's office? Did anyone get braces? Did anyone get contact lenses?

And If We Have Very Low Medical Expenses?

Congratulations, but keep records anyway. The schools who use the PROFILE form will still see the amount you put down, and you may have to answer questions about these items on the schools' own aid forms. You might as well give the FAOs a realistic sense of what your monthly bills look like.

Last Medical Point

We recommend that if you don't have medical expenses in excess of 4% of your total taxable and untaxable income each year, you might consider postponing some discretionary medical procedures and advancing others, in order to bunch your deductions together and pass the 4% mark during one particular year. This might seem at first to fly in the face of conventional wisdom. Facing the burden of college, many parents' first thought would be to put off braces for a younger child, for example. In fact, if you are in a base income year, it makes much more sense to get them now. Once you reach the 4% threshold, each dollar in excess may increase your aid eligibility by 47 cents.

Finally, if you anticipate large medical bills in the near future, you should certainly let the colleges know what's coming up.

Elementary and Secondary School Tuition

If your college-bound child has a younger brother or sister who is attending a private elementary or secondary school, you may be able to get a deduction for part of the tuition you pay for the private school. Neither the federal nor the institutional methodologies provide an automatic deduction, but the PROFILE form and many of the individual college aid forms do ask questions about this category. The FAOs are supposed to use their judgment in deciding whether to make any deduction for younger children's tuition.

Obviously, you can't include the private high school tuition of the child who is *now* applying to college, because next year the student won't be there anymore. You are also not allowed to include the cost of pre-school or college tuition of other siblings. (Don't worry if you have more than one child in college at the same time; this will be taken into account elsewhere.) When you write down the amount you pay in elementary and secondary school tuition, remember to subtract any scholarship money you receive.

Two Special Circumstances

Because of the vagaries of the base income year, two special cases come up from time to time. The first case: You have a son or daughter entering college next year and another several years younger who has been in public school up to now, but who is about to switch to a private school at the same time. As we've already explained, financial aid is always a year behind. The aid you get this year is based on your income and expenses from last year. Although the PROFILE form now asks about tuition expenses for siblings in the base year and the current calendar year, you will be listing tuition only from September through December of the current year for that particular sibling. Therefore, we recommend a separate note be sent to the FAOs explaining the full tuition for the entire academic year of that child. Sometimes the FAOs will make an adjustment if you let them know about it.

Second, and more amusing: You have two children who are one year apart. Let's call the elder Jane. Next year she will be a sophomore in college. The younger is called Joe, and next year he will start his freshman year of college. It is December, and we are filling out his PROFILE form. Remember, Joe's first base income year was the last calendar year, which includes the spring term when he was a junior in high school and Jane was a senior in high school. If Jane went to private high school, according to the instructions, you can include six months (the spring term) of Jane's senior year of high school tuition on Joe's aid form for his freshman year.

This may seem a little crazy, since Jane is older than Joe, and won't even have been in high school for over a year by the time Joe gets to college, but when you think about it, it is no more crazy than not being able to get credit for the full year's tuition in our first example. Some schools won't take this figure into account anyway, but it won't get you into trouble to try. You are merely following the directions.

Keeping Track of Information

What makes all this complicated is that some of the schools you will be applying to will require just the FAFSA (which does not ask about medical expenses and siblings' tuition), others will also require the PROFILE form (which asks about medical expenses and siblings' tuition) and others will have their own forms as well. It's easy to forget which schools know what information.

If you apply to a school that requires only the FAFSA, they will not see any of the information you filled out on your PROFILE form. If that school does not ask questions about items such as unreimbursed medical expenses on their own aid form, and you consider this information important, you should send it to the school under separate cover.

In addition, some state grant aid programs (Pennsylvania's PHEAA program comes to mind) will increase award amounts if you send them proof of high medical expenses.

Good News for a Few Parents

The IRS will not allow you to deduct child support payments from your taxable income (although they do allow you to deduct alimony payments). However, the colleges do allow a deduction for the payment of child support, under both the federal and the institutional methodology. The same is true for any part of your taxable income that consists of financial aid received by a parent in school, or living allowances received by the parent under the National and Community Service Act of 1990.

So Far So Good

Now that you've given the need analysis people all this information, they will add up all your taxable and untaxable income and then subtract all the expenses and adjustments they have decided to allow. What's left is your available income.

Available income will be assessed on a sliding scale. If your available income is zero (or less), the parents' contribution from income will be zero. If your available income is greater, the contribution will be greater. The parents' contribution from income can go only as high as 47% of available income.

If you are applying to colleges that require the PROFILE form (and thus use the institutional methodology) the parents' contribution from income may be higher or lower than it would be under the federal methodology.

Income and Expenses:
How the Methodologies Differ

FEDERAL METHODOLOGY
- Excludes medical/dental expenses
- Income protection allowance based on poverty line figures from the 1960s, adjusted for inflation
- Excludes amounts withheld from wages for dependent care and medical spending accounts.

INSTITUTIONAL METHODOLOGY
- Provides an allowance for unreimbursed medical and dental expenses in excess of 4% of income
- Income protection allowance based on current consumer expenditure survey data
- Gives colleges the option of adding back losses that appear on lines 12, 13, 14, 17, 18, and 21 of the 1996 IRS 1040
- Gives colleges the option of making an allowance for elementary/secondary tuition paid for the student's siblings
- No automatic zero—EFC

ASSETS AND LIABILITIES

Now that the need analysis companies know about last year's available income, they want to see your assets and liabilities. On the standardized financial aid forms, these two items are joined at the hip. The need analysis computers subtract what is owed on the assets from what they are worth. In a nutshell, the strategies you will find in this chapter are designed to make the value of your assets look as small as possible, and the debts against your assets as large as possible.

What Counts as an Asset?

Cash, checking and savings accounts, money market accounts, CDs, U.S. Savings Bonds, stocks, other bonds, mutual funds, trusts, ownership interests in businesses, and the current market value of real estate holdings other than your home.

None of these items appear directly on your tax return. However, your tax return will still provide the colleges with an excellent way to verify these assets. How? Most assets create income and/or tax deductions, both of which do appear on your 1040 in the form of capital gains, capital losses, interest, dividends, and itemized deductions under schedule A.

Assets in retirement provisions such as IRAs, Keoghs, and 401(k)s, for example, don't have to be listed on the standardized form (though as we have already said, voluntary tax-deductible *contributions* to retirement provisions made during base income years must be listed under income). Cars are also excluded from the formula and don't have to be listed on the form.

What About My Home?

Under the federal methodology, the value of your home is no longer considered part of your assets. This is great news and will help many families who own their own home to qualify for a Pell Grant and other federal aid programs. However, many colleges are using the more stringent institutional methodology to award their *own* funds. Under this formula, the value of your home will *not* be excluded from your assets.

Which schools will exclude the value of your home? It's safe to say that most state schools will do so. If a school asks you to complete the PROFILE form and/or asks you for the value of your home on their own aid form, then most likely the value of the home is going to be treated like other assets. You can bet that the highly selective private colleges that meet a high percentage of their financial aid students' need, will be looking closely at home equity. Other private colleges may or may not.

However, even if you're considering colleges that have decided to look at home value, the news is not all bad. Some of these institutions have elected to cap the value of your home at three times the parents' total yearly income. In other words, at these schools if you earned $50,000 last year, the value of your home (for assessment purposes) will be considered to be no more than $150,000—even if you own a home worth $200,000.

Which schools will be capping home value this year? At present there is no list available. However, the schools most likely to cap home value are the highly selective colleges that have large amounts of their own money to award, and that meet a high percentage of need.

One of the questions you may want to ask the FAO at any school you are considering is which of the three ways they will treat home value—not at all, at three times income, or at full value.

Under the federal methodology, the definition of "home" is the primary residence. If you own a vacation home in addition to your primary residence, the vacation home will not be excluded from your assets. If you own a vacation home, and you rent your primary residence, the value of the vacation home will still not be excluded under the federal formula—as it is considered "other real estate."

What About My Farm?

The value of your farm is not included as an asset under the federal methodology provided that the family lives on the farm and you can claim on Schedule F of the IRS 1040 that you "materially participated in the farm's operation." The Feds call this type of farm a "family farm." We'll discuss how to handle this situation in part three, "Filling Out the Standardized Forms." Under the institutional methodology, the value of any farm property is considered an asset.

How Much Are My Assets Worth?

To repeat, the need analysis form is a snapshot of your financial picture. The value of most assets (with the exception of money in the bank) changes constantly, as financial markets rise and fall. The colleges want to know the value of your assets *on the day* you fill out the form.

Remember, This Is One Snapshot for Which You Don't Want to Look Your Best

When people sit down to fill out financial statements they have a tendency to want to put their best foot forward. After all, most of the time when you fill out one of these forms it is because you are applying for a credit card, or a bank loan, or hoping to be accepted by a country club or an exclusive condominium. Trying to look as fiscally healthy as possible has become almost automatic. However, you have to remember that in this case you are applying for financial aid. They aren't going to give it to you if you don't let them see the whole picture, warts and all. On the financial aid form, you don't want to gloss over your debts.

What Counts as a Debt?

The only debts that are considered under the financial aid formulas are debts against the specific assets listed on the aid forms.

For example, you do NOT get credit for: unsecured loans, personal loans, educational loans like Stafford or PLUS loans for college, consumer debt such as outstanding credit card balances, or auto loans. If you have any debt of these types, you should realize that it will NOT be subtracted from your assets under the financial aid formulas.

It will be to your advantage to minimize these types of debt during the college years. In fact, you may want to convert these loans into debts that do get credit under the financial aid formulas.

You DO get credit for: margin loans, passbook loans, as well as home equity loans, first mortgages, and second mortgages on "other real estate." Of course, you will only get credit for debts on your *primary* residence, if the college has decided to look at your home value.

> *Tip #13: Convert debts that are not counted by the aid formulas into types of debt that do count.*

Let's go through the different types of assets you have to report and discuss strategies for minimizing the *appearance* of those assets.

Cash, Checking Accounts, Savings Accounts

The need analysis forms ask you to list any money in your accounts on the day you fill out the forms. However, you can't list this money if it isn't there.

We are not counseling you to go on a spending spree, but if you were planning to make a major purchase in the near future, you might as well make it *now*. If roof repairs are looming, if you can prepay your summer vacation, if you were going to buy a new car sometime in the next year, do it now, and pay cash. You were going to make these purchases anyway. By speeding up the purchase, you reduce the appearance of your cash assets.

> *Tip #14: If you were going to buy soon, buy now and use cash.*

Another way to reduce assets in the bank is to use the cash to pay off a liability that the colleges refuse to look at.

Plastic Debt

If you have credit card debt, your need analysis form won't give a realistic picture of your net worth, because as far as the colleges are concerned, plastic debt doesn't exist. You could owe thousands of dollars on your VISA card, but the aid formula does not allow you to subtract this debt from your assets, or to subtract the interest on the debt from your income.

Any financial adviser will tell you that if you have any money in the bank at all, it is crazy not to pay off your credit card debt. Recently we had one parent say to us, "But it makes me feel secure to have $7,000 in the bank. I know I could pay my $2,000 MasterCard bill, but then I would have only $5,000 left."

There are three reasons why this is wrong-headed thinking.

First, any way you look at it, that parent really did have only $5,000. It is a complete illusion to think that you have more money just because you can see it in your bank account at the moment.

Second, this guy's $2,000 credit card debt was costing him a lot of money—19% each year. This was 19% that could not be deducted from income on his taxes or on his financial aid form. Meanwhile, the $2,000 he was keeping in the bank because it made him feel better, was earning all of 2% after taxes. He was being taken to the cleaners.

Third, and most important, by paying off his credit card debt he could reduce his net assets on the need analysis form, and pick up some more aid.

> *Tip #15: Use cash in the bank to pay off credit card balances. This will reduce your assets and thus increase your eligibility for aid.*

Your Tax Bill

If you did not have enough tax withheld from your wages this year, and you will end up owing the IRS money, consider speeding up the completion of your taxes so that you can send in your return—with a check—before you complete the need analysis form.

If you are self-employed, you might consider prepaying your next quarterly estimate. The IRS is always pleased to receive the money early. You will lose out on the interest the money would have earned if it had stayed in your account a little longer, but this will probably be offset by your increased aid eligibility.

> *Tip #16: Use cash in the bank to pay off tax bills to reduce your assets and increase your eligibility for aid.*

You will notice on the FAFSA that below the item "cash, savings, and checking accounts," there is no corresponding item for debts as there are for the other asset categories on the form. For the most part, you can't have debts on these kinds of assets. There is one exception.

Passbook Loans

With a passbook loan, you use your savings account as collateral for a loan. This is a legitimate debt against your asset. To get credit for the debt, you must list your savings account and the debt against it under "other real estate and investments" (on the FAFSA) and under "investments" (on the PROFILE form).

Some parents suggest that they simply subtract the value of the passbook loan from the value of their passbook account and list it on the line that mentions savings accounts. This is a very bad idea. The schools will be able to tell (by the interest the account earns) that your savings account has more money in it than you say. Essentially, the need analysis companies want you to give them all the raw data and let *them* do the subtraction. They don't trust you to do the subtracting for them.

IRAs, Keoghs, 401(k)s, 403(b)s

In most cases, money that you contribute to a retirement provision —such as an IRA, Keogh, 401(k), or 403(b)—*before* the base income years begin is completely sheltered from the FAOs. That money isn't part of the snapshot; they can't touch it.

However, as we stated in our chapter on income, contributions made *during* base income years are a different story. While the IRS may allow you to deduct retirement provisions from your current income, the financial aid formula does not; during base income years, voluntary contributions to these plans will be assessed just like regular income.

This does not mean that retirement provisions are a complete waste of time during the college years. To see the big picture, it helps to remember that the aid formula assesses both your income and your assets. Let's say a family had $30,000 in income last year. The FAOs will assess the $30,000 as income. Then, if any of that $30,000 is left in the bank on the day the family fills out the need analysis form, it will also be assessed a second time as an asset. However, if that family had made a contribution to an IRA before filling out the need analysis form, the contribution would have been assessed only once—as untaxed income. It couldn't have been listed as an asset because it wasn't there.

A contribution to a retirement provision during the base income years will always be assessed as income, but it will never be assessed as an asset—so long as you make the contribution before you fill out the need analysis form.

Thus retirement provisions are still a good way to shelter assets while building your retirement fund and getting a tax deduction all at the same time. If you can afford to keep contributing during college years, it will be to your benefit. But when during the year should you make the contribution?

Timing on IRA Contributions

The IRS allows you to make contributions to an IRA from January 1 of one year through April 15 of the following year. Many people wait until after they've done their taxes in March or April to make a contribution to an IRA for the preceding year. Unfortunately, if you make the contribution *after* you fill out the financial aid form, the money won't be shielded from the FAOs.

In fact it makes sense to make retirement provisions as soon as possible in a calendar year. Not only will you shelter the money itself from assessment as an asset but you will also shelter the *interest* earned by that money: If you leave that money in a regular bank account for most of the year, the interest will have to be reported on the need analysis form as regular income. Your AGI will be larger, and your financial aid package will be correspondingly smaller. By making the contribution early in the year, the interest earned by that contribution will be out-of-bounds to the FAOs. How much money are we talking about? A married couple that makes an allowable IRA contribution of $4,000 on January 1 of a base income year instead of April 15 of the next year can increase its aid eligibility by as much as $250 each year.

> *Tip #17: Make your contributions to retirement provisions as early in the year as possible.*

Other Retirement Provision Strategies

Let's say it's January of a new year. You go to see your accountant and she says, "You've got some extra money. Let's make an IRA contribution. Which year do you want to take the contribution in?" Remember, the IRS allows you to make contributions to an IRA from January 1 (well, realistically January 2; the banks and brokerage houses are all closed on January 1) all the way through April 15 of the next year. That means there are three and a half months during which you can contribute to either the preceding year or the year you are in now. In which year do you make the contribution?

If Possible, Contribute to Both Years

Let's say this is January of your child's senior year in high school. You are just about to fill out a need analysis form. From January 2 through April 15, you can contribute to the year that has just ended (in this case, the base income year) and the year that is just beginning. If you are married, you and your spouse can make an IRA contribution of up to $4,000 toward last year, and $4,000 toward the year that has just begun. By making these contributions before you sign the need analysis form, you completely shelter $8,000 in assets from the scrutiny of the FAOs. This is such a good deal that you might even want to consider making an IRA contribution even if it isn't tax deductible.

We Don't Have $8,000. We Might Not Even Have Enough to Make IRA Contributions Every Year

Many people don't contribute the maximum allowed amount into their retirement accounts every year. Many people don't contribute *anything* in a given year. Sometimes, of course, you just haven't got it. Other times, it is a matter of which year it makes the most sense tax-wise to make the contribution:

During College Years, Some Tax Strategies Have to Change

Why shouldn't you make retirement contributions based solely on tax considerations? It's all in the numbers. Remember our IRA example from the "Expenses" section of this chapter? Given a choice of making a tax-deductible contribution to an IRA in a base income year or a non–base income year, you were better off making the contribution in the non–base income year. Tax-wise, there was no real difference, but by *concentrating* your taxes into the base income year, you effectively raised your expenses during the year the colleges were looking at it, and thus lowered your expected family contribution.

Parents and accountants find this hard to believe. "How could an IRA contribution possibly hurt a family's chances for aid?" they demand.

Federal income tax is an expense that is deducted from your total income under the aid formula. A tax-deductible retirement provision contribution *reduces* your tax. Reduced taxes increase your available income, and thus increase the amount of money the colleges think you can afford to fork over for tuition next year.

You're Saying Parents Should Try to Pay More Taxes?

Never. But by *concentrating* your taxes into the base income years, you can end up paying the same amount in taxes over the course of time while *lowering* the amount you have to pay for college.

The Big Picture

Extrapolating from this, if you were to load up on contributions to retirement provisions over the course of several years prior to the first base income year, and then avoided contributions to retirement provisions completely during the base income years, you could end up paying about the same amount in taxes over the years, but you would have made yourself eligible for far more financial aid.

Tip #18a: If you can, try to load up your contributions to retirement provisions in the years prior to base income years.

Let's take the hypothetical case of Mr. Jones. Mr. Jones is doing pretty well: He has a substantial regular savings account, and every year he contributes $1,000 to his 401(k) plan at work. Over the next eight years, he figures he will be able to contribute $8,000 to the retirement provision. His daughter is entering college in five years. By the first base income year, Mr. Jones will have sheltered only $4,000 in his retirement plan. The FAOs will assess his entire regular savings account at the maximum asset rate. His $1,000 401(k) contribution for that year will lower his taxes a bit, which means that his available income will be just a bit higher, which will raise his EFC.

Consider what would have happened if Mr. Jones had contributed the same $8,000 to his 401(k) but had arranged to lump it all into the four years *before* the first base income year. Over the eight years his total tax bill would turn out to be about the same as before, but everything else would be very different. Now he would have $8,000 sheltered in his retirement plan. In order to make the contributions over only four years, he would probably have to take some money out of his savings account—but that's actually good news because it would reduce his assets in the eyes of the FAOs. During the four base income years, Mr. Jones wouldn't have to contribute to his retirement fund at all—this means that the taxes he has concentrated into these years would lower his EFC.

Mr. Jones had only $8,000 to contribute over eight years. However, by changing the timing of his contributions, he made them much more valuable. This strategy will work only if your voluntary contributions to retirement provisions are tax deductible. If you won't qualify for the tax deductions, you won't be able to concentrate your taxes into the base income years.

The Big, Big Picture

Mr. Jones (like most of us) could not afford to contribute the maximum amounts allowed by the law to retirement provisions; therefore it made sense to plan the timing of the contributions to get the most aid. However, if you can afford to make maximum contributions to IRAs, Keoghs, 401(k)s, or 401(b)s in every single year, it is in your interest to do so. This will enable you to shelter the largest amount of assets, and also build a sizable retirement fund.

However, Before You Frame the Picture

The only reason not to follow the advice we've just given you is if you have income just over $50,000 and no one in the household has to file the long form. In this case, by making contributions to retirement provisions *during* the base income years, you could lower your AGI below the $50,000 magic number for the simplified needs test. As we said earlier, anyone who meets the simplified needs test will have all assets excluded for federal aid purposes.

You would have to work out the numbers very closely on this to see if it really makes sense. Factors to consider: how much you have in the way of assets; does the school look at your assets anyway in awarding their own aid funds; the difference in your EFC using the simplified needs test vs. not using the simplified needs test. Since these factors are all pretty complicated, consider discussing this with a financial aid consultant.

> *Tip #18b: If a contribution to a retirement provision will lower your AGI below $50,000, and you meet all other criteria for the simplified needs test, you should load up your contributions to retirement provisions during the base income years.*

Prying Colleges

Although the law doesn't allow the need analysis forms to ask questions about the money in parents' retirement provisions, a few private colleges ask for this information on their own forms. Short of refusing to apply to these colleges, there is nothing you can do but supply the information gracefully. Unless you have retirement provisions in the hundreds of thousands of dollars, however, there should be no effect on your family contribution.

They Won't Give Aid to *Us*— We Own Our Own Home

One of the biggest myths about financial aid is that parents who own their own home will not qualify for aid. This is not the case at all. As we have already mentioned, the federal methodology (used to award Pell Grants and other federal aid programs) does not look at home equity anymore. While many private colleges and some state universities continue to use home equity in determining eligibility for their *own* aid programs, it has been our experience that most homeowners—even in this situation—do get aid. In some cases, this will be true even if they have several properties, if they apply for it in the right way.

Real Estate Strategies

Because we know that many of our readers will be applying to schools that assess home equity in awarding the funds under their own control, the next few sections of this chapter will suggest strategies that focus on both your primary residence and any other real estate you may own.

If none of the schools you are considering assess home equity, then the following strategies will apply only to your other real estate holdings.

Valuing the Property—Be Realistic

Figuring out the value of your home can be difficult. Is it worth what your neighbors down the street sold theirs for last week? Is it worth what someone offered you three years ago? Is it worth the appraised value on your insurance policy? Figuring out the value of other properties can be even more difficult, especially if you rarely see them.

You want to try to be as accurate as possible. The temptation to over-represent the value of your real estate should be firmly controlled. The forms are asking for the value of the property if you had to sell it right this minute, today—not what you would get for it if you had a leisurely six months to find a buyer. If you had to sell it in a hurry—at firesale prices—how much is it worth? Remember also that there are always attendant costs when you sell a property: painting and remodeling, possible early payment penalties for liquidating your mortgage, real estate agent's commission. If the colleges want to know what your real estate is worth, these costs should be taken into account. Be realistic. Inflating the price of your property beyond what it is really worth will reduce your aid eligibility.

At the same time, you don't want to under-represent the value either. The colleges have verification procedures to prevent parents from lowballing. One of the procedures: the PROFILE form asks when you purchased your home and how much you paid for it. The analysis computer will then feed these numbers into the Federal Housing Index Multiplier to see whether your current valuation is within reasonable norms.

Equity

Ultimately, what your real estate is worth is much less important than how much equity you've built up in it. The need analysis computer takes the current market value of your real estate and subtracts what you owe on it (mortgages, home equity loan balances, debts secured by the home). What is left is the equity you've built up. Let's assume for a moment that two families are looking at a private college that considers home equity as an asset. All other things being equal, the family with a $100,000 house fully paid up would probably pay a higher family contribution to that college than the family with a $300,000 house with a $250,000 mortgage. Sounds crazy? Not really. The first family has built up equity of $100,000; the second family has equity of only $50,000.

Parents often don't remember when they are filling out the need analysis forms that their first mortgage need not be their only debt against their property. Did you, for example, borrow money from your parents to make a down payment? Have you taken out a home improvement loan? Have you borrowed against a home equity loan line of credit? Is there a sewer assessment? All of these are also legitimate debts against the value of your real estate.

If you are a part-owner in any property, obviously you should list only your share of the equity in that property.

The Home Equity Loan: A Possible Triple Play

One of the smarter ways to pay for college is the home equity loan. A home equity loan is a line of credit, secured, most likely, by the equity in your home. Of course, it is also possible to get a home equity loan using one of your other properties as collateral. You draw checks against this line of credit, up to the full value of the loan, but you pay no interest until you write a check, and you pay interest only on the amount that you actually borrow.

There are three possible benefits to a home equity loan. First, in most cases you get a tax deduction for the interest you pay. Few other types of debt are now tax deductible. Second, you temporarily reduce the equity in your property, which, in turn, lowers your net assets, which lowers your family contribution—provided, of course, that the loan is taken against a property that is being considered an asset by the college. Third, because it is a secured loan, the interest rates are fairly low. As always, you should consult with your accountant or financial planner on this.

If you have any outstanding loans that cannot be used as a deduction under the financial aid formulas (personal loans, car loans, large credit card balances, etc.), it might make sense to use a home equity line of credit to pay off these other obligations. The interest rate will probably be lower, you will most likely be able to deduct the interest payments on your tax return, and the value of one of your prime assets may look smaller to the FAOs.

Which Property Should I Borrow Against?

If you have only one property, the decision is easy. Borrow against your one property. You'll almost certainly get a tax deduction and a low interest rate. Whether you will reduce your equity in the eyes of the FAOs depends on whether they have decided to assess the value of the primary residence—and if so whether they are choosing to assess it at full market value or at a lower rate.

If your college is actually going to follow the federal methodology, a home equity loan on a primary residence would no longer help you to qualify for more aid (although the tax and interest savings still may make it a good idea). If you own two homes, take out the loan on the second residence instead.

If your prospective colleges are using the institutional methodology *and* electing to cap home value at three times income (and many private colleges will be), the effective-ness of our strategy will depend on how much equity you have in your home. Let's take a family with income of $60,000 and a home valued at $200,000, with a $100,000 mortgage. At schools that choose to use the optional cap on home value proposed by CSS, the maximum value of this family's home would be three times $60,000 or $180,000. The colleges will subtract the $100,000 debt from the $180,000 asset and decree that the family has equity of $80,000—which the colleges feel is available to help pay for college, and will assess at a rate of up to 5.65% per year. In this case, it would still make sense to take out a home equity loan to reduce the appearance of equity in the house.

However, let's take a family with a combined income of $60,000, a home valued at $300,000 and a mortgage of $200,000. If the schools choose to cap home value, the maximum value of the house (for assessment purposes) is $180,000. The colleges then subtract the mortgage of $200,000. In this case, there is, in fact, no equity at all in the home as far as the colleges are concerned. Thus, if this family took out a home equity loan on their primary residence, it would not reduce their assets in the eyes of the colleges (since as far as the colleges were concerned, the family had no equity in the house in the first place). To reduce the appearance of their assets, this family could borrow instead against a second home, other real estate, or their stock portfolio.

If the schools you are considering use the CSS cap on home value, this makes our tips #2 through #11 (which describe ways to lower the appearance of your Adjusted Gross Income) even more important. Lowering your AGI will keep your capped home value down, and thus protect more of the value of your home from the FAOs.

> *Tip #19a: Take out a home equity loan to pay for college and/or to consolidate debt not taken into account in the aid formulas.*

A home equity loan is not something to be done lightly. Unlike unsecured loans and credit card balances, a home equity loan uses your real estate as collateral. If you default, the bank can foreclose. Nonetheless, if you have a low mortgage to begin with and your income seems stable, this is an excellent alternative.

A Home Equity Loan vs. a Second Mortgage

When you take out a second mortgage, the bank writes you a check for a fixed amount, and you begin paying it back immediately with interest. Parents sometimes ask, "Isn't a second mortgage just as good as a home equity loan?" It depends on what you're going to do with the money you get from the loan. If you put it in the bank to pay for college bills as they come due, then a second mortgage is not as good at all. Consider: You are paying interest on the entire amount of the loan, but you aren't really using it yet. The money will earn interest, but it will not earn nearly as much interest as you are paying out. For financial aid purposes, the interest you earn will be considered income, yet the interest you are paying on the second mortgage will not be taken into account as an expense.

Even worse, if the money you received from your second mortgage is just sitting in the bank, the debt does not reduce your net assets either. The reduced equity in your house will be offset by the increased money in your bank account. Under these circumstances, a home equity line of credit loan is a much better deal. You pay interest only when you withdraw money, and you withdraw only what you need.

But if the school you select has opted *not* to look at home equity, then a second mortgage becomes the worst deal in the world. You will have taken an asset that the college could not touch and converted it into an asset with no protection at all. This could actually raise your EFC by several thousand dollars.

Should We Buy a House Now?

We're all for it if you want to buy a house, but don't think of it as an automatic strategy for reducing your assets in the eyes of the FAOs. If the school assesses home equity, then exchanging the money in your bank account for a down payment on a house just shifts your assets around, rather than making them disappear. Your net assets will be exactly the same with or without the house (at least until the house starts appreciating in value). On top of that, your monthly housing costs will probably increase. As you may remember from the "Expenses" section of this chapter, you don't get credit in the aid formulas for mortgage payments.

However, if the schools uses the federal methodology excluding home value, then a first-time home purchase could make a lot of sense. You would be exchanging an unprotected asset for an asset that could not be touched.

By the same token, it might also make sense to prepay or pay down the mortgage on your primary residence since this will reduce your net assets in the federal formula.

> *Tip 19b: If the school your child is attending uses the federal methodology, consider buying a primary residence if you currently rent. If you already own your primary residence, consider liquidating unprotected assets to prepay your home mortgage.*

The Perils of Inheritance and Gifts from Grandparents

Many accountants suggest that elderly parents put assets in their children's name. In this way, the elderly parents more readily qualify for government benefits such as Medicare; they avoid having their investments eaten up by catastrophic illness; and, if they are wealthy, their heirs avoid having their inheritance eaten up by estate taxes.

If a grandparent is contemplating putting assets in the parents' name, the parents should at least consider the possible financial aid consequences before accepting. Obviously, such a transfer will inflate your assets and possibly your income as well (the interest on monetary assets could be considerable). In many cases, while the grandparents may have transferred their assets to the parents, the parents do not feel that this money really belongs to them yet. When grandparents decide to move to a nursing home, or need health care not provided by insurance, the parents often pay the expenses. Since the money is not really yours to spend, you may feel dismayed when the colleges ask you to pony it up for tuition.

If it is possible to delay the transfer of assets until you no longer have to complete aid forms, you might wish to do so. Or perhaps the assets could be put in the name of another relative who does not have college-age children. If that is impossible, you should explain to the FAOs that this money really does not yet belong to you.

An even worse situation arises when grandparents transfer assets to the grandchild's name. These assets will be assessed at a much higher rate than those of the parents (35% versus a maximum of 5.65%). If the only possible choice left to you is to put the grandparents' gift in the name of the parent or the child, it is better to put it in the parents' name.

Trusts

While trusts have much to recommend them, their effect on the financial aid formulas can be disastrous. We are not speaking of the general feeling among FAOs that "trust fund babies don't need aid" (although this is a pervasive feeling).

The real problem is that the FAOs assume the entire amount in the trust is available to be tapped even if the trust has been set up so that the principal can't be touched. Let's see how this works:

Suppose your child Johnny has a $10,000 trust, which has been prudently set up so that he can't touch the principal, a common practice. He gets a payment from the trust every year until he reaches age 25, at which time he gets the remaining balance in the trust. Parents often set up trusts this way under the mistaken impression that the colleges will thus never be able to get at the principal.

However, because the money is in his name, it is assessed for his freshman year at 35%, or $3,500. Never mind that Johnny can't get $3,500 out of the trust. He, or more likely you, will have to come up with the money from somewhere else.

Next year, the need analysis company looks at the trust again, and sees that it still contains $10,000. So it gets assessed at 35% again, and again Johnny gets up to $3,500 less in aid.

If this continues for the four years of college, and it will, Johnny's $10,000 asset may have cost you $14,000 in aid. The trust may have prevented you from getting aid entirely, but couldn't actually be used to pay for college.

Put Not Your Trust in Trusts

If you are counting on any kind of financial aid and you have any control over a trust that is being set up for your child, prevent it from happening. If a grandparent wants to help pay for schooling, the best way to do this is to wait until the child has finished college. Then the grandparent can help pay back the student loans when they become due.

If a trust has to be set up, make sure at least that it is set up so that the principal money can be withdrawn if necessary. You might also consider setting the trust up in *your own* name. Parents' assets are assessed at the much lower rate of 5.65% each year.

Setting up a trust that matures just as your child is entering college would at least ensure that the money could be used to pay for tuition. However, if the trust is sizable, you may be jeopardizing any chance to receive financial aid.

If Grandmother wants to provide for Johnny's *entire* education, but doesn't want to wait until after graduation, perhaps a better idea would be for her to take advantage of one of the prepayment plans being offered by a growing number of colleges. We generally don't think a prepayment plan makes economic sense (see chapter 8), but in this one case, it would be infinitely better than a restrictive trust.

Direct Payments to the School

If you are in the happy position of having a rich uncle who wants to pay for part of your child's college education, he can avoid paying gift tax on the money (even if it is above the $10,000 annual limit) by writing the check directly to the school. However, he and you should realize that if your uncle is paying less than the entire amount of the tuition, this won't necessarily save *you* any money.

If you are eligible for aid and you receive any money from a third party toward college, the FAOs will treat this money like a scholarship. They will simply reduce the amount of *aid* they were going to give you by the size of your uncle's payment. Your family contribution will probably remain exactly the same.

If your uncle wants to be of maximum help, he could wait until your child is finished with college and *then* give you the money. If you were going to qualify for aid, this would ensure that you actually got it. You can then use your uncle's money to pay off any loans you've taken out along the way.

Stocks, Bonds, Money Market Accounts, and CDs

The need analysis forms ask for the value of your assets on the day you fill out the forms. For stocks and bonds, you can find the prices by consulting the market listings in a newspaper or your broker. Remember that bonds are not worth their face value until they mature. Until that time, they are worth only what someone is willing to pay for them at a given moment.

The need analysis companies will subtract debts against these assets. However, the only real debt you can show against these types of assets is a margin debt.

Many parents shudder when they hear the word *margin*. "Oh, that's just for people who really play the market," they say. In fact, this is not true at all, and margin debt may be one of the more sensible approaches to paying for college if you run out of liquid assets. Here's how it works:

In most cases, you set up a margin account with a brokerage firm. Using stock that you own as collateral, they will lend you a certain amount of money. Traditionally, you would then use this money to buy more stock. However, there are no rules that say you have to buy stock—these days, the brokerage firms are just as happy to cut you a check for the full amount of the loan.

Because this is a secured loan based on the value of your stock portfolio, the interest rates are far superior to unsecured personal loans. You still own the stock, and it continues to do whatever it was going to do. (Out of all the long-term investment possibilities, the stock market has been the single best way to build principal over the past 40 years.) In most cases, you get to deduct the interest expense against your income on your tax return. And—here's the beauty part—you get to deduct the entire loan from your assets on the need analysis forms.

Margin Can Pay for College

If you own stocks or bonds and you need the money to pay for college, it may make sense to borrow against these assets rather than to sell them. If you sell the investment and write the college a check, the money is gone forever. By borrowing on margin, you can avoid capital gains (which will raise your AGI) and still retain your assets.

A margin loan is a bet that the value of your stock will increase faster than the interest you are paying on the loan (and based on long-term past performance, this is a reasonable bet). Even if you don't make money on the deal, it will cost far less than an unsecured personal loan, and your assets will still be there when your child walks back from the podium with his diploma and tells you he wants to go to graduate school.

Margin allows you to avoid paying taxes on capital gains, keep your investment working for you, and reduce your assets in the eyes of the FAOs.

> *Tip # 20: Use a margin loan to pay for college and reduce the* appearance *of your assets.*

A major drawback to this type of loan is that if the stock market declines drastically, you may be asked to put up additional stock as collateral, or even (it would have to be a very drastic decline) pay back part of the money you borrowed. If you were unable to put up additional stock or money—or if you couldn't make the loan payments—you could lose the stock you put up as collateral. This is the kind of calculated risk you should discuss with your broker or accountant before you jump in.

Doesn't This Margin Strategy Conflict with What You Said Earlier?

In the "Income" section of this chapter we suggested that you avoid margin debt as an investment strategy. How then can we turn around now and say it's a good strategy for paying for college? Whether margin makes sense for you depends on what you're using it for. If you are using it to purchase more stock, this should be avoided as it will overstate your investment income and therefore your AGI.

On the other hand, if you do not have sufficient income or liquid assets (such as savings, checking, or money market accounts) to pay the college bills, margin debt is infinitely preferable to:

(a) borrowing at high rates from loan sources that are not considered debts under the aid formulas and/or

(b) selling off assets that will generate capital gains during a base income year.

Mortgages Held

This category has nothing to do with the mortgage you have on your house. It refers to a situation in which you are acting as a bank and someone else is making monthly payments to you. This situation might have come up if you sold your house to a person who could not get a mortgage from a bank. If you were anxious to make the sale, you might agree to act as the banker. You receive an initial down payment, and then monthly installments until the buyer has paid off the agreed price of the house plus interest. The exact terminology for this is an installment or land sale contract.

If you are the holder of a mortgage, the amount owed to you is considered a part of your assets. However, you should not write down the entire amount that is owed to you. A mortgage, installment contract, or land sale contract is worth only what the market will pay for it at any particular moment. If you had to sell that mortgage right now, it might not be worth its face value. You should consult a real estate professional or a banker who is familiar with second mortgage markets (yes, there actually is a market in second mortgages) to find out the current market value of your investment.

Ownership of a Business

If you are the owner or part-owner of a business, you must report the company's assets and liabilities (or your share of its assets and liabilities) on the aid form. From this, the colleges will determine your business's net worth. Net worth is NOT the same thing as what you would get if you sold the business; it does not include goodwill; it has nothing to do with gross receipts.

The net worth of a business consists of the cash on hand, receivables, furniture, property, and inventory held, minus accounts payable, debts, and mortgages. In most cases you can find the figures you will need from the company's year-end balance sheet, or a corporate income tax return (IRS forms 1120 or 1120S).

The main thing to realize here is that just like when you are assessing the value of your real estate, there is no point getting carried away with your valuation of your company. Business owners are rightfully proud of what they have accomplished, but this is not the time to brag. The higher your assets, the worse your chances of receiving aid. The FAOs are interested in only selected portions of your balance sheet. Don't look any further than they do.

For example, if your company is part of the service industry, it may have a very small net worth, even if it is extremely successful. Let's assume for a moment that you own a small advertising agency. Like most service industry companies, you would have no real inventory to speak of, little in the way of property, and, because you're putting your profits back into the company, not much money in the bank. The net worth of this company, as far as the need analysis form is concerned, would be almost nil—even if it were one of the most well-respected small firms on Madison Avenue.

Business Assets Are Much Better Than Personal Assets

Because the FAOs acknowledge that businesses need operating capital, their net worth is assessed much less harshly than personal assets. For example, of the first $85,000 in net worth, the colleges count only 40 cents on the dollar.

Thus if you own at least 5% of the stock in a small corporation, it may be possible to call yourself a part-owner and list the value of your stock as a business asset on the aid form instead of as a personal investment. How much difference would this make? If you had $40,000 in stock in a small, privately held corporation, you could find yourself eligible for up to $1,300 per year in increased aid simply by listing this stock as a business asset rather than as a personal asset.

Real Estate as Business

Can you turn your various real estate properties into a business? It depends. If you own several properties, receive a significant portion of your income from your properties, and spend a significant proportion of your time managing the real estate, then you probably can.

If you own your own business and the building in which you conduct business, then you certainly can. If you rent out one or more properties and file business tax returns, then you perhaps can. Some schools will want to see extensive documentation before they will buy this strategy. The benefits, of course, are enormous. Business assets are assessed much less severely by the formula. Listing your real estate holdings as a business could reduce your expected family contribution by thousands of dollars—if the FAOs buy it.

Ownership of a Farm

If you live on your farm and can claim on Schedule F of your IRS 1040 that you "materially participated in the farm's operation," the equity in the farm will be protected under the federal methodology. While the federal FAFSA form will still ask you questions about your farm assets and liabilities, the instructions to the form tell you not to include the "family farm."

Unfortunately, the institutional methodology used by many private colleges and some state schools will assess your farm equity, regardless of where you live.

If you are filling out the PROFILE form, be sure not to count the value of your farmhouse twice. If you list it under "home," then there is no need to count it again as part of your farm property.

All of our other strategies for ownership of a business apply to ownership of a farm as well.

Limited Partnerships

Under the aid formulas, limited partnerships are also considered assets. Determining a value for limited partnerships can be difficult. If you can't sell your interest in the partnership, and the other general partners are unable to buy back your shares, then it isn't worth anything at the moment, and you should list this worth as "zero." Again, the FAOs may not buy this strategy, but let them tell you that you can't do it.

The Business/Farm Supplement

Some schools ask the owners of businesses and farms to fill out a standardized form that asks about your business or farm net worth and income in greater detail. We will discuss this, as well as some more complicated strategies in the "Special Topics" chapter of this book.

Asset Protection Allowance

After the need analysis company has added up all your assets and subtracted allowable debts, they make one final subtraction, called the Asset Protection Allowance.

This number, based on the age of the older custodial parent (or custodial stepparent), is how much of your net assets can be exempted from the financial aid assessment. The older you are, the more the need analysis company allows you. Below is a chart that will give you a rough idea of the asset protection allowance permitted at various ages under the federal methodology. According to the Department of Education, this allowance is calculated to yield the same amount of money as "the present cost of an annuity which, when combined with social security benefits, would provide at age 65 a moderate level of living for a retired couple or single person." Of course, their idea of "a moderate level of living" probably means a more spartan existence than you had in mind. The CSS institutional methodology asset protection allowance for next year will be slightly different but has not been released as of this writing.

ASSET PROTECTION ALLOWANCE (approximate)		
Age	Two-Parent Family	One-Parent Family
39 or less	$33,100	$23,200
40–44	$37,300	$26,000
45–49	$42,400	$29,000
50–54	$48,300	$32,700
55–59	$55,900	$36,900
60–64	$65,400	$42,300
65 or more	$72,400	$46,100

After subtracting the asset protection allowance, the remaining assets are assessed on a sliding scale (depending on income). The maximum assessment on parents' assets is 5.65%. In other words, the most you will have to contribute is slightly more than $5\frac{1}{2}$ cents for each additional dollar of assets.

Parents with few assets worry that the colleges will take what little they have. In fact, a family with low income and, say, $5,000 in assets would almost certainly not have to make any contribution from assets at all. If your total net assets are less than your protection allowance, then your assets will not be touched by the FAOs.

This is how the colleges treat assets held by the parent. Now, the entire process will be repeated for the child.

Assets and Liabilities:
How the Methodologies Differ

THE FEDERAL METHODOLOGY
- Does not assess home value
- Does not assess farm value provided the family lives on the farm and can claim on Schedule F of the IRS 1040 that they "materially participated in the farm's operation"
- Asset protection table based on present cost of an annuity
- Provides for exclusion of all assets if you meet the simplified needs test

THE INSTITUTIONAL METHODOLOGY
- Assesses home value, but offers colleges the option of capping home value at three times income
- Assesses farm equity, even if you live on the farm
- Asset protection allowance based on current consumer expenditure survey data
- All assets are assessed, regardless of whether or not you meet the simplified needs test

STUDENT ASSETS AND LIABILITIES

Need analysis companies ask precisely the same questions about students' income and assets that they do about the parents' income and assets, but there is one major difference in the way students' money is treated.

Colleges take a much larger cut of students' money. A student's assets are assessed at a whopping rate of 35% each year (versus a ceiling of 5.65% on parents' assets). A student's income is assessed by up to 50% (versus a ceiling of 47% on parents' income).

Student Income

Under the federal formula, there is no longer a minimum contribution from student income, and the first $1,750 (after tax) dollars earned by a dependent student are excluded from the federal formula.

Thus an incoming freshman can earn about $1,980 before he will be assessed one penny. Once he crosses the $1,980 threshold, his additional income will be assessed at a rate of 50%. If he then saves his money, it will also be assessed as an asset at a rate of

35%. Thus, if he banks his 1,981st dollar, 50 cents of it will be assessed as income and 35 cents of it will be assessed as an asset. The extra dollar he earned could cost him 85 cents in reduced aid. While this is much better than the old ridiculous rule under which the same child would have been assessed $1.05 for each dollar earned over a certain amount, most students will still be better off devoting their extra time to their studies once they have hit the $1,980 mark.

And that's only if the college is using the federal formula. If your child attends a private college that uses the CSS institutional methodology, she will be responsible for a minimum freshman year contribution of $900 ($1,100 as an upperclassman) and there is no $1,750 income protection allowance. A student at a private college will owe only the minimum contribution as long as she keeps her income below $2,037 as a freshman and $2,490 as an upperclassman. Over $2,037, she may be losing 85 cents in aid eligibility on each additional dollar she earns and saves.

> *Tip #21a: For a student who hopes to receive aid from a school using the federal methodology, it doesn't make sense to have income higher than $1,980.*
>
> *Tip #21b: For a student who hopes to receive aid from a school using the CSS institutional methodology, it doesn't make sense to have income higher than $2,037 for an incoming freshman, or $2,490 for an upperclassman.*

The current assessment rates have set up a bizarre situation, in which the best way a student receiving financial aid can help his parents pay for college is by not working very much. If your family has no chance of receiving aid, then by all means encourage your child to make as much money as possible. However, any student who might qualify for aid will find that most of the money he earns will just be canceled out by the money he loses from his aid package.

Under current rules, it makes more sense for students receiving financial aid to earn the minimum amount of money the college will allow, and concentrate on doing as well as possible in school. Most aid is dependent at least in part on the student's grades. A high GPA ensures that the same or better aid package will be available next year; a good GPA also helps students to find better-paying jobs when they graduate so they can pay back their student loans.

There is only one type of job that really benefits a student who receives financial aid:

The Federal Work-Study Program (FWS)

The Federal Work-Study program, funded by Uncle Sam, pays students to work, perhaps in the college library, the dining hall, even sometimes in nearby off-campus businesses. Work-study earnings, while subject to income tax, are excluded from the financial aid formulas and will not decrease your aid. The money a student earns through work-study goes either toward tuition or toward the student's living and travel expenses. It does not count as part of the $900 ($1,100 for an upperclassman) minimum contribution from income that each student is expected to earn during the summer.

Because they are excluded from the financial aid formula, work-study wages are in effect worth much more than wages from a regular job. For an upperclassman receiving aid who has already earned $1,980 from non-FWS jobs, a work-study job paying minimum wage makes more sense than a $7.00 per hour regular job off-campus.

It's Too Late.
My Daughter Already Earned $3,000 Last Year!

Earning extra money is not the end of the world. Just remind her that as much as $1,350 of that $3,000 will have to go to the college. If she buys a car with it, she—or you—will have to come up with the money from some other source. You might also want to remind the colleges that while your daughter managed to earn $3,000 as a senior in high school, she is unlikely to earn that much again now that she is in college and has a tough work load. They might bear this in mind when they are allocating aid for the coming year. Some schools (Cornell is one) specifically ask you if your child will be earning less money in future years.

Student Income and Taxes:
Not Necessarily Joined at the Hip

When does a student have to file a tax return? Generally, a student who is being claimed as an exemption on his parents' tax return has to file if he has gross income of over $650 and at least one dollar of that income is unearned income (i.e., interest or dividends). If the student has NO unearned income at all, he can earn up to $4,000 in wages reported on a W-2 form before he is required to file. If the student is working as an independent contractor (with earnings reported to the IRS on a 1099), there are special rules to follow. Ask your accountant if the student has to file.

The rules used to be more lenient. The IRS is cracking down on parents who are sheltering assets by putting them in the child's name. If your child has any investment income at all, his standard deduction can drop from $4,000 to as low as $650.

A student who is not being claimed as a dependent on her parents' taxes can have income up to $6,550 without filing a tax return, provided that she gets no more than $400 net earnings from self-employment.

As long as your children are under 24 years old, and are full-time students, they can be claimed as dependents on the parents' tax return, whether they filed income taxes or not, and regardless of how much money they earned.

You should also realize that the colleges' criteria for who can be considered an independent student are much tougher than the IRS's. A student could have been filing a separate return for years, taking her own exemption, and paying taxes like anyone else, but that does not necessarily mean that she will qualify as an independent under the financial aid formula.

Can My Child Go the Independent Route?

If the colleges decide that a student is no longer a dependent of his parents, then the colleges won't assess the parents' income and assets at all. Since independent students are young and don't earn much money, they get large amounts of financial aid. The key point to grasp here is that it is the federal government and the colleges themselves who get to decide who is dependent and who is independent, and it is obviously in their best interest to decide that the student is still dependent.

We will discuss the criteria for becoming an independent student in part three, "Filling Out the Standardized Forms," and in chapter 9, "Special Topics," but don't get your hopes up. The rules are tough, and getting tougher all the time.

Student Assets

Accountants and other financial counselors love to advise parents to "put their assets in the kid's name."

As a tax reduction strategy, this is pretty good advice, since your child is almost certainly in a lower bracket than you are. Unfortunately, as many parents learn the hard way, following this advice during college years is virtually economic suicide.

Parental assets are assessed by the colleges at a top rate of 5.65% each year, after subtracting your protection allowance. Your child's assets, on the other hand, will be hit up for 35% each year, *and your child has no protection allowance at all*. Any potential tax benefits of putting assets in the child's name can be completely wiped out by the huge reduction you will see in your aid package.

> *Tip #22: If you think you will qualify for financial aid, do not put assets in the child's name.*

Even worse, some of the assets in the child's name can be hit twice each year: first, colleges take 35% off the top of the entire amount of the asset; second, the colleges take up to 50 cents out of every dollar in income generated by the asset.

Let's say a parent puts $10,000 in the child's name and invests it in a bond fund that pays 7%. When he fills out the need analysis form, he enters the $700 interest the fund earned that year under the student's income; because the $700 was reinvested in the bond fund, the fund now has $10,700 in it, so he enters $10,700 under the student's assets. The need analysis company assesses the $10,700 asset at 35% (in this case $3,745). The need analysis company also assesses the $700 income at a rate of up to 50% (in this case, $350). Note that the $700 income got assessed twice—35% as an asset, and 50% as income, for a total of 85%. That $700 in income may have cost the family $595 in lost aid.

It's Too Late. I Put Assets in My Son's Name!

If you have already transferred assets to your child in the form of a Uniform Gifts to Minors Act (UGMA) account, or a custodial account, or a trust, you should pause and consider three things before you strangle your accountant.

1. You may not have been eligible for need-based aid in the first place. If you weren't going to qualify for aid anyway, those assets are in just the right place, and your accountant is a genius.
2. You may have been offered only a subsidized Stafford loan. If you were going to qualify only for minimal need-based aid in the form of student loans, the tax benefits of keeping assets in the child's name may well exceed the aid benefits, and you did just the right thing.
3. Even if it turns out that putting assets in your child's name was a bad mistake, you can't simply undo the error by pulling the money out of your child's account now. When you liquidate a custodial account, the IRS can disallow the gift, come after you for back taxes and back interest, and tax the money at the *parents'* tax rate from the time the funds were first transferred to the child.

Is There Anything We Can Do to Get Assets Back in Our Name?

There may be, but this situation is much too complicated for us to give general advice. You should consult with a competent financial adviser who has a sound understanding of both the tax code and the ins and outs of financial aid.

Student Income and Assets: How the Methodologies Differ

THE FEDERAL METHODOLOGY
- First $1,750 in student's after-tax income is sheltered for a dependent student
- No minimum contribution from income

THE INSTITUTIONAL METHODOLOGY
- No income protection allowance
- Minimum contribution from income: $900 for incoming freshmen, $1,100 for upperclassmen

PUTTING IT ALL TOGETHER

Making an Estimate of How Much You Will Be Expected to Pay

After receiving all your financial data, the need analysis service crunches the numbers to arrive at your family contribution:

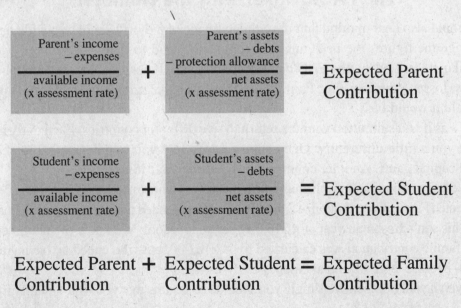

$$\frac{\text{Parent's income} - \text{expenses}}{\substack{\text{available income} \\ \text{(x assessment rate)}}} + \frac{\substack{\text{Parent's assets} \\ - \text{debts} \\ - \text{protection allowance}}}{\substack{\text{net assets} \\ \text{(x assessment rate)}}} = \text{Expected Parent Contribution}$$

$$\frac{\text{Student's income} - \text{expenses}}{\substack{\text{available income} \\ \text{(x assessment rate)}}} + \frac{\text{Student's assets} - \text{debts}}{\substack{\text{net assets} \\ \text{(x assessment rate)}}} = \text{Expected Student Contribution}$$

Expected Parent Contribution **+** Expected Student Contribution **=** Expected Family Contribution

If you have read this book carefully up to now, you know that behind the apparent simplicity of the chart above lies a wealth of hidden options that can save—or cost—you money.

By using the worksheet at the back of this book, you can get a rough approximation of what your Expected Family Contribution will be under both the federal and the institutional methodology. Bear in mind that it will be just that—an approximation. Our worksheet uses the same formula(s) used by the need analysis companies, but because you will be estimating many of the numbers there is little likelihood that it will be exact.

Parents always want the bottom line. "How much will I have to pay?" they ask, as if there were one number fixed in stone for their family. In fact, you will see as you begin to play with your numbers that there are numerous ways to present yourselves to the colleges. By using the strategies we have outlined in part two of this book, you can radically change the financial snapshot that will determine your Expected Family Contribution.

Your bottom line will also be determined in part by whether you choose schools that use the federal or the institutional methodology to award institutional aid. In most cases, the federal formula will come up with a lower EFC. We'll discuss this in more detail in our chapters on "How to Pick Colleges" and "The Offer."

Filling out our worksheet will be a quite different experience from filling out the need analysis form. The need analysis form asks you for your raw data, but does not allow you to do the calculations to determine your family contribution.

The FAOs Tinker with the Numbers

You should also bear in mind that the college financial aid officers have a wide latitude to change the figures the need analysis companies send to them. If a school wants a particular student badly, the FAO can sweeten the pot. If a school has a strict policy on business losses, your Expected Family Contribution at that school may be higher than the Feds said it would be.

It's as if you submitted your tax return to five different countries. Each of them will look at you a little differently. One country may allow you to have capital losses that exceed capital gains. Another country may disallow your losses.

We know of one parent with unusual circumstances whose need analysis form generated an Expected Family Contribution of $46,000 but who still ended up getting $7,000 in financial aid for his son's freshman year at a $16,000-per-year school. We know of another couple whose family contribution was calculated to be $10,000, but who ended up having to pay $15,000 because there was no aid money left.

Even if your numbers look high, you should not assume that you won't qualify for aid.

CHAPTER FOUR

How to Pick Colleges

How to Pick Colleges—
with Financial Aid in Mind

Richard Freedman, a former guidance counselor at prestigious Hunter College High School in New York City, used to keep a copy of *Who's Who* handy in his office. When parents came in with visions of Ivy dancing in their eyes, he invited them to look up famous people they admired in *Who's Who*. It turned out that their heroes almost never attended Ivy League schools.

We aren't suggesting that Ivy League schools are no good, or that your child should not apply to one of them, but it is worth noting (even as you look at the $28,500 price tag) that many important, interesting people managed, and are still managing, to get good educations elsewhere—and for less money.

There are many factors that go into a decision to apply to a particular college, and one factor that cannot be ignored is money. You and your child are about to make a business decision, and it's vital that you keep a clear head. How much are you willing to pay for what level of quality of education under what circumstances? It is possible to pay $28,500 per year for a worthless education, and possible to pay $5,000 per year for an outstanding education. Price is not always synonymous with quality. The real determining factor in the kind of education a student comes away with is how seriously the student took the experience.

This Is a Joint Decision . . .

Many parents feel that it is somehow their duty to shield their children from the harsh economic realities of higher education. It is a form of need-blind application, in which parents do their level best to remain blind to their own needs. They allow their children to apply to any school they like, without thinking through the consequences of what an acceptance at that school would mean. Taking on large amounts of debt should be a rational rather than an emotional decision, and any important decision like this should involve the student as well. Especially if money is a concern, your child should be included in every step of the decision making, from computing a rough estimate of the expected family contribution to picking colleges with a view toward financial aid.

. . . That You Must Make in the Dark

One of the frustrating parts about applying to college is that you have to apply without really knowing what it is going to cost. Well, of course you do know the sticker price, but as we've already said, the vast majority of families don't actually pay the sticker price. The $64,000 question is what kind of aid package the different schools will give you to reduce that sticker price.

The process has been made even more difficult by the Justice Department investigation into possible violations of anti-trust law by many of the highly selective colleges, including the Ivies. For years, the FAOs from these schools would get together at an annual "overlap" meeting to compare notes on students who were going to be accepted by more than one of these colleges. After these meetings, there was usually an amazing similarity between the financial aid packages offered to an individual student by the competing colleges. While the Justice Department has recently worked out an agreement with the colleges on this matter, it remains to be seen to what extent colleges will be sharing information with each other after this experience.

Therefore, financial aid offers are still likely to differ by many thousands of dollars. Any counselor who says he can predict the precise amount and type of aid you will receive at one of these selective schools is lying. Thus applying for college is something of a financial crapshoot.

Applying to More Schools

Many counselors feel that it is now necessary to apply to more schools than before, to ensure that one of them will give you a good deal.

One good offer can frequently lead to others. If you have received a nice package from school A, you can go to a comparable school B that your child is more interested in, and negotiate an improved package. For the same reason, even if your child has been accepted "early action" or "early notification" by her first-choice school, you might want to apply to several other schools as well.

An early action or early notification acceptance (unlike an "early decision" acceptance) does not bind the student to go to that school. The college is just letting you know early on that you have a spot if you want it. Your child has just been accepted by her first-choice school, which is great news, but you won't receive an aid package for several months. If the college knows that you applied only to one school, they will be under no pressure to come up with a good aid package. However, if you have received several offers, you may find that the first choice will be willing to match a rival school's package.

Students who need financial aid should always apply to a variety of colleges. Perhaps one or two of these should be "reach" schools at which the student is less certain of admission; the student should also apply to several schools that not only fit his academic profile but also have good reputations for meeting students' "remaining need"; finally, the student should apply to what we call a "financial safety school."

The Financial Safety School

Now it may well be that your child will ultimately get into his or her first choice (over 70% of last year's applicants to colleges in the United States *were* accepted by their first-choice school). Just as important, your child's first choice may even give you a financial aid package that is acceptable to you. However, part of picking colleges entails selecting second, third, fourth, and fifth choices as well.

This is an opportunity for your child to get to know several schools better. Students sometimes seem to pick their first-choice schools out of thin air. We have often seen students change their minds as they actually go to visit the schools and read the literature. If money is a consideration, discuss this openly with your child. Look at the relative merits of the schools as compared to their price tags, and discuss what sacrifices both the parent and the student would have to make in order to send the student to one of the more expensive schools if the aid package you get is low.

At least one of the schools you apply to should be a "financial safety school." There are three factors to take into account when picking a financial safety school. You want to pick a school that . . .

(A) . . . THE STUDENT IS PRETTY MUCH GUARANTEED TO GET INTO.

What is an admissions safety school for one student may be a reach for another. Force yourself to be dispassionate. A good way to figure out a student's chances for admission is to look up the median SAT scores and class ranking of last year's freshman class (available in most college guides). A particular college qualifies as a safety school if the student who is applying is in the top 25% of the students who were admitted to the college last year.

(B) . . . YOU CAN AFFORD EVEN IF YOU RECEIVED NO AID AT ALL.

For most families, of course, this means some sort of state or community college. There are some extremely fine public colleges, whose educational opportunities rival those of many of the best private colleges.

(C) . . . THE STUDENT IS WILLING TO ATTEND.

We've met some students who freely admit they wouldn't be caught dead going to their safety school. As far as we are concerned, these students either haven't looked hard enough to find a safety school they would enjoy, or they have unreasonable expectations about what the experience of college is supposed to be.

Let's examine what you might be looking for in a financial safety school based on a rough approximation of your Expected Family Contribution.

Federal vs. Institutional

In the previous chapters we have constantly referred to the differences between the federal and the institutional methodologies. By now you have probably figured out that in most cases the federal methodology is kinder on a parent's pocketbook than the institutional methodology. However, before you start looking only at schools that use the federal methodology, there are a number of points to be made:

First, a college that uses the institutional methodology must still award federal money such as the Pell and the subsidized Stafford loan using the federal criteria. Thus, the institutional methodology will only affect funds under the institution's direct control—principally, the school's private grant money, but also some federal money under campus control such as the SEOG grant, the Federal Work-Study program, and the Perkins loan.

Second, families may find that the difference in aid packages from two schools using the different methodologies is actually not very significant. Families who don't have a lot of equity built up in their primary residence, who don't show business or capital losses, or losses on property rental may not notice much difference at all.

Third, most of the competitive schools will be using the institutional methodology this year to award the funds under their control. It would severely limit your choice of colleges to apply only to schools that use the federal methodology.

The best way to find out which methodology is being used at a particular school is to ask an FAO at that school. However, as a rough guide, if the school wants you to fill out the PROFILE form, then it will most likely be using the institutional methodology.

Should We Apply Only to Schools that Use the Federal Methodology?

No. There are so many other factors that determine an aid package—demographics, special talents, academic performance, just to name a few. Any of these factors could make an FAO decide to award merit-based aid or to be more generous in awarding need-based funds. However, if money is a concern, then it makes sense to apply to a financial safety school.

If You Have Extremely High Need

If your Expected Family Contribution is in the $700 to $3,000 range, a good safety school would be a public university or community college located in your own state. This type of school has two advantages. First, the likelihood that you will be eligible for state aid is extremely good. Second, your child may be able to live at home and commute, thus saving many of the expenses of room and board.

However, a student with high need should not neglect to apply to private colleges as well, preferably colleges where that student will be in demand. If the student has good grades, or some other desirable attribute, the student may receive an aid package that makes an expensive private school cheaper to attend than the local community college. Remember, by good grades we are not necessarily talking straight As. At many colleges, there are scholarships available for students with a B average and combined SAT scores of over 1,000 (or the equivalent on the ACT). We've even seen students with C averages and high need get generous aid packages at some private colleges.

If You Have High Need

We are frequently amazed at how often families with high need choose an out-of-state public university as their safety school. For most families with an EFC of between $3,000 and $8,000, an out-of-state public university is the most expensive option they could possibly choose. Why? First, students from out-of-state are charged a lot more. Second, much of the financial aid at these schools is earmarked for in-state students. Third, you will most likely not be able to take aid from your own state across state lines. Fourth, if the student is likely to fit into the top half of the entering class, he will probably get a better deal from a private college.

Families with limited means have difficulty imagining that they could get an aid package of $25,000 per year, but in fact this is not out of the bounds of reality at all. Choose schools with high endowments where the child will be in the top quarter of the entering class.

Naturally, you can't depend on a huge package from a private college, so again, a financial safety school is a must. For families with high need, the best financial safety school is probably still an in-state public university or community college.

If You Have Moderate Need

A family with an expected family contribution of from $8,000 to $16,000 is in a tough position. This is a lot of money to have to come up with every year, perhaps more than you feel you can afford. As Jayme Stewart, a counselor at York Preparatory in New York City, says, "A four-year private school education is not an inalienable right guaranteed by the Constitution."

A family with moderate need might want to choose two financial safety schools consisting of either in-state or out-of-state public universities. Depending on your circumstances, either choice may actually cost you *less* than your EFC.

Financial planning is particularly vital to moderate-need families. The strategies we have outlined in the previous chapters can make a much bigger difference in the size of your aid package than you probably think, and may make it possible for your child to attend a private college. For private colleges, you should again be looking at several schools where the student will be considered desirable and stands a good chance of getting institutional grants and scholarships.

Preferential packaging is particularly important to moderate-need families, as is the practice of applying to a wide variety of schools. By applying to more schools, you increase the likelihood that one of the schools will give you a particularly good package. You can then either accept the offer or use it to try to get a better deal at another college.

If You Have Low Need

A family with an EFC of between $17,000 and $30,000 must decide how much it is willing to pay for what kind of education, and how much debt it is willing to take on. If you are willing to go into debt, then your financial safety school becomes merely a regular safety school.

If you are unlikely to get aid, some of the advice we have given in this book to people who want aid does not apply to you; for example, you might be well advised to put some assets into the child's name, you might want to set up a trust for the child, and the child should be earning as much money as possible in the years before and during college.

However, even families with low need should apply for aid. For one thing, with the cost of college being what it is, you may still qualify for some. You also have to look ahead four years. Perhaps your situation will change; for example, you might have only one child in college now, but next year you might have two.

Finally, as enrollment drops across the country, some private colleges are having trouble filling their classrooms. The FAOs at many of these schools seem to be more and more willing to play "let's make a deal." As a result, a family's final family contribution may end up being several thousand dollars less than was calculated by the need analysis company. If you have used our worksheets in the back of the book to determine your Expected Family Contribution, you should bear this in mind before you decide that your EFC is too high to bother applying for aid.

The Public Ivies

Over the past few years, the cost of some of the best public universities has skyrocketed, to the point at which an out-of-state resident can pay more to attend a public university than a private college. At the University of Michigan and the University of Vermont, for example, the cost to an out-of-state student is over $20,000 per year—hardly a bargain, even if the quality of education is high. However these and other "public ivies" remain good deals to in-state residents.

In the past, it was relatively easy to change your state of residence and qualify for lower tuition and state aid. However, in recent years, it has become almost impossible for an undergraduate student to pull this off, unless the entire family moves to that state.

Nevertheless, some of the "public ivies" remain bargains for everyone—University of Virginia, University of North Carolina at Chapel Hill, University of Wisconsin (Madison) and SUNY Binghamton are all first-class schools with undervalued price tags.

What to Look for in a Private College

If you are selecting a private college with financial aid in mind, there are some criteria you should bear in mind as you look at the colleges:

- What is the average percentage of need met? You can find this statistic in most college guides. A high percentage is a sign that the school is committed to meeting as much of a student's "need" as possible. This statistic should not be misunderstood, however, for it is based on an average. A school that normally meets only a low percentage of need may come through with a spectacular offer for a student the school really wants. Another school that normally meets a very high percentage of need may make a very poor offer to a student the school considers marginal.

- Does the student have something this particular school wants? Is the student a legacy? Is he a track star applying to a school known for its track stars? Is she a physics genius applying to a school known for its physics department?

- How does the student compare academically to last year's incoming class? If this is a reach school for the student, the aid package may not be outstanding.

- Some colleges are very open about their academic wants; they mention right up front in their promotional literature that a student with SAT scores above x and a GPA of above y will receive a full scholarship.

- What percentage of gift aid is NOT based on need? If a student has an excellent academic record, this statistic might give some indication of whether she will be eligible to receive non-need scholarships. Of course, this statistic might be misleading for the same reasons we mentioned above.

- What is the school's endowment per student? If the school is on its last legs financially, then it may not be able to offer a great aid package—to say nothing of whether it will remain open long enough for the student to graduate. Don't necessarily be scared if a small school has a small endowment—take a closer look at what that actually means. Earlham College in Indiana has a small endowment compared to, say, Harvard, but it has a very high endowment *per student*.

- Will the school use the institutional methodology in awarding aid under the school's direct control?

A General Note of Caution

Take the statistics in the college guides with a grain of salt. These statistics may show general trends, but (like all statistics) they are subject to interpretation. First of all, the information presented in these books usually comes from the colleges themselves, and as far as we know, is never checked.

Second, a particularly affluent (or poor) pool of applicants could skew the statistics. It would be easier for a school to meet a high percentage of need if the applicants to that school tend to be well off.

CHAPTER FIVE

What the Student Can Do

What the *Student* Can Do

Until now, most of our discussion has concerned what *the parent* can do to pay for college. Income and asset strategies, tax strategies, home equity loans—these are subjects that have little relevance for high school students. After all, in many cases, they have no income or assets, pay no taxes, and almost certainly don't own their own home. Is there anything *the student* can do to help pay for college?

The most obvious idea would seem to be for the student to get a job. However, under "Student Income and Assets" in chapter 3 we explained that earning more than a certain dollar amount will decrease a student's aid faster than the earnings can be deposited in the student's bank account. After $1,980, every dollar a college freshman earns and saves can decrease his aid eligibility by 85 cents. Of course, if his family is not eligible for aid, the student should be out there earning as much as possible; but if his family stands a chance of qualifying for aid, the student's time would be better spent (at least under the current ridiculous law) by making the most of his educational opportunities.

There are, however, some very tangible ways a student can help pay for college. The first of these may make it sound like we've been paid off by high school teachers, but here goes anyway:

Study Like Crazy

It's the gospel truth. Good grades make a student desirable to the colleges. Yes, this will help you get in, but in these budget-tight times, good grades also translate directly into dollars and cents. As we said in chapter 2, every tenth of a point a student raises her high school GPA can save her thousands of dollars in student loans she won't have to pay back later.

Even at the prestigious Ivy League schools, where students are supposedly awarded aid based only on their "need," applicants with high academic achievement do get preferential packaging—award packages with a higher percentage of grants and a lower percentage of loans.

If a student's dream is to attend an expensive private college, it isn't going too far to expect the student to contribute to help make that dream a reality. Parents are about to invest a sizable portion of all the money they have ever been able to save. It seems only fair that the student should be prepared to invest in his own future as well. And the single most productive way a student can invest in his future is by doing as well as possible during high school.

There are some colleges out there who state up front, "If you have a GPA of more than 3.5 and SATs of 1200 or above, we will offer you a full scholarship." There are other schools (more and more in recent years) that give out large merit-based grants, irrespective of need. These grants are not necessarily just for geniuses. We know of several colleges that award merit-based grants for students with B averages.

Take an SAT Review Course

Nothing can change a student's fortune *faster* than a big increase on the SAT. Look at it this way: it takes four years to accumulate your grades from high school. It takes six weeks to take a prep course. The latest study by FAIRTEST, published in *The New York Times,* showed that students who took these prep courses had an average improvement of over 100 points.

Every ten points a student can raise his score on the SAT can save his family thousands of dollars by increasing his desirability in the eyes of the FAOs, and hence, increasing the size of the aid packages they offer him. This is too important to leave to chance.

There are many companies that offer test preparation, some affordable and some quite expensive. We, of course, are partial to The Princeton Review course, which at the moment is getting average score improvements of about 150 points. If there are no preparation courses offered in your area, we suggest you at least buy a book put out by ETS called *10 SATs*. This will provide the student with actual SAT sections to practice on. If money is a consideration, don't lose heart: even some test prep companies offer financial aid.

Take AP Courses

Many high schools offer advanced placement (AP) courses. By passing an advanced placement test at the end of the year, a student can earn college credits without paying college tuition. Not all schools accept AP credits, but many do, again enabling a student to save his family literally thousands of dollars. Some students are able to skip the entire freshman year in this way, thus cutting the entire cost of their college education by one quarter. Consult with the colleges you are interested in to see if they accept AP credits, and with your high school to see which AP courses are offered, and how to sign up.

Condense Your College Education

You have to be a little crazy to try this, but for motivated students it is sometimes possible to complete a four-year education in three years. The family may not realize big savings on the tuition itself (since some schools charge by the credit) but there will be savings on room and board, and the student will be able to get out into the work force that much sooner.

A more reasonable goal might be to reduce time in college by half a year. By attending summer school (which is often less expensive than the regular terms) a student can reduce her time on campus by one full semester.

Even at half a year, this strategy may take its toll on the student. Academics are only one part of the college experience, and by accelerating the process, a student may lose out on some of the opportunities and friendships that make the college years meaningful.

Defer Admission

Many schools allow students to defer admission for a year. If the family is financially strapped, a student could use this year to earn money. You should always remember that at least under current law, student earnings above a certain dollar amount will reduce aid eligibility—thus for many students, this strategy could backfire. However, if the college the student really wishes to attend decides the family is not eligible for aid, and the family cannot shoulder the entire cost of college, this might be the only way the student could make up the difference. Be extremely careful in making a decision like this. If there is no reasonable plan for how you can meet the entire *four years'* worth of college bills, it may not make sense to begin the first year.

Go to School Part-Time

Some schools allow students to attend college part-time so that they can earn money while they are in school. Points to be aware of:

- Student loans become due as early as six months after the student stops taking classes or goes below half-time status. If the student takes too much time off between classes, she may have to start paying off the loans, even though she's still in school.

- The financial aid available for part-time students is much reduced. Particularly if the student is attending less than half-time, there will be little chance of substantial aid.

- Any money the student earns is going to be assessed by the colleges at a very high rate, thus reducing aid eligibility. You should consider carefully whether a job will actually help pay for college. It will depend on whether your family was judged eligible for aid, and what kind of package you have been offered. If you were not eligible, or if the aid package left you with a substantial piece of "unmet need," then part-time study may make sense. However, before you take that course of action, ask the FAO what would happen if the student earned, say, $15,000 after taxes this year. Would the student's aid package remain the same, or would the extra income simply reduce the aid package by $15,000?

Transfer in Later: Option 1

If a family is on a very tight budget, a good way to finance a four-year college education is to start with a two-year college education. Two-year community colleges or junior colleges, where the average tuition in 1995–96 was just $1,387, represent an outstanding way to save money. A student with a good academic record at a community college (perhaps earned while still living at home) can then transfer to a slightly more expensive state college for two more years to earn a BA. The total cost would be only a fraction of the cost of a private college, and still thousands of dollars less than that of a four-year program at the state college.

Transfer in Later: Option 2

If a student really has her heart set on a particular private college but the family cannot afford the costs of four years' tuition, there is another option: The student could go to a public college for the first two years and then transfer into the private school. The student will get the private college degree at a much more affordable price. Obviously, the student would have to get accepted by the private school as a transfer student, and this can be quite difficult. Outstanding grades are a given. We will go into this strategy in more detail in chapter 8, "Innovative Payment Options."

Transfer in Later: Option 3
Generic College, Designer Graduate School

Extending the previous strategy, a student could attend a good public university during all four of the undergraduate years, and then go to a top-of-the-line private graduate school. The undergraduate savings would be huge, but again, whether the student attends a private or a public undergraduate college, a compelling academic record is always very important to ensure acceptance.

The Senior Year

The family will complete its last standardized need analysis form in the spring of the student's junior year of college. Once that form has been filed, there are no longer any financial aid considerations to worry about. During the summer between junior and senior year, students who want to help out with the last year's tuition can earn unlimited amounts of money without hurting their eligibility for financial aid.

Of course, if the student goes straight on to graduate school, then the senior year of college becomes the first base income year for graduate school, and the process begins again.

CHAPTER SIX

State Aid

States sometimes don't get the credit they deserve for their most pervasive and sweeping form of financial aid: an affordable college education for in-state residents through public state university programs. These programs are still terrific values (as we explored in chapter 4, "How to Pick Colleges") and in some cases, the quality of education is at least as good as it is at the best private colleges.

However, it is the other kind of state aid that we are going to discuss here. It comes in the form of need-based and merit-based grants and loans to qualifying students who attend public *or* private colleges and universities within their own state. All 50 states have need-based financial aid programs for their residents, and more than 25 states now have merit-based awards as well. While some states are richer than others, and all states are feeling a fiscal crunch right now, the amount of money available for state aid is substantial; in many states—California, Illinois, and New York, to name a few—students can qualify for more than $3,000 each year in grant money alone.

To qualify for this aid a student must generally attend a public university or private college within the student's state of legal residence. A few states have reciprocal agreements with specific other states that allow you to take aid with you to another state. For example, if you qualify for Pennsylvania state aid, you are allowed to use that aid at any approved school in another state, except for Maryland, New Jersey, and New York.

Even If You Don't Qualify for Federal Aid, You May Qualify for State Aid

Because of the differences between the state aid formulas and the federal formula, it is sometimes easier to qualify for state aid. Federal aid is based on your adjusted gross income (along with information about your assets). In some states, however, aid is based solely on your taxable income (the AGI minus deductions) *without reference to your assets*.

Thus if you miss out on federal aid because you have been industrious and managed to save enough to make investments, you may be able to qualify for state money anyway. In some states, it is possible to own a mansion, a business, and sizable investments, and—as long as your *taxable* income is within state parameters—still qualify for thousands of dollars in aid.

There are too many states with too many different types of programs and formulas for us to go into each one separately. Suffice it to say that state aid is one of the more overlooked ways for middle- and upper-middle-class families to help pay for college. We estimate that thousands of these parents, under the impression they make too much money, never even apply.

How to Apply for State Aid

Some states use the data you supply on the federal FAFSA form to award their aid. Other states require you to complete a supplemental aid form that is processed directly by that state's higher education agency.

Confused? Very. Your high school guidance counselor should have the correct forms for your situation. If, for some reason, forms are not available at your high school, or your guidance counselor doesn't seem to know what is what, contact your state agency (a list of all the state agencies with their addresses and phone numbers is at the end of this chapter).

The only time the forms you find at your high school might not be the right forms for you is when the student goes to school in one state but lives in another. If this is the case, again contact your state agency.

If your family is eligible for state financial aid, your state grant will appear as part of the aid packages you receive from the colleges sometime before April 15. Obviously, unless your state has reciprocal agreements, the state money will appear only in the aid packages from colleges in your own state. Families that are pondering several offers from schools within their own state, sometimes notice that the amount of state money they were offered at each of the schools differs. This might be because aid is based not just on need, but also on the size of tuition at different schools. A more expensive school will often trigger a larger grant. However, if you applied to two comparably priced schools within your own state, and one school gives you significantly less state aid than another, then something is amiss because you should be getting approximately the same amount of state aid at similarly priced schools.

Alternative State Loans

Some states make guaranteed student loans much like the Stafford loans provided by the federal government. These are sometimes called "special loans." Again, if your state offers these loans and if you qualify, they will appear as part of your aid package.

Establishing Residency in a State

In-state rates are much cheaper than out-of-state rates at public universities; at the University of Vermont, for example, an out-of-state student pays $10,092 more than an in-state resident. So it should come as no surprise that students have tried over the years to establish residency in the state of the public university they were attending. Until recently, it was much easier for a student to establish residency in a state if he wished to take advantage of the in-state rates. It has since become much more difficult, with the exception of one or two states. We will discuss establishing residency in greater detail in the "Special Topics" chapter.

The State Agencies

Alabama
Alabama Commission on
Higher Education
P.O. Box 302000
Montgomery, AL 36130-2000
(334) 242-1998

Alaska
Alaska Commission on Postsecondary
Education
3030 Vintage Blvd.
Juneau, AK 99801-7109
(907) 465-2962

Arizona
Arizona Commission for Postsecondary
Education
2020 North Central Avenue
Suite 275
Phoenix, AZ 85004
(602) 229-2590

Arkansas
Arkansas Department of
Higher Education
114 East Capitol
Little Rock, AR 72201-3818
(501) 324-9300

California
California Student Aid
Commission
Customer Service
P.O. Box 510845
Sacramento, CA 94245-0845
(916) 445-0880

Colorado
Colorado Commission on Higher
Education
1300 Broadway, 2nd Floor
Denver, CO 80203
(303) 866-2723

Connecticut
Connecticut Department of Higher
Education
61 Woodland Street
Hartford, CT 06105
(203) 566-2618

Delaware
Delaware Higher Education Commission
Carvel State Office Building
820 North French Street
Wilmington, DE 19801
(302) 577-3240

District of Columbia
Department of Human Services
Offices of Postsecondary Education,
Research and Assistance
2100 Martin Luther King, Jr. Avenue SE,
Suite 401
Washington, DC 20020
(202) 727-3688

Florida
Florida Department of Education
Office of Student Financial Assistance
1344 Florida Educational Center
Tallahassee, FL 32399-0400
(904) 487-0049

Georgia
Georgia Student Finance
Commission
State Loans & Grants Division
2082 East Exchange Place
Suite 200
Tucker, GA 30084
(770) 414-3200

Hawaii
Hawaii State Postsecondary Education
Commission
2444 Dole Street, Room 209
Honolulu, HI 96822
(808) 956-8213

Idaho
Office of the State Board
of Education
P.O. Box 83720
Boise, ID 83720-0037
(208) 334-2270

Illinois
Illinois Student Assistance Commission
1755 Lake Cook Road
Deerfield, IL 60015
(708) 948-8500

Indiana
State Student Assistance
Commission of Indiana
ISTA Center Building
150 West Market Street
Suite 500
Indianapolis, IN 46204
(317) 232-2350

Iowa
Iowa College Student Aid
Commission
200 Tenth Street
4th Floor
Des Moines, IA 50309-3609
(800) 383-4222

Kansas
Kansas Association of Student
Financial Aid Administrators
Kansas Board of Regents
700 S.W. Harrison
Suite 1410
Topeka, KS 66603
(913) 296-3517

Kentucky
Kentucky Higher Education
Assistance Authority
1050 U.S. 127 South
Suite 102
Frankfort, KY 40601
(800) 928-8926

Louisiana
Louisiana Student Financial
Assistance Commission
Office of Student Financial
Assistance
P.O. Box 91202
Baton Rouge, LA 70821-9202
(800) 259-5626

Maine

Finance Authority of Maine
Maine Education Assistance
Division
119 State House Station
One Weston Court
Augusta, ME 04333
(207) 287-2183

Maryland

Maryland Higher Education Commission
Scholarship Administration
The Jeffrey Building
16 Francis Street
Annapolis, MD 21401-1781
(410) 974-5370

Massachusetts

Commonwealth of Massachusetts
Office of Student Financial Assistance
330 Stuart Street, Suite 304
Boston, MA 02116
(617) 727-9420

Michigan

Michigan Higher Education
Assistance Authority
Office of Scholarships and Grants
P.O. Box 30462
Lansing, MI 48909-7962
(517) 373-3394

Minnesota

Minnesota Higher Education
Services Office
Suite 400, Capitol Square
550 Cedar Street
St. Paul, MN 55101
(800) 657-3866

Mississippi

Mississippi Postsecondary Education
Financial Assistance Board
3825 Ridgewood Road
Jackson, MS 39211-6453
(601) 982-6663

Missouri

Missouri Coordinating Board for Higher
Education
3515 Amazonas
Jefferson City, MO 65109
(800) 473-6757

Montana

Montana Guaranteed
Student Loan Program
2500 Broadway
Helena, MT 59620-3103
(800) 537-7508
(For grants, contact college's aid office)

Nebraska

Nebraska Coordinating Commission for
Postsecondary Education
P.O. Box 95005
Lincoln, NE 68509-5005
(402) 471-2847

Nevada

State Department of Education
Capitol Complex
700 E. Fifth Street
Carson City, NV 89710
(702) 687-9227

New Hampshire
New Hampshire Postsecondary
Education Commission
2 Industrial Park Drive
Concord, NH 03301-8512
(603) 271-2555

New Jersey
Office of Student Assistance
4 Quakerbridge Plaza CN 540
Trenton, NJ 08625
(609) 588-3268

New Mexico
New Mexico Commission
on Higher Education
1068 Cerrillos Road
Santa Fe, NM 87501
(800) 279-9777

New York
New York State Higher Education
Services Corporation
99 Washington Avenue
Albany, NY 12255
(518) 474-5642

North Carolina
North Carolina State Education
Assistance Authority
P.O. Box 2688
Chapel Hill, NC 27515-2688
(919) 549-8614

North Dakota
North Dakota University
Systems
Tenth Floor, State Capitol
600 E. Boulevard Avenue
Bismarck, ND 58505
(701) 328-4114

Ohio
Ohio Student Aid Commission
State Grants and Scholarship Dept.
309 S. Fourth Street
Columbus, OH 43215
(800) 837-6752

Oklahoma
State Regents for Higher Education
500 Education Blvd.
State Capital Complex
Oklahoma City, OK 73105
(800) 858-1840

Oregon
Oregon State Scholarship Commission
1500 Valley River Drive
Suite 100
Eugene, OR 97401
(503) 687-7395

Pennsylvania
Pennsylvania Higher Education
Assistance Agency
1200 North 7th Street
Harrisburg, PA 17102
(717) 720-2800

Rhode Island
Rhode Island Higher Education
Assistance Authority
560 Jefferson Boulevard
Warwick, RI 02886
(800) 922-9855

South Carolina
South Carolina Higher Education
Tuition Grants Commission
P.O. Box 12159
Columbia, SC 29211
(803) 734-1200

South Dakota
Dept. of Ed. and Cultural Affairs
Office of the Secretary
700 Governors Drive
Pierre, SD 57501-2291
(605) 773-3134

Tennessee
Tennessee Student Assistance Corporation
Parkway Towers, Suite 1950
404 James Robertson Parkway
Nashville, TN 37243-0820
(615) 741-1346

Texas
Texas Higher Education
Coordinating Board
P.O. Box 12788
Capitol Station
Austin, TX 78711
(512) 483-6340

Utah
Utah State Board of Regents
Utah System of Higher
Education
355 West North Temple
#3 Triad Center, Suite 550
Salt Lake City, UT 84180-1205
(801) 321-7100

Vermont
Vermont Student
Assistance Corporation
Champlain Mill
P.O. Box 2000
Winooski, VT 05404-2601
(800) 642-3177

Virginia
State Council of Higher
Education for Virginia
James Monroe Building
101 North Fourteenth Street
Richmond, VA 23219
(804) 225-2141

Washington
Washington State Higher
Education Coordinating Board
917 Lakeridge Way
P.O. Box 43430
Olympia, WA 98504-3430
(360) 753-7850

West Virginia
Central Office of the State College &
University Systems of West Virginia
P.O. Box 4007
3110 MacCorkle Avenue SE
Charleston, WV 25364
(304) 347-1211

Wisconsin
Higher Education Aids Board
131 West Wilson Street
Suite 902
P.O. Box 7885
Madison, WI 53707-7885
(608) 267-2206

Wyoming
University of Wyoming
Student Financial Operations
Box 3923
Room 172 Knight Hall
Laramie, WY 82071
(307) 766-3214

American Samoa
American Samoa Community
College Board of Higher
Education
P.O. Box 2609
Pago Pago, AS 96799-2609
(684) 699-9155

Guam
University of Guam
Financial Aid Office
UOG Station
Mangilao, GU 96923
(671) 734-4469

Northern Mariana Islands
Northern Marianas College
P.O. Box 1250
Saipan, MP 96950
(670) 234-5498

Puerto Rico
Council on Higher Education
Box 23305-UPR Station
Rio Piedras, PR 00931
(809) 758-3350

**Trust Territory of the
Pacific Islands**
Palau Community College
P.O. Box 9
Koror, Republic of Palau, TT 96940
(680) 488-2471

Virgin Islands
Virgin Islands Board of Education
Storre Gronne Gade #1
P.O. Box 11900
St. Thomas, VI 00801
(809) 774-4546

CHAPTER SEVEN

Looking for a Financial Aid Consulting Service

Do the Form Even If He Doesn't Want To

Accountants want you to come back to see them next year. Even if your accountant hates preparing need analysis forms and even if he knows very little about the financial aid process, he will probably tell you that he'll do the forms for you. He's afraid that if he says no, you'll go to another accountant and he'll lose your regular business.

Why You May Not Want to Let Him

At stake are tens of thousands of dollars. You do not want to be your accountant's guinea pig. If your need analysis form is his first, or even his tenth, you may not get the best aid package possible.

Of course there are accountants, tax lawyers, and financial planners who have made it their business to learn the ins and outs of financial aid. The problem is finding out whether you are dealing with one of these knowledgeable experts or a rank beginner *before* you place your child's future in his hands. How do you find a competent person?

Ask Your Friends for Referrals

There is no licensing organization in this field, and asking your local Better Business Bureau about prospects will only reveal the most egregiously bad apples. The best way to find a good aid consultant is to ask your friends for a referral. Some questions to ask your friends:

- Did the consultant give them the forms in time to meet deadlines?

- Was he available throughout the year for planning?

- Did he give them an idea of what their Expected Family Contribution would be, and was it reasonably correct?

- Did he provide them with strategies to maximize aid for the coming year?

It's always hard to know what kind of packages a family would have received had they *not* gone to a professional for help, which makes objective comparison difficult. However, if your friends came away from the experience feeling that the professional knew the process inside and out and that they had been well taken care of, then you are probably in good hands.

Fees can be expensive, but if a professional can find you ways to increase your aid eligibility by thousands of dollars, even a relatively expensive fee is a bargain.

Be leery of professionals who try to sell you financial products. They may be more interested in selling you financial investment instruments you may or may not need than in getting you the most aid. You should also be suspicious if a consultant promises that you'll receive a certain amount of aid before reviewing your situation. And pass immediately on any professional who tries to steer you toward anything illegal. Please report any unprofessional behavior to the Better Business Bureau immediately.

Some Questions to Ask the Professional

Before you engage anyone to give you financial aid advice, you might want to ask a few of the following questions:

- What is the name of the state grants awarded here in _____?

Any professional who does financial aid consulting should certainly know the name of the state grants offered by your home state. Each state calls its grant something else, and each state has its own set of rules as to who qualifies for these grants. If the professional doesn't even know the names of the grants, he probably doesn't know the rules under which they are dispensed either.

- Should we put assets in the child's name?

A competent professional should know that student's assets are assessed at a much higher rate than parents' assets. If the family is eligible for aid, putting money in the child's name can be a very expensive mistake.

- Which year's income and assets do the colleges look at?

To determine what a family can afford to pay for college in the academic year of 1997–98, for example, the colleges look at the income from the *previous* year; in this case, 1996. They look at assets as of the day the need analysis form is completed.

- What is the difference between a Stafford loan and a PLUS loan?

Both are sponsored by the federal government, but the Stafford loan is made to students, while the PLUS loan is made to parents.

- Could you explain a couple of terms for us?

Go to the glossary and pick a few terms at random. An experienced professional should have no difficulty defining those terms.

One Question Not to Ask:

• Could you tell us if we qualify for aid?

Of course this is the one question you really want answered, but no competent consultant could answer this question without a detailed analysis of your situation.

If you've decided to fill out the forms yourself, the next section will provide a line-by-line guide to help you do just that.

PART THREE

Filling out the Standardized Forms

Filling Out the Forms

Any prospective U.S. college student who wants to be considered for financial aid must complete the Free Application for Federal Student Aid (FAFSA). If you are applying to private colleges (as well as a few state schools) you will probably also have to complete the Financial Aid PROFILE form.

Just in case you thought all this was too simple, there are also two different processors of the FAFSA and each puts out its own version of the form. Each processor will currently accept and process any version of the FAFSA. The two processors for the 1997–98 forms are the American College Testing Program (which will primarily handle FAFSAs distributed in the East and the South) and INET (which will mostly handle those FAFSAs for the Midwestern and Western parts of the United States).

While individual colleges may prefer that you use one processor over another, it really doesn't matter which processor you use since they must all analyze your information using the federally mandated methodology. Your EFC will be exactly the same.

After you finish filling out your form or forms, you mail them back to the need analysis company, which then sends out reports to you and the colleges you designate. Based on the FAFSA data, you will receive a report called the Student Aid Report or SAR. If you also file the PROFILE form, you will receive an "Acknowledgment" and a "Data Confirmation Report" from the CSS which lists the schools to which your PROFILE was sent and summarizes the data submitted respectively.

In this part of the book, we will give you line-by-line instructions for filling out the 1997–98 version of the FAFSA and the core questions of the 1997–98 PROFILE form.

First Step: Decide Which Form(s) to Fill Out

As your child narrows down his choice of colleges, you should find out which financial aid forms are required by each of the schools. Don't rely on the popular college guides sold in stores for this information. These books sometimes get their facts wrong, and can contain incorrect or outdated information. You also shouldn't rely on information you receive over the telephone from the schools themselves. We are amazed at how often schools have given us misleading or wrong information over the telephone. If you must rely on information given over the telephone, get the name and title of the person you're talking to. In the financial aid process, Murphy's Law is in full effect, and when things do go wrong, remember, it will always be your fault.

The best filing requirement and deadline information comes from the annual college-published bulletins. When applying to several schools you should keep in mind that you are only allowed to file one FAFSA form per year. You don't have to fill out a separate FAFSA for each college being considered. The form will have a space where you can list the schools to which you are applying.

What if one school wants you to fill out the one version of the FAFSA, and another wants you to fill out another version? Since you can fill out only one FAFSA per year, you'll just have to pick one version of the form. Regardless of what the colleges say they prefer, they will *accept* any version of the FAFSA.

Sometimes the Schools Have Their Own Aid Applications as Well

To make things even more confusing, some of the schools have supplemental financial aid forms for you to fill out in addition to the forms we've just mentioned. For example, anyone applying for financial aid at Cornell must complete the Cornell University financial aid application (form 2E) in addition to the FAFSA and the PROFILE form. Carefully check through the admissions applications of the schools to which your child is applying to see if there are any supplemental aid forms that you need to complete. Supplemental forms are very important and must be sent directly to the individual colleges. For now, we are going to talk only about the FAFSA and the PROFILE form.

Filling Out the Right Form

Make sure you are using the most up-to-date version of the form. Don't laugh. We've seen parents fill out last year's form. This can happen because the processing of the next academic year's need analysis form overlaps for four months with the processing of the current academic year's form. If you fill out the wrong form during those four months, the need analysis company will assume you are applying for the year already under way and you will be up the proverbial creek. The form you want will have an academic year written at the top that should correspond to the academic year for which you want to receive aid.

The forms also change color from year to year. The 1996–97 FAFSA was red and white; the 1997–98 FAFSA will be green and white. The 1996–97 PROFILE Registration materials were turquoise and white; the 1997–98 PROFILE Registration materials will be purple and yellow. For your information, the PROFILE form replaced the Financial Aid Form (FAF) which the CSS printed for the last time for the 1995–96 academic year.

Second Step: Know Your Deadlines

Missing a financial aid deadline is worse than missing a mortgage payment. Your bank will probably give you another chance; the colleges probably will not. Schools process their financial aid candidates in batches. At most schools student aid applications are collected in a pile up until the "priority filing deadline," and then assessed in one batch. If you send in your application three weeks early, you will not be better off than someone who just makes the deadline. However, if your application arrives a day late, it could sit unopened in a small pile of late applications until the entire first batch has been given aid. Then, if there is anything left in their coffers, the FAOs look at the second batch on a rolling basis.

Tip #23: Determine early on which forms you must file, and when they are due.

Meeting Deadlines

There are so many different deadlines to remember during the process of applying for college admission and financial aid that the only way to keep everything straight is to write it all down in one place. We suggest that you use the chart that appears on the following page.

You should realize that the deadlines for the FAFSA and the PROFILE form may be different for a particular school. While the FAFSA cannot be filed until after January 1, the PROFILE can be filed as soon as you receive it in the mail. A few private colleges (Middlebury College in Vermont is one that comes to mind) have in the past required the completion of the PROFILE by mid to late December. The earliest FAFSA deadline we've ever seen was the first week in January.

Since most of our readers apply only to schools that either do not require the PROFILE or do not require completion of the PROFILE until after January 1, much of the information in the remainder of this book assumes you will first complete the FAFSA and then the PROFILE if it is required. However, if you must file the PROFILE prior to January 1, you will have to file your completed PROFILE before the FAFSA.

COLLEGE	Admissions deadline	Which standardized need analysis forms (FAFSA, PROFILE) are required? When are they due at the processor?	Is there an individual aid form required? If so, when?	Are income tax returns required? When?	Any other forms required? (divorced/separated statement, business/ farm supplement, etc.) When are they due?	Name of contact FAO at college & phone number

As with Taxes, Filing Close to the Deadline Is Better

Conventional tax logic says that filing on April 15 reduces your chance of an audit. The same logic applies to financial aid applications. Even if you apply as early as you possibly can, the FAOs will not be able to start awarding aid until after the priority filing deadline. While they're waiting for the deadline, they will have time to examine early filers with a fine-tooth comb. Why give the schools extra time to think up embarrassing questions to ask you?

But Don't Miss It

Use the deadline chart on the previous page to note every deadline that you will have to meet for financial aid. This information can be found in the individual college bulletins.

There Are Three Types of Financial Aid Deadlines

1. The school says your application must be mailed (and postmarked) by a particular date.

   Send the form by registered mail, return receipt requested, and make sure the postal worker shows you the postmark on the envelope before you leave the post office.

2. Your application must be received and "date stamped" by the need analysis company by a particular date.

   In this case, you must factor in delivery time. Again, send the application by registered mail, return receipt requested. If you are mailing the standardized form close to this type of deadline, use the U.S. Postal Service's Express Mail service (return receipt requested). You cannot use Federal Express or any of the other private carriers because standardized forms must be sent to a post office box.

3. Your standardized application must be processed and the results sent to the school by a certain date.

   To be on the safe side allow six weeks' processing time. If the deadline is March 15, for example, then you should send the form to the need analysis company by February 1.

The Earliest School's Financial Aid Deadline Is YOUR Deadline

In effect, the earliest school's deadline by which a standardized need analysis form must have been sent to or received by the need analysis company becomes your overall deadline. Once the need analysis company has your numbers, it sends them to all the schools you designated.

One thing to be careful about: The instructions for the FAFSA say that you have until late June of the next year (that is, almost until the end of the academic year for which you want aid) to fill out the form. What they mean is that the need analysis company is willing to *process* the form until this date, but by then there will be virtually no money left at almost any college in the land. Many private colleges need your financial information by February 15 of the prior academic year (these are generally type 1 or type 2 deadlines). Some selective private colleges want the information as early as December 15.

The Standardized Form Deadlines May Be Different from the Individual Aid Form Deadlines

If you are applying to a school that asks you to fill out their own separate supplemental financial aid form in addition to a standardized form, make sure you know the deadlines for both. Unfortunately, the deadlines are usually different. Even if they are the same, the standardized form may have a postmark deadline while the college form has a receipt deadline, or vice versa. The only way to keep all this straight is to read each college's bulletin carefully and then use a deadline chart like the one we provide on page 130.

If You Are Filling Out Common Admissions Applications

Forty or fifty colleges currently belong to "common admissions application" programs. The idea is that you can fill out one admissions form and use it to apply to any of the member schools. Unfortunately, most of the schools involved have their own supplemental financial aid applications, with differing deadlines. If you will be using the common application for admissions, be sure to request individual admissions packets from each of the schools anyway—these will contain the individual financial aid forms, filing requirements, and deadline information.

Supplemental Forms at the Highly Selective Colleges

The Ivy League schools, the "little Ivies," and many other selective schools, have rather extensive financial aid forms of their own. The quantity of paperwork may seem daunting at first, but when you start answering the questions you will begin to notice that many of the questions on the forms are identical—designed to get more detailed responses to the questions already asked on the FAFSA and the PROFILE form and to discover inconsistencies in your responses. Individual schools may also ask a few questions that may strike you as bizarre. For example, Amherst wants to know if the student applicant is "given to drinking, gambling, or smoking." This is less Big Brotherish than it sounds. The FAOs are just trying to find recipients for a rather dated scholarship. We wouldn't dream of spoiling the fun by telling you which way to answer the question.

Third Step: If At Least One School Requires The Profile Form, Register With The CSS

Many private colleges and a handful of state schools will require completion of the CSS Financial Aid PROFILE form in addition to the FAFSA. While original FAFSA forms are widely available in high school guidance offices and college financial aid offices, the PROFILE form can only be obtained by registering with the CSS and paying a processing fee. Registration for the 1997-98 PROFILE can be done only by telephone, the World Wide Web, or electronic transmission via a computer network available at some schools. Purple and yellow 1997-98 PROFILE Registration materials are available in high school guidance offices or the financial aid offices of those schools which will be requiring the form. It is important to note that not all schools which require the PROFILE have their CSS code numbers printed in the PROFILE Registration materials. You should therefore carefully review each college's financial aid requirements in order to determine which ones need the PROFILE information.

A few weeks after you have registered, the student will be sent a customized PROFILE packet which will contain the following:

1. A personalized cover letter with detailed guidelines for completing the PROFILE form.

2. The core questions of the PROFILE form (Sections A through P). These questions involve the basic data requested by all the schools which require the PROFILE form. On pages 157–170, we will provide you with line-by-line tips for completing these core questions.

3. The institutional questions if they are required by one or more of the schools or programs involved. In addition to the core questions, the CSS has a pool of about 200 other optional questions and have downloaded these into their computer system. These "institutional questions" were culled from old versions of individual college aid forms as well as from requests submitted by FAOs at various schools. Based upon the college or program codes that you list on

Question 15 of the Registration form, the CSS will generate the appropriate institutional questions required by those schools. These questions will appear in Section Q of the PROFILE form.

4. Optional supplements. Based upon your response to Questions 7, 12, and 13 on the Registration form, you may receive a Graduate/ Professional Student Information Supplement, a Divorced/Separated Parent's Statement and/or a Business/Farm Supplement. (We discuss these supplements on pages 211–212, 215, and 220 in chapter 9.) These supplements should be completed and then sent directly only to those aid offices that require the particular form. Signed photo-copies are accepted by the FAOs. In the rare instance that you do not receive a supplement with the PROFILE packet and you know it's required of you by one of the colleges (consult each school's own financial aid requirement information), contact the FAOs involved and request the missing supplement directly. Do not automatically assume the CSS will send you all the required supplements.

5. An invoice for the processing fee. (Sent only if you did not provide credit card information when you registered).

Not Too Early

While counseling thousands of individual clients over the past 11 years, we've noticed that many families fit into two distinct categories: those who like to do things right away and those who like to wait until the last minute. When handling the PROFILE Registration process, either course of action could get you into trouble.

You can register with the CSS anytime after September 15, 1996 for the 1997–98 version of the PROFILE. However, since the PROFILE questions in Section Q are customized to the particular colleges you listed on the Registration form, you may not get all the necessary questions in your PROFILE packet if you register with the CSS before the student has finalized the list of colleges under consideration. While students can always have the CSS send the PROFILE information to additional schools, the processor will never provide any additional institutional questions that may be required by the additional schools, but were never previously asked. As a result, the additional schools may never receive all the necessary data they require. Unless the college requests the completion of the PROFILE form in the early fall for an Early Decision application (see page 225), it is a good idea to wait to register until late November when the student's list of colleges is better known. If your child is still unsure at that time whether or not they will apply to a college that requires the PROFILE form, it would be a good idea to list them on the Registration form just to be on the safe side.

Worksheet

Complete this worksheet before calling CSS to register for your customized PROFILE Application.

1 Student's name:

☐☐☐☐☐☐☐☐☐☐☐☐☐☐☐☐
Last

☐☐☐☐☐☐☐☐☐☐☐☐☐☐ ☐
First   M.I.

2 Student's permanent mailing address (mail will be sent to this address):

☐☐☐☐☐☐☐☐☐☐☐☐☐☐☐☐☐☐☐☐☐☐☐☐
Number, street, and apartment number

☐☐☐☐☐☐☐☐☐☐☐☐☐☐☐ ☐☐ ☐☐☐☐☐
City   State   Zip

3 Student's home telephone number:

☐☐☐ – ☐☐☐ – ☐☐☐☐
Area code

4 Student's title (optional):

☐ Mr.   ☐ Miss, Ms., or Mrs.

5 Student's date of birth:

☐☐ ☐☐ ☐☐
Month Day Year

6 Student's social security number:

☐☐☐ – ☐☐ – ☐☐☐☐

7 What will be the student's year in school during 1997–98? (check one)

☐ 1st year (never previously attended college)

☐ 1st year (previously attended college)

☐ 2nd year

☐ 3rd year

☐ 4th year

☐ 5th year or more undergraduate

☐ first-year graduate/professional (beyond a bachelor's degree)

☐ second-year graduate/professional

☐ third-year graduate/professional

☐ fourth-year or more graduate/professional

8 What is the student's current marital status? (check one)

☐ unmarried (single, divorced, widowed)

☐ married

☐ separated

9 Is the student a veteran of the U.S. Armed Forces?

☐ Yes   ☐ No

10 Is the student an orphan, or a ward of the court, or was the student a ward of the court until age 18?

☐ Yes   ☐ No

Worksheet (continued)

11 Does the student have legal dependents (other than a spouse) that fit the definition in the instructions?

☐ Yes   ☐ No

12 Are the student's natural or adoptive parents separated or divorced?

☐ Yes   ☐ No

13 Do the student's parents own all or a part of a business or farm?

☐ Yes   ☐ No

14 What will be the student's 1997–98 financial aid status?

☐ First-time applicant, entering student (including transfer student)

☐ Renewal applicant, continuing student

☐ First-time applicant, continuing student

15 Colleges, universities, and programs to receive PROFILE information. Write in the Code Number and Housing Code for up to 10 schools to which the student wants CSS to send information. Use only the CSS Code List. At least one code must be entered.

CSS Code No.   Housing Code*

1. ☐☐☐☐   ☐
2. ☐☐☐☐   ☐
3. ☐☐☐☐   ☐
4. ☐☐☐☐   ☐
5. ☐☐☐☐   ☐
6. ☐☐☐☐   ☐
7. ☐☐☐☐   ☐   *Housing Codes for 1997–98.
8. ☐☐☐☐   ☐   (Enter only one code per school.)
              1=Campus housing
9. ☐☐☐☐   ☐   2=Off-campus housing
              3=With parents
10. ☐☐☐☐ ☐   4=With relatives

16 Fee and type of payment

A. Registration Fee (Non-refundable) $ 5.00

B. Schools' and Programs' Processing Fee
(Multiply number from Question 15 above
by $14.50. Enter result. Must be
at least $14.50) $_____

C. Express Delivery Service (optional)
(Enter $10.00 to receive service.) $_____

Total (Add amounts on lines A–C) $_____

Have your credit card information available when you call CSS.

Check one: ☐ MasterCard   ☐ VISA   ☐ American Express

☐☐☐☐☐☐☐☐☐☐☐☐☐☐☐☐☐ ☐☐/☐☐
Credit Card Number   Expiration Date (Month/Year)

This form has been reprinted with permission. It is for information purposes only. Do not send in.

Not Too Late

In years past, you could locate, complete, and mail a CSS FAF form the day it was due and still meet your deadline. Eleventh hour procrastinators who try this approach with the PROFILE procedures will not be so lucky. While the CSS will provide a Federal Express delivery option (at an added cost of $10.00) for tardy families, it may still take seven days or more to get your customized PROFILE packet after you register, even with this option.

Completing The Registration Form

The 16 registration questions are rather self-explanatory. However, we caution you to carefully read and follow the instructions in the registration materials. There are also a few additional tips to keep in mind:

- Be extremely careful when providing the code numbers for the colleges and programs (question 15).

- If you are applying to more than ten schools that require the PROFILE form, you should list those ten schools with the earliest deadlines on the Registration form. When you receive the PRO-FILE packet, the CSS will provide information on how to add additional schools.

- If you are applying to more than ten schools which require the PROFILE form and/or you decide to apply to any additional schools that require the PROFILE form after you have registered, you should contact each FAO at those schools after you get the PRO-FILE packet. Mention to the FAOs that their school is not listed on the PROFILE form and ask them the institutional question numbers they require for Section Q of the form. If all of these questions are not printed on your PROFILE form, ask the FAO how to proceed. This will insure that these additional schools get all the necessary information.

Fourth Step: Decide Whether You Can Get Your Taxes Done in Time to Fill Out the FAFSA and/or the PROFILE Form

If your child is applying to any of the prestigious private colleges, getting your taxes prepared in time for the deadline is a forlorn hope. Federal law mandates that you must receive all of your W-2 forms by January 31. Even assuming that you actually have all the documents you need by the 31st, it would still be almost impossible to get your taxes and your financial aid forms filled out by the January deadlines favored by many schools.

How are you supposed to fill out your financial aid forms if you haven't done your taxes yet?

You Estimate

Regardless of what anyone says, do *not* miss the financial aid form filing deadline just because your taxes aren't completed. It is a perfectly accepted practice for you to estimate your earnings on the financial aid forms. The colleges know their deadlines are too early for most people to have completed their taxes. You will have the opportunity to revise your estimates later if you were wrong.

If your estimates are going to be wrong, err in your own favor. Slightly underestimate income and slightly overestimate expenses in order to come up with a slightly lower EFC. It is always easier to let them take away aid than it is to get them to give you more.

However, you should not pull your estimate out of thin air. Most colleges will want you to send them revised figures as soon as possible. When you receive your SAR report based on the data from the FAFSA it will contain instructions for revising your numbers, if that is necessary.

To estimate, you will need a blank copy of this year's tax form and all of the records that you would use to fill out your taxes. In essence, you will be doing a rough version of your taxes as you fill out the need analysis form. It is extremely helpful to have a copy of last year's tax return available as well so that you can use it as a checklist. So, for example, when you get to line 9 (dividend income) of this year's 1040, you can look at last year's return. Most people's financial situations don't change that radically from one year to the next. If your stock portfolio has remained basically the same, this year's dividend income should roughly coincide with last year's figure. If your situation has changed, it will be a reminder to call your broker for a statement of your dividend income if it hasn't arrived yet.

Whether you have already completed your taxes or are estimating them now, we hope you took or will take advantage of the strategies we've discussed previously.

Fifth Step: Gathering Together All Your Financial Records

It would be much better if you were not reading this chapter on the day of the deadline, because this is going to take more time than you think—if you want to maximize your aid. A ten-year-old child can fill out the form, but *HOW you fill it out will determine your aid package*. You can begin gathering together all this information in December.

Here are the records you will need:

IF YOU HAVE ALREADY COMPLETED YOUR TAXES

1. Completed federal tax return (all schedules)
2. W-2 forms
3. Records of untaxed income (social security payments received, welfare payments, tax-exempt interest income, etc.)
4. Bank statements
5. Brokerage statements
6. Mortgage statements
7. Student's social security number and driver's license (if available)
8. If you are an owner of a business, the business's financial statements or corporate tax return
9. Any other investment statements and records
10. Record of child support paid to or received by former spouse
11. Records of medical and dental expenses (must have been actually paid or charged on your credit card during the base income year)

IF YOU HAVE NOT COMPLETED YOUR TAXES

1. A blank copy of the 1996 federal income tax form
2. A copy of your federal return for last year (all schedules)
3. W-2 form (if unavailable, you can probably get your employer to tell you the numbers, or you can figure them out for yourself from pay stubs. Remember to include any bonuses or overtime you received.)
4. Any 1099s (statements sent by an employer, brokerage house, bank, or the government to report income earned as an independent contractor, dividends, interest, unemployment benefits, or a refund on state and local taxes from the prior year)
5. If you are self-employed, a record of all income received, and a record of all IRS-deductible business expenses

6. Records of untaxed income (social security payments received, welfare payments, tax-exempt interest, etc.)
7. Bank statements
8. Brokerage statements
9. Mortgage statements
10. Student's social security number and driver's license (if available)
11. If you are an owner of a business, the business's financial statements or corporate tax return
12. Any other investment statements and records
13. Record of child support paid to or received by former spouse
14. Records of medical and dental expenses (must have been actually paid or charged on your credit card during the base income year)

A Word on Confidentiality

The information you supply will go directly to the financial aid office and will stay there. You can trust them to keep information confidential. No one else at the school will see your personal data. And no one else at the school—not professors, students, or administrators—will know who is getting financial aid and who isn't.

Some parents are reluctant to share intimate details with a stranger. No matter how spectacular the details of your private life are, the FAOs have seen worse. And frankly, the FAOs are too busy coping with the needs of thousands of students to have time to make value judgments.

Currently the only way the IRS can see a copy of your need analysis form is by getting a subpoena, although the laws could change soon. There has been talk in the past few years about letting government agencies share data bases.

Photocopy, Photocopy, Photocopy

Before you even touch the form you are using, make a photocopy of it. You will use the copy to work on. Once you are satisfied with all of your entries, you can transfer the information carefully onto the real form. Only the original form will be accepted by the need analysis companies. When you've finished, make a photocopy of the completed form and put it in a safe place. If you are in the habit of just dumping all of your financial records at your accountant's office, change your habits for the next four years. Photocopy every conceivably relevant document, and *then* dump them at your accountant's office.

Read ALL the Instructions

You should read all the instructions on the form before you begin work. In many cases, these instructions will be sketchy or misleading. Hopefully this book will clarify what the forms do not.

Be careful not to mix up the various versions of the forms and their instructions. If you have decided that you need to fill out the one processor's version of the FAFSA, don't use the instructions for another version of the form.

Some versions of the FAFSA ask you to use a #2 pencil, others ask that you use black pen. Use what they ask you to. If you use the wrong writing implement, your need analysis will be delayed until they return your original form and you send them another one. Next year, when you fill out the form again for the sophomore year, don't get cocky. Read the instructions just as carefully. Sometimes the rules change from year to year. If the processor suddenly decided to switch to pen from pencil, you could get badly hurt. We have also seen cases in which the college FAOs told parents to use the wrong writing implement for a version of the FAFSA. The instructions for that particular version of the form supersede any instructions from the FAOs.

If there is a box to check, use the kind of check they ask for. If they want a ●, don't give them a ✓ instead. Writing in the margins is forbidden. You are also not allowed to give a range of numbers for a particular item. For example, you cannot write down $700–$800. It must be $750. Use whole dollar amounts only. Do not include cents or decimals. When writing down the numeric equivalent of a single-digit date, you must enter a digit for each box. Thus, January 5, 1974 would look like this: 01-05-1974.

Don't Skip

Finally, don't skip any question unless the instructions specifically tell you that you can. If you do not own a business, for example, put down "0" for that asset and "0" for what is owed on it. If you leave certain items blank, they will just send the form back to you to correct. You can't afford to lose the time that takes.

Let's Begin

You will find draft versions of the 1997–98 FAFSA and PROFILE form on pages 268–275. We don't anticipate any major changes in the ordering of the questions on the final version of these forms, but you can never tell. We will inform you of any significant changes to the forms or rules regarding financial aid if you are on our mailing list. Send the postcard bound into this book and we'll add your name to it.

Note: The IRS line reference numbers on the draft versions of the FAFSA and the PROFILE form printed at the back of this book may not correspond to the numbers on the 1996 tax returns. This is because the drafts had not yet taken into account the possible changes to the 1996 IRS line numbers. The IRS line reference numbers will be changed on the final versions of the FAFSA and the PROFILE form.

FILLING OUT THE 1997–98 FAFSA

Section A—You (the student)

1–3. **Your name.** By this, they mean the student's name. On need analysis forms, "you" always refers to the student. This name must agree exactly (down to the middle initial) with the name listed on the student's social security card. It should also agree with the name of the student on the admissions application. If the first name is listed as Giovanni on the social security card, don't write down John on the need analysis form.

If you have two children applying for aid, you must fill out two separate forms, even though the information will be largely identical. Do this even if the children are planning to attend the same college.

Your title. Mr. ◯ Miss, Ms. or Mrs. ◯—This question is optional. The only reason we can think of for answering it is if the first name of the student is ambiguous. It is just possible that if the FAOs decided incorrectly that "Leslie" is a boy, the application could be delayed if "Leslie" is a female and the records show that "Leslie" had not registered for Selective Service.

4–7. **Address.** Do not use the student's address at boarding school or any other temporary address. Much of the mail you will receive from the colleges will be time sensitive. It's important that you get it quickly. When filling out question 6—your home state—use the abbreviations listed on page 2 of the FAFSA instructions.

8. **Your social security number.** By this they mean the student's social security number. These days, all students are required to have one. If your child does not have one, get one immediately; your form will be returned unprocessed if you do not complete this item. If you can't get a number in time for the deadlines, call the need analysis company. If your child does have one, be careful copying the social security number onto the form and make sure it agrees with the number on the admissions application. At the larger schools students are called up on the computer by social security number. The Department of Education will now check your number against the social security database. If the number doesn't match the name, there will be no aid until the problem is corrected and it does match.

9. **Your date of birth**. Again, this is the *student's* date of birth.

10. **Your permanent home phone.** Remember to include the area code.

11. **Your state of legal residence.** This can be quite important if you are applying to state schools. Look up the correct abbreviation for the student's state of residence in the instructions that come with the forms.

12. **Date you began living in your state of legal residence**. This is a double check to see if you really meet the residency requirements of the state you put down in question 11. For a student who moved to this state on March 5, 1985, write, "03, 05, 85" not "3, 5, 85." If the student has always lived in the state, list his birthdate.

13–14. **Your driver's license**. This question is presumably here so that there is some means of tracking the student down later for student loan payments. When you copy down the license number itself, do not include dashes or spaces even if you see them on your license. If the student doesn't have a valid license, write "NONE" in the license number space.

15–16. **Are you a U.S. citizen?** To get federal aid the student must be either a U.S. citizen or an eligible noncitizen (in most cases, the holder of a green card, although there are some exceptions. Consult the instructions for the FAFSA). If the student will have a green card by the time she starts school, but doesn't have one on the day you fill out the form, you should contact the financial aid offices of the schools she is interested in for further instructions on how to proceed.

   If the student is not a U.S. citizen or eligible noncitizen you may also have to complete special "international student" aid forms. Ask the FAOs for details at the schools to which you are applying.

17–18. **As of today, are you married?** This refers to the *student's* marital status, not the parents'. If the student is married, separated, widowed or divorced, answer question 18 as well; otherwise, leave it blank. Note : If you filled in oval 2 for question 17, then all student income and asset questions for sections F and G of the FAFSA (as well as Sections B, C, D, and E of the PROFILE, if required) must include information regarding the student's spouse as well.

19. **Will you have your first bachelor's degree before July 1, 1997?** For most students, of course, the answer will be no.

Section B—Education Background

20–21. **High school diploma information.** You either graduated from high school or you earned your GED. You can't have done both. Fill in the date in the correct space. Leave these blank if you did neither.

22–23. **Parents' education.** These questions do not affect federal or institutional aid. They may affect state aid in a handful of cases. These questions relate to the natural parents of the student—not the stepparents. These questions refer to the highest grade completed, not the highest program. Thus, if the student's father attended only one year of college, fill in oval 3, "college or beyond," in question 22.

Section C—Your Plans

24–28. **Your expected enrollment status.** It is better from a financial aid standpoint to be attending full-time or at least more than half-time. You will receive more aid. If you aren't sure what constitutes full-time, three-quarter time or half-time, consult your FAO about what your status will be. Answer each of the five questions, and remember to fill in the oval for "Not enrolled" if applicable.

29. **Your course of study. 30–31. Your degree certificate code, and the date you expect to receive it.** For questions 29 and 30, write in the code for "Other/undecided" unless you are absolutely sure (the codes can be found on page 3 of the instructions). This is especially important if you are applying to widely divergent programs at different schools; for example, if you are applying to the Cornell School of Hotel Management and the Columbia School of Engineering, or if you are planning a double major. For question 31, if you are unsure, use a later date. Be sure to write down all four digits for the year.

32. **Your grade level during the 1997–98 school year?** If your child will be enrolling for the first time as a freshman, he should fill in oval 1 even if he took college courses while he was in high school. This question is used to determine annual borrowing limits for student loans and refers to the student's academic standing at school, not the number of years he's been attending college.

List the grade level the student has attained at the start of the academic year, rather than the level the student *will* attain during the year. For example, a student who in the fall term will be a second semester sophomore should fill in oval 3 ("2nd year/sophomore") even though she will be a junior by midyear.

33–35. **Other types of financial aid you're interested in**. You would like the colleges to come up with their best offer before you start to commit yourself. Because of this, we recommend that you answer "yes" to each question. This does not commit you; you can change your mind later. These questions have no effect on grant or scholarship eligibility.

36. **Do you plan to attend the same college in 1997–98?** If the student is in high school or never attended college prior to the 1997–98 academic year, leave this blank. If the student attended a particular college, then stopped for a while, and now plans to re-enroll at the same school, fill in the "Yes" oval.

37. **Dependents**. This question is asking if the *student* has any dependents for whom childcare will be paid. If this is not the case, write in 00.

38–39. **Veterans' Education Benefits.** For most families questions 38 and 39 will not be applicable. If this is the case for you, put down "0" for question 38 and "00" for question 39. If you expect to receive veterans' benefits, note that this question is asking about educational benefits only.

Section D—Student Status

These questions are here to establish whether a student is independent or dependent. (A dependent student receives financial help from her family. An independent student does not.) The colleges would prefer that all their students were dependent. Independent students are much more expensive for a school since they usually require more financial aid.

Of course it would be wonderful if your child could establish that he is independent, but there are several tough criteria to meet and they get tougher all the time. If a student can answer "yes" to any of the **questions 40–45**, then he is undoubtedly independent for federal aid purposes for the 1997–98 academic year.

40. Were you born before January 1, 1974?

41. Are you a veteran of the U.S. Armed Forces?

42. Will you be enrolled in a graduate or professional program (beyond a bachelor's degree) in 1997–98?

43. Are you married?

44. Are you an orphan or a ward of the court, or were you a ward of the court until age 18?

45. Do you have legal dependents (other than a spouse) that fit the definition on page 4 of the FAFSA instruction booklet?

If you answered "Yes" to any of these questions, according to federal guidelines, you are an independent student and you can skip the parents' green-shaded questions on the rest of the form.

If you answer "No" to each of the questions from 40–45, then most likely the child will be considered a dependent student—in which case you get to skip the gray-shaded independent student questions on the rest of the form. To be absolutely sure that you are answering these questions correctly, read the FAFSA instructions very carefully.

All students, whether dependent or independent, have to fill out the unshaded sections of the form.

The one exception to these rules would be for certain graduate health profession students. Graduate students who apply for federal aid from programs under title VII of the Public Health Service Act must give information about their parents, even if they filled in "yes" to any of the questions in Section D. In this instance, we suggest you contact the FAOs at the schools to which you are applying and inquire about this before you fill out the forms.

A few years ago, claiming that the child was an independent student was a popular financial aid loophole that many parents took advantage of. The colleges and the government have since cracked down and every year the rules get more stringent. If you can go the independent route, be prepared to provide extensive documentation—i.e., birth certificate (proving you will be over 24 by the time you receive aid), marriage license, discharge papers, etc. You should also be aware that many schools have even tougher criteria for proving independence than the federal guidelines. Some colleges require independent students to fill out the parent information on the PROFILE form (not the FAFSA) even if they do fit the federal guidelines, and a few will insist that parents are still responsible for some portion of their child's tuition.

In very rare circumstances, the FAOs can use their professional judgment to decide that a student is independent even if the student doesn't completely fit the federal criteria.

Section E—Household Information

If the student is independent, you don't have to answer questions 48–52 related to parents. If the student is dependent, you can skip questions 46 and 47 in this section.

Since we realize that the majority of our readers will be completing the FAFSA for dependent students, we are going to deviate from the order of questions, and describe the parent questions first.

48. **What is your parents' current marital status?** Given the state of modern relationships in this country, this is a complicated question. For financial aid purposes, "parent" means the person or persons the child lived with most during the past 12 months—known as the custodial parent(s)—or if both parents are dead, the legal guardian. (For the definition of "legal guardian," refer to page 9 of the FAFSA instructions.) This is not necessarily the same parent who claims the child on a tax return or the person who was awarded custody by the courts. If you are divorced or separated, please read chapter 9 of this book, "Special Topics."

   "Marital status" refers to the custodial parents' status RIGHT NOW.

   - **single**—If the natural parents of the child never married each other, or anyone else, ever, this is the oval you fill in. This is not asking if you are single *again*.

   - **married**—If the natural parents of the student are still married, fill in "married." If the custodial parent was divorced or widowed and has since remarried, also fill in "married." In this case, for the remaining questions the stepparent will be considered the other parent.

   - **separated**—If the natural parents are separated, fill in "separated." You do not need to have a legal separation agreement to be considered separated under the aid formula. If the custodial parent was divorced or widowed, remarried, and is now separated *again,* fill in "separated."

   - **divorced**—If the parent with whom the child lives is divorced and has not remarried, fill in "divorced." If the custodial parent was divorced or widowed, got married and divorced *again,* fill in "divorced."

   - **widowed**—If the custodial parent is widowed, and has not since remarried, fill in "widowed."

49. **Parents' state of legal residence.** Be sure to use the correct abbreviation.

50. **Date parents became legal residents.** Use the earliest date that either of the student's custodial parents (or stepparent) began living in the state.

51. **Number of family members.** This question is used to determine the income protection allowance. You would like this number to be as high as possible. The more family members, the higher your allowance. Include the student whose name is on the application, custodial parents (this includes a steppar-

ent as long as he or she is living in the household), younger siblings, older siblings (even if they don't live at home so long as they are receiving more than half of their support from the custodial parents or they are not yet considered "independent" for federal aid purposes for the 1997–98 academic year), grandparents or other individuals (if they live in the household and get more than half support from the custodial parents and will continue to get this support during the 1997–98 academic year), and newborn babies (even if they are not yet born when you are filling out the form).

The number of family members does not have to agree with the number of exemptions you took on your taxes for the past year, but if it doesn't, the colleges will probably ask why. That's okay. Just be prepared to explain.

52. **Number of college students in the family.** One of the myths about college is that it is better not to have two kids in school at the same time. In fact, if you qualify for aid, the more members of your family who can attend college at the same time, the better. In addition to being enrolled at least half time (6 credits or more per semester or the equivalent), the other family member must be "working toward a degree or certificate leading to a recognized education credential at a college that is eligible to participate in any of the federal student aid programs" (though the family member need not be receiving any aid). The student applying for aid should always be included even if he is attending college less than half-time.

In theory, the parents' expected contribution stays the same regardless of how many students are in school. If you have one daughter in school, you will be expected to pay the full amount of the parents' contribution toward her tuition. If you have two daughters in college at the same time, the two colleges will usually divide the parents' contribution between them and make up the difference with a larger aid package. For example, let's suppose that Mr. and Mrs. Jones have two sons, Frank and Tom. Last year, only Frank was attending college. The Joneses' expected contribution was judged to be $9,000, and they paid the full $9,000 to Frank's college. This year both Frank and Tom will be in college, but the Joneses' expected contribution is still just $9,000. Each school will receive $4,500 and will try to make up the difference with additional aid. In effect, the Joneses are getting two educations for the price of one.

In addition, some parents who might not have qualified for aid with only one child in college find that with two children in school at the same time, they do qualify for substantial amounts of aid. This is why it is worth applying for aid each year, even if you were refused the first time.

If one of your children is trying to decide whether to take a year off from college, this might be a factor when it comes time to make that decision. You want as much overlap as possible.

Parents can also be college students. In fact, if one parent has always dreamed about going back to school, this might be the time to do it. As long as the parent attends college at least half-time in an approved program of study, he or she will be considered a college student under the federal methodology. Individual schools may disallow this tactic but it is certainly worth a try, for it could substantially reduce the price of both sets of education. (Note: Even if the colleges nix this strategy, it could still help both college students— younger and older—to become eligible for Stafford loans and/or the Pell Grant.)

You have to answer **questions 46 and 47** only if you are an independent student. The strategy here is the same as it will be for questions 51 and 52: the more family members the better; the more family members in college the better. Compared to question 51, question 46 has a slightly more rigid definition of which children can be considered to be members of the household. Therefore, if you are completing the gray sections of the form, be sure to read the FAFSA instructions related to this section carefully.

Section F—1996 Income, Earnings, and Benefits

(See chapter 3 for our suggested strategies.) Each of the questions in this section must be answered by both the parents and the student, unless the student is independent, in which case you can skip questions 65–76. If you are separated, divorced, or widowed, and you have not since remarried, put "0" for all the spouse items. Do not leave any items blank. If you are separated but continue to file a joint tax return, write down only your proportionate share of the income on your joint return, and your proportionate share of the taxes that were paid. The same holds true if you were recently widowed.

Note: The FAFSA now begins asking two sets of interlocking questions that apply both to the parent and to the student. The questions are the same, although the numbering is different. For simplicity's sake, we are pairing up the questions. Thus, for example, we will address question 55—the adjusted gross income for the student—and question 67— the adjusted gross income for the parent—simultaneously.

53. **and 65. Type of U.S. income tax return.** Most parents will probably be using the 1040 form just because their tax situation is no longer simple. If children can avoid filing a tax return at all, it will be to the family's advantage. If your child must file, use the simplest form possible. If both the parent *and* the child can file the 1040A or the 1040EZ form, it may be to your advantage to do so in order to qualify for the Simplified Needs Test (which excludes your assets from the federal formula). If you are going to be estimating on the FAFSA, you may at least want to figure out which IRS form you will eventually be using. By saying here on the FAFSA that you intend to file the 1040, you will disqualify yourself

from the Simplified Needs Test during the initial processing. Even if you later end up filing the short form and qualify for the Simplified Needs Test, you may find that the colleges have given away the bulk of their available aid, and will not be able to increase your package.

By the same token, if you say here that you intend to use the short form and then eventually file the long form, you may lose your Simplified Needs status, and with it, a substantial piece of change in the form of reduced aid.

Note: If you file or will file an IRS 1040-TEL, which involves filing by telephone (available in some states), fill in the oval for completed or estimated 1040A or 1040EZ.

a. If you have already filed a 1040EZ or a 1040A, fill in oval 1. Note: If you file a 1040 but were eligible to file a 1040A or 1040EZ, fill in oval 1 as well, but be sure to reread our section on the Simplified Needs Test (pages 39–43).
b. If you have already filed a 1040, fill in oval 2.
c. If you are estimating, and plan to file the 1040EZ or 1040A, fill in oval 3.
d. If you are estimating, and plan to file the 1040, fill in oval 4.
e. If you are not filing a return, fill in oval 5 and skip to question 57 (for the student) or 69 (for the parent.)

If you filed a foreign tax return, consult the "Special Topics" chapter.

54. **and 66. Total number of exemptions.** Eventually, this number is going to have to agree with the number of exemptions you take on your taxes. If you filed or will file an IRS 1040 EZ, consult the FAFSA instructions (p. 6) for guidelines on how to answer this question.

A custodial parent who is still filing jointly with someone else (let's say, for example, that you are separated from your husband, but are not yet divorced, or you are recently widowed) should write down only the proportionate share of income, exemptions, and taxes that belong to the custodial parent.

Even if your child is a millionaire child star, you are allowed to claim him as a dependent on your tax return until he is 24 years old, provided he is a full-time student. Of course if he is a millionaire, he will probably want the $2,550 personal exemption for himself. Since *most* kids earn less than their parents, most families will be better off putting "0"s in the child's exemption box on the aid form (and on his tax return), and adding his exemption to the parents' exemption box.

55. and 67. Adjusted gross income. If you've already filed your taxes, just copy the appropriate line requested from your federal return. For example, if you filed the 1040, the AGI is on line 31.

If you have not yet filed your taxes, then now is the time to bring all the tax-planning strategies we've discussed in earlier chapters to bear in order to make your AGI as small as possible. Refer to our chapters on income and expenses for specifics.

Use the worksheet we provide at the back of this book (called Table 3). Remember to save all worksheets as well as copies of all documentation. Last year's returns can be very helpful in reminding you of all the different kinds of income and expenses you have had in the past. A blank copy of this year's federal tax form is important in case there have been any changes in the tax law or in the line numbers for the various items on the tax form itself. The same process must be duplicated for the student's income.

Veterans of the financial aid process may recall that prior to the 1994–95 academic year, they were told to exclude need-based financial aid (including work-study earnings) from the AGI figure they listed on the aid form. The government changed its mind, and now asks for this information in a separate question (64 for students, 76 for parents) which we will cover later on.

56. and 68. U.S. income tax paid. See pages 59–61 for our suggested strategies. If you have already filed an income tax return, you should write down the total federal income taxes that you paid. The FAFSA form will tell you where to find this on your tax return. Do not include self-employment tax.

If you are estimating, remember that this number is not necessarily the same as the amount your employer withheld. You may have to pay more or less than your withholdings. Remember also that you paid taxes even if you got a refund. Every year we see at least one family who, because they received a refund, put down "0" for their U.S. income tax paid. The amount of federal taxes you paid will be a deduction in the aid formula, so it is in your interest to report all of it.

The need analysis companies always seem to catch errors in the parents' favor, but we cannot remember the last time we saw them *notify* a parent of an error that would save the parents money. Chances are, if you make an error such as underreporting your tax bill, your mistake could cost you money for four years.

Self-employed parents, who make quarterly estimated payments to the IRS, sometimes forget that a large part of the money they send to the IRS is self-employment tax, which should not be included here. Although *this* mistake would be in your favor, the FAOs would almost certainly catch it, causing delays and frustration.

Even if there is no time to get your taxes done in time to complete the need analysis form, your accountant may be able to give you an estimate of your tax liability. If this is the case, we hope that you examine his work in light of the strategies we have outlined. If his plan includes transferring assets or income to the child, please give him your copy of this book and ask him to think again.

If you do your own taxes, you will in effect be creating a pro forma tax return, which you will probably be able to use (with some minor adjustments) once you've received all your W-2s and 1099s in the mail.

ADD UP

father's income (less deferred compensation)

mother's income (less deferred compensation)

all other taxable income

THEN SUBTRACT

adjustments to income

itemized deductions (or the standard deduction)

number of exemptions multiplied by $2,550

The result is an estimate of your taxable income. Now consult the tax tables in the federal tax instructions to determine what the tax on that estimate would be. Be careful to use the *current* year's tax tables.

57., 58., 69., and 70. Income earned from work. See pages 43–45 and 61–62 for suggested strategies. Parents always ask, "We already gave them our adjusted gross income. Why do they want to know our income earned from work?"

Although they don't look like it, these are *expense* questions. The only purpose of these questions is to compute how much social security tax you paid (the computer will subtract this from your income) and to see whether you qualify for the employment allowance. Therefore, you want these numbers to be as high as possible.

This is about the time we hear screams of alarm from our clients. "Why are you including my 401(k) contributions? Whose side are you on?" We *know* these questions are in the "income" section of the form, but trust us, these are expense questions. The higher this number, the lower your contribution to college will be. Include everything: wages (line 7 from the 1040), business income from schedule C (line 12 from the 1040), income from nonlimited business partnerships (listed as part of schedule E), and deferred compensation contributed in the past year to 401(k) plans, 403(b) plans, or tax-deferred annuities (this can usually be found in box 13 of your W-2, or possibly on your year-end pay stub).

If you had a loss from business income or from partnerships, don't subtract the loss from your total earned income. This will underreport the amount of social security tax you paid.

Again, in prior years when answering these questions you could deduct Work-Study earnings. This is no longer the case. These earnings will be recognized in a later question.

Finally, questions 69 and 70 are not supposed to add up to question 67, your adjusted gross income. The same holds true for 57 and 58: these should not necessarily equal 55. The sum of your income earned from work and your spouse's income earned from work could be higher or lower than your AGI.

59–63., 71–75. Untaxed income. See pages 55–57 for our suggested strategies. This is where you must report all the income that the IRS lets you shelter.

If you or your child did not receive the earned income credit, social security benefits, AFDC, AFC, or child support, write in "0" for 59–62 and for 71–74. Skip our explanations of these questions, and go straight to 63 and 75. Note: For dependent students, 59–63 will most likely be zero.

59. and 71. Earned Income Credit. This question involves a tax credit given by the IRS to certain lower income individuals who earn at least some of their income from work. If you have already completed your 1996 federal income tax return, simply refer to the IRS line references listed on the original FAFSA and answer accordingly. If you have not yet completed your tax return, ask your accountant or consult the IRS worksheets in the tax return instruction booklet to determine the amount of the credit, if any. Of course, if your income is too high to qualify for the credit, write in "0" for this question.

60. and 72. Social security benefits. This question is not about the social security tax (FICA) that you paid on your income; it is about social security benefits you or your children may have *received* for the entire year.

Part of social security benefits may be taxable. If this is true for you, be sure to subtract the taxable portion from the total benefits to come up with the untaxed portion. Be careful not to double-count.

Payments made to you for your children are considered part of *your* income for financial aid purposes and should not be listed in the student section. This is to your advantage because parents' income is assessed less heavily than a child's. Unfortunately, you must include as part of parents' income the benefits you received for your other children as well.

Let's see how this works with a slightly oversimplified example. Let's say that Dad has retired and is receiving $10,000 in social security benefits each year (85% of which is taxable). His two daughters are also receiving $4,000 apiece in social security benefits. Mom works and earns $45,000 a year. The family has no other income. The family's total *taxable* income is $53,500 (Mom's $45,000 plus the $8,500 taxable portion of Dad's $10,000). The family's total *untaxed* income is $9,500 (the two daughters' $4,000 apiece, plus the $1,500 untaxable portion of Dad's $10,000).

61. and 73. Aid to Families with Dependent Children. If you are receiving these benefits you will receive a statement from the agency. List the annual amount here.

62. and 74. Child support received. As we've said before, the amount you write here should include only the money you actually received during the year, not what was promised.

63. and 75. Other untaxed income. The instructions to the FAFSA form include a fairly complete worksheet for this item. Some things to bear in mind:

- As we've mentioned before, IRA contributions are not necessarily deductible. If you and your spouse are not already an active participant

If you (or your spouse if filing a joint return) were covered by a retirement plan—		
Your filing status is	**And your modified AGI is**	**You can take**
Single, head of household, or married filing separately and lived apart from your spouse for all of 1995	$25,000 or less	Full IRA deduction
	Over $25,000 but less than $35,000	Partial IRA deduction
	$35,000 or more	No IRA deduction
Married filing jointly or qualifying widow(er)	$40,000 or less	Full IRA deduction
	Over $40,000 but less than $50,000	Partial IRA deduction
	$50,000 or more	No IRA deduction
Married filing separately and lived with your spouse at any time during 1995*	Over 0 but less than $10,000	Partial IRA deduction
	$10,000 or more	No IRA deduction

* If married filing separately and you were not covered by a plan but your spouse was, you are considered covered by a plan unless you lived apart from your spouse for all of 1995.

The above chart was based on the rules in effect for 1995.

in an employer or self-employed retirement plan, then IRA contributions are fully deductible up to the $2,000 per person maximum. If you are an active participant in a retirement plan then your contribution may be fully or partly deductible, depending on your income.

To determine whether you qualify for a deduction in 1996, consult your accountant or the IRS instructions for the 1996 forms.

Realize that nondeductible portions need not be listed. However, the tax-deductible portion of your retirement contributions is considered untaxed income. It is that tax-deductible portion of your IRA contribution that must be included on the FAFSA worksheet. This number should correspond to the sum of lines 23a and 23b on your 1040.

- You should not include legitimate rollovers of IRAs or pension funds.

- It may be tempting to think about not reporting your tax-free income, but do not give in to temptation. The schools are extremely good at reading between the lines and IRS reporting requirements change from year to year. What doesn't need to be reported this year might very well be reportable next year. You should also bear in mind that the odds of being "verified" by the colleges are much greater than the odds of being audited by the IRS.

64. and 76. Title IV income exclusions—The FAFSA instructions provide a worksheet to help you answer this question. For students, the most common item they will report will be federal work-study income. For parents, the most common item will probably be child support paid.

Section G—Asset Information

Before completing this section, you should go to page 7 of the FAFSA instructions and complete the appropriate worksheet: Worksheet A for independent students or Worksheet B for dependent students. This is the criteria for the Simplified Needs Test. Even if you can check "No" and have income below $50,000, which will exclude all assets from the analysis for federal aid, you should contact the FAOs at all of the schools you are considering. Ask them if they want you to complete Section G anyway, since some schools do not recognize the Simplified Needs Test when awarding their own aid funds.

77–83. and 85–91. The value of your assets. We don't intend to repeat all the advice we gave under "Assets and Liabilities" in chapter 3. Look through that chapter again—it could save you some serious money. Remember not to list retirement provisions such as IRA accounts. Under the federal financial aid formulas, assets in retirement provisions are protected from assessment. Also, remember that you are not allowed to list credit card debt.

Be careful not to double-count assets. An asset belongs to you or to your child. Don't list it twice. If you have set up an account in trust for your child, it is legally part of *your* assets as long as *your* social security number is listed as the taxpayer I.D. However, if the asset is under the child's name, it will be assessed severely. Consider consulting a financial adviser who understands the aid process to discuss your options.

If you have a passbook loan, remember to list the account as part of "other real estate and investments value" rather than under "cash, savings, and checking accounts." Also remember to list the outstanding amount of the passbook loan as part of "other real estate and investments debt." Do not include your home if it is your primary residence.

If you own real estate but you rent your primary residence, include the real estate as part of "other real estate and investments value," and the debt against that real estate under "other real estate and investments debts."

Owners of businesses and farms should also read our advice on this subject (in the Special Topics chapter) before they answer these questions. Remember that if you are a part-owner, you should list only your share of the assets and liabilities. Also, if you live on a farm and can claim on Schedule F of your 1040 form that you "materially participated in the farm's operation," the value and debt of the "family farm" should not be included on the FAFSA.

For dependent students, there is one more question still to answer:

84. The age of the older parent. See page 87 for our suggested strategies. This is one of the few times when you don't want to lie about your age. The purpose of this question is to determine your asset protection allowance.

This question, like all the questions on the need analysis form, refers only to "parents" living in the household. For example, if a student lives with his biological mother, age 42, and a stepfather, age 45, it is the stepfather's age that should be listed here.

Section H—Releases and Signatures

92–103. What college(s) do you plan to attend in 1997–98? List all the schools (up to six) to which you want the data sent. Write down the complete unabbreviated name of the colleges. List only one school per line and don't cross out or skip any lines. You have a choice of writing in the complete address of the school or of looking up the six-digit code of the school (to be published in a book that will be available at your high school guidance office, financial aid office, or public library by the time the forms are out). The feds say that using the codes will speed up processing time. On the other hand, if you make a mistake when you write down the code, your information will not be sent to the school you wanted and you may not find out about the snafu until it is too late. Either way, we recommend that you take great care in writing down the information on the FAFSA. If you are applying to a particular branch or division of a university, be sure to specify that as well or use the correct code for that branch or division.

If you are applying to more than six schools, you should first list those schools with the earliest FAFSA deadlines. After your FAFSA has been processed, there are ways you can have the data sent to the colleges you were not able to list on the FAFSA. (If you are applying to any schools in your home state, we recommend that you list at least one of them first here.)

At the far right of this section you must list the correct housing codes for each school: 1 = on-campus, 2 = off-campus, 3 = with parents, 4 = with relatives other than parents. If you aren't sure, list code 1 since the cost of attendance will be higher if you are living on campus.

104. **Do you give the U.S. Department of Education permission to send information from this form to other agencies?** Leave this question blank. In some states, you may have to apply separately for state aid, but leaving the "No" oval blank will expedite the process.

105. **Do you give Selective Service permission to register you?** To receive federal aid, males 18 years old and older are required to register. You can fill in this oval only if the student is already 18 (but not yet 26) and has not yet registered. Since few students are just turning 18 when the FAFSA is completed, it is probably best to put a reminder in your calendar for your son to go to the post office and register the week he turns 18. (Since there is no draft at present, this only involves filling out a form.)

- A note for potential conscientious objectors: by registering for the Selective Service, you are not expressing a willingness to serve. The first step in the process of achieving conscientious objector status is to register.

106–107. Certification. Signatures are required of all individuals who give information on the form, including a stepparent. Simply by signing the FAFSA, you are applying for all types of federal aid, including the Pell Grant. When you sign, you are affirming that to the best of your knowledge, the information you have supplied is true and complete. An unwitting mistake will not be grounds for electrocution. However, a deliberate lie is fraud—a federal crime.

You cannot sign, or mail in, this form until January 1. (You might have won the lottery on December 31.) Be sure to enter the date and fill in the correct year for question 107.

On the bottom of page 1 of the FAFSA instruction booklet, there is a box concerning "unusual circumstances." With the exception of a family member who recently became unemployed (also sometimes referred to as a dislocated worker), we have already discussed these items in previous chapters. Recently unemployed workers will be covered in the "Special Topics" chapter, as well as in our instructions on how to fill out the PROFILE form (section L) which follows.

Section I—Preparer's Use Only

108–110. FAFSA preparer information. You can skip this section if you are filling out the FAFSA on your own. The only person who would have to fill out this section is someone other than the student, the student's spouse, or the student's parents or stepparents. For example, if the form were filled out by a financial aid consultant, a tax preparer, a high school guidance counselor, or a financial aid officer, then this person would have to complete this section and sign off on the form.

Some FAOs have already hinted to parents that the appearance of a preparer's name on the form will make the application subject to much closer scrutiny. Aside from the questionable legality of such a practice by the school, at the time of this writing the Department of Education had not yet determined if they would release this information to the schools. In addition, details as to what constitutes a "preparer" and at what point someone must sign on the form have not yet been completely clarified.

That does it for the FAFSA. Congratulations! If none of the schools to which you are applying require the PROFILE form, skip ahead to page 171, "Are You Done?" Otherwise, let's go to the PROFILE form.

FILLING OUT THE 1997–98 PROFILE FORM

If you are required to fill out the PROFILE as well as the FAFSA, be sure to read the instructions for the PROFILE carefully. Double-check to be sure that you are using the correct writing implement—it may not be the same implement you used for the FAFSA. Also, be sure to complete the response areas they way they tell you to in the PROFILE instructions. Many of the questions on the PROFILE will correspond exactly to the questions on the FAFSA. If the responses don't match exactly, you can expect inquiries from your FAO. To help you avoid inconsistencies, we are going to refer you to the corresponding FAFSA questions.

Note: The version of the 1997–98 PROFILE which appears on pages 272–275 of this book is the most recent draft that was available at the time of this book's publication. We have been told that there may be a few small changes in the final version of the form. Before you start completing the PROFILE, you should first read any special instructions that appear on the top of page 1 of the form. Depending on the student's status, you may be instructed to skip certain questions and/or sections of the PROFILE.

If the student is already in college, you may be given a renewal version of the PROFILE to complete. The numbers for the questions on the renewal version may be different from the ones listed in this book since there are usually some extra questions in the beginning of the Renewal form. However after you complete these preliminary questions, which are rather simple, the order of the questions will be the same on the Renewal PROFILE, so you should not have much difficulty utilizing our tips that follow.

PROFILE Section A—Student's Information

PROFILE 1.   How many family members will the student (and spouse) support in 1997–98? If the student is an independent, your answer will be the same as FAFSA 46. If the student is dependent, most likely you were advised to skip questions 1 and 2.

PROFILE 2.   Of the number in 1, how many will be in college at least half-time for at least one term in 1997–98? For independent students, your response will be similar to FAFSA 47.

PROFILE 3.   What is the student's state of legal residence? Same as FAFSA 11.

PROFILE 4.   What is the student's citizenship status? If you filled in oval 1 for FAFSA 15–16, you should fill in oval 1 on question 4a of the PROFILE form. If the student is a permanent resident, fill in oval 2 for question 4a. If the student is not a U.S citizen or permanent resident, fill in oval 3 for question 4a and be sure you answer 4b and 4c as well. U.S. citizens and permanent residents should be sure to leave questions 4b and 4c blank.

PROFILE 5.   Type of U.S. Tax return. Same as FAFSA 53. If you filled in oval 5, you should skip PROFILE questions 6 through 9. Note: The ordering of the response ovals for the PROFILE is different from the FAFSA for this question.

PROFILE Section B— Student's 1996 Income & Benefits

PROFILE 6.   Total number of exemptions. Same as FAFSA 54.

PROFILE 7.   Adjusted Gross Income. Same as FAFSA 55.

PROFILE 8.   U.S. income tax paid. Same as FAFSA 56.

PROFILE 9.   Itemized deductions. Most students do not itemize deductions. As such, your most likely answer for this question will be "0." If the student did or will itemize deductions, your answer to this question will be the same as the bottom line of Schedule A of the IRS 1040 form.

PROFILE 10 and 11.   Income earned from work Same as FAFSA 57 and 58 respectively.

PROFILE 12.   Student dividend and interest income. This question is being asked to detect the presence of student assets during the base income year. The number here should agree with dividend and interest income reported to the IRS.

PROFILE 13.   Untaxed income and benefits. PROFILE 13a same as FAFSA 60; PROFILE 13b same as FAFSA 61; PROFILE 13c same as FAFSA 62; PROFILE 13d same as FAFSA 59. For PROFILE 13e complete the worksheet on page 4 of the PROFILE instruction booklet—in most cases your answer will be the same as FAFSA 63.

PROFILE 14. **Earnings from Work–Study or other need-based aid plus taxable grant or scholarship aid.** If you answered "0" for FAFSA 64, then answer "0" for this one as well. Otherwise, refer to the FAFSA Worksheet #3 which you completed in order to answer FAFSA 64. Add together lines 1 and 2 only in the Student/Spouse column of the worksheet and write down the total on the PROFILE form.

PROFILE Section C—Student's Assets

PROFILE 15. **Cash, savings, and checking accounts.** Same as FAFSA 77.

PROFILE 16. **Retirement accounts.** Most student's don't have IRAs, Keoghs or other retirement accounts, so most likely your answer for this will be "0." If the student does have any funds in these types of accounts, remember to list their value as of December 31, 1996 and not their value on the day you completed the PROFILE form.

PROFILE 17. **Student investments.** Instead of asking separate questions about "value" and "debt" as the FAFSA does, the PROFILE asks you to list "what is it worth today" and "what is owed on it" in the same question. With the exception of trusts, include the same investments listed as part of FAFSA 78 and debts against investments listed as part of FAFSA 79. (Information regarding trusts will be listed in PROFILE Section D.) The answers to this PROFILE question will not necessarily be the same as FAFSA 78 and FAFSA 79 if the student owns other real estate and/or has a trust.

PROFILE 18. **Home.** If the student does not own his or her primary residence, enter "0". Don't worry, the value of the parent's home will be listed later in the form.

PROFILE 19. **Other real estate.** Include any real estate owned by the student that you included as part of FAFSA 78 and any debts against that real estate included as part of FAFSA 79. If the student does not have any trusts, the sum of the "worth" columns from PROFILE 17 and 19 must equal FAFSA 78. The sum of the "what is owed on it" columns in PROFILE 17 and 19 must equal FAFSA 79.

PROFILE 20. **Business and Farm.** In contrast to the FAFSA, on the PROFILE form farm value includes the value of a "family farm." If the student owns any farm property at all, its "worth" and "what is owed on it" should be included here as well as the value and debt of any business listed in FAFSA 80 and 81.

PROFILE 21.   Is the student living on the farm? If the student does not own any farm property, leave this question blank. If you fill in the "no" oval for PROFILE 21, then your answer under the "what is it worth" column for PROFILE 20 must equal the sum of FAFSA 80 and 82; your answer under the "what is owed on it" column for PROFILE 20 must equal the sum of FAFSA 81 and 83.

PROFILE 22.   If the student owns a home, give year of purchase and purchase price. If you answered "0" in the "worth" column for PROFILE 18, leave this blank. Otherwise, answer accordingly. As we'll explain in more detail in our comments regarding PROFILE 40, this question is an audit check to be sure you have not lowballed the value of real estate.

PROFILE Section D—Student's Trust Information

PROFILE 23.   Trust information. If you included the value of any trusts as part of FAFSA 78, then you should complete questions 23a through 23c. Otherwise, list "0" in 23a and skip 23b and 23c. You should realize that when the word *trust* is used for this question, it is not referring to a regular type of bank account that is maintained by one person "in trust for" another person.

PROFILE Section E—Student's 1996 Expenses

PROFILE 24.   Child support paid. If you listed "0" as your answer for FAFSA 64, then your answer here should be "0" as well. Otherwise, go back to the FAFSA Worksheet #3 and list the amount you entered under the Student/ Spouse column for line 4.

PROFILE 25.   Student's medical and dental expenses. If parents paid the medical and dental expenses for the student, don't include them here—do refer to the PROFILE instructions before answering this one. This question is primarily for independent students.

PROFILE Section F—Student's Expected Resources

PROFILE 26.   Veteran's benefits. Same as FAFSA 38–39.

PROFILE 27a–d. Student's Expected Summer/School Year Income. See pages 88–91 for our suggested strategies. In light of what we have said in our section on student income, we suggest you aim for "0" during the school year (remember not to include work-study earnings in this projection) and as close as possible to the minimum amount the colleges ask you to earn during the summer months under the institutional methodology ($900 for a freshman, $1,100 for an upperclassman). Always estimate on the low side. Since this is a PROFILE question, most likely the school will use the CSS institutional methodology to determine the student's contribution from income. Be slightly conservative with your estimates for questions 27b–27d. If the student is unmarried, list "0"s for number 27b. If the student doesn't expect any income other than from work, write in "0"s for 27c and 27d as well.

PROFILE 27e. Outside grants and scholarships, etc. See page 203. When answering this question you should not include any awards, unless you are absolutely sure you will be receiving the money. If the student has not received an official notification for any outside organization at the time you are completing the PROFILE form, then list "0."

PROFILE 27f. Employer tuition benefits. If there will be no tuition benefits, enter "0." If there will be benefits, but the amount of the benefits will be based upon the school attended, list the least benefit that you would receive (considering all the colleges to which you applied that require the PROFILE form).

PROFILE 27g. Contribution from the student's parent(s). For dependent students, the best way to answer this question is to use the worksheets at the back of this book to determine an estimate of the parents' expected contribution per student under the institutional methodology (Line T of the IM column on page 261)—and then understate it by 20%. In the past, parents who have written down a higher figure on this question than the amount that was later determined by the need analysis companies to be their expected contribution were deemed responsible to pay the higher figure. Independent students should list only a minimal figure if any help is expected; otherwise list "0."

PROFILE 27h. Contributions from others. Before answering this question, you should review the section "Direct Payments to the School" on page 82.

PROFILE Section G—Parents' Household Income

Before proceeding further, you should refer to the appropriate page in the PROFILE instruction booklet. Even students who are not required to answer the green-shaded sections of the FAFSA form may have to complete sections G to O of the PROFILE form.

PROFILE 28. **Household size.** Same as FAFSA 51.

PROFILE 29. **Number in college.** Same as FAFSA 52.

PROFILE 30. **Parents in college.** This question is asked so that the processor can calculate how many dependent children are in college. As you may recall, the Institutional Methodology only recognizes dependent children as college students when calculating the parent's expected contribution per child to college costs. When answering this question, remember that they are referring to the parents (stepparents) included as part of the household size you listed in PROFILE 28. If you fill in oval 2 or 3 for this question, you should make sure that these parents were included as part of your answer for PROFILE 29 and FAFSA 52.

PROFILE 31. **Parents' marital status.** Same as FAFSA 48.

PROFILE 32. **Parents' state of legal residence.** Same as FAFSA 49.

PROFILE Section H—Parents' Expenses

For this section of the PROFILE form, you are required to answer the questions relating to the calendar year 1996 as well as 1997. Use annual figures only, and enter zero whenever appropriate.

PROFILE 33. **Child support paid.** If your answer for FAFSA 76 is "0," then list "0" for the 1996 column and answer the question involving 1997 accordingly. Otherwise, you should refer to line 4 of the Parent's column of the FAFSA Worksheet #3 which you completed to assist you with FAFSA 76 and list the same dollar amount under the 1996 column. Then, give your best estimate for 1997. Note: Independent students who were not required to answer the green-shaded sections of the FAFSA should refer to the PROFILE instructions for this question.

PROFILE 34. **Repayment of parents' educational debt.** Be sure to read the instructions carefully for this one, and only include payments on those loans specifically mentioned.

PROFILE 35.   Medical and dental expenses not paid by insurance. See pages 64–65 for our suggested strategies. These expenses are among the most underreported by parents. Use all the IRS allowable expenses. This includes medical or dental expenses you've charged on a credit card during the year, even if you haven't paid for them yet. We find that many families forget about health insurance premiums deducted from their paychecks along with medical-related transportation costs. In addition, many members of organized labor forget to include the medical portion of their union dues. Many parents assume that if their total gross medical expenses aren't higher than 4% of their total taxable and untaxable income (at which point the colleges may allow a deduction) then there is no point in writing down the figure for unreimbursed medical expenses at all. This is not true. Even if you don't qualify for a deduction, the schools ought to have a fair idea of what you are really spending. Remember, if you are self-employed or own at least 2% of the shares of an S corporation, you may have already taken the self-employed medical insurance deduction on line 26 of the 1040 form. Be sure to exclude 30% of your medical insurance premiums if you've already deducted them there. After you have figured out 1996 expenses, project 1997 as best you can.

PROFILE 36.   Elementary, junior high, and high school tuition for dependent children. See pages 65–66 for our suggested strategies. These are calendar year payments, not academic year payments. As the instructions say, you can't include private school tuition for the child who is now applying to college. You also cannot include money spent on after-school programs such as Hebrew school or music lessons. If your child is a music prodigy and you anticipate that the private music lessons will continue during college, this can be explained in a separate letter to the colleges.

PROFILE Section I—Parents' Assets

PROFILE 37.   Cash, savings, and checking accounts. Same as FAFSA 85.

PROFILE 38.   Parents' monthly home mortgage/rental payment. Include all monthly mortgage payments (first and second) on a house, condominium, or cooperative apartment, maintenance fees, real estate taxes (if paid directly to the bank), home equity loan payments, and rent. Not that it will do you any good. These numbers are not factored into the formula.

PROFILE 39. Investments. Include investments listed as part of FAFSA 86 and debts against investments listed as part of FAFSA 87. However, the answers to this PROFILE question will not necessarily be the same as these two FAFSA items if the parents own other real estate.

PROFILE 40a. Home. Refer to our strategies in chapter 3 regarding home value and debts on the home (pages 76–80). If you rent your primary residence but own other real estate, list "0"s for item 40a. You will include the value of this real estate as part of question 43a.

PROFILE 40b–c. If parents own a home, give year purchased and price. This is a check on the value of your home, which you list in question 40a. By using the Federal Housing Index Multiplier the colleges can see if you have lowballed the value of your house. If you inherited the house, the purchase price is "0." If you built the house yourself, the purchase price is the cost of the house plus the cost of the land.

PROFILE 41. Business. Same as FAFSA 88 and 89.

PROFILE 42. Farm. In contrast to the FAFSA, on the PROFILE form farm value includes the value of a "family farm." If the parents own any farm property at all, its "worth" and "what is owed on it" should be listed here and you should then answer 42b as well. Do not include the farmhouse as part of 42a if it has already been listed in question 40a. If you answer "no" to 42b, then your answers to 42a should be the same as FAFSA 90 and 91.

PROFILE 43. Other real estate. Include any real estate owned by the parent that you included as part of FAFSA 86 and any debts against that real estate listed in FAFSA 87. The sum of the "worth" columns from PROFILE 39 and 43a must equal FAFSA 86. The sum of the "what is owed on it" columns in PROFILE 39 and 43a must equal FAFSA 87. If you own more than one piece of other real estate, you should list the appropriate information for one of the properties in 43b and 43c. Later in Section P of the PROFILE, you should break out the individual elements (worth, debt, year of purchase, and purchase price) for each of the properties.

Section J—Parent's 1995 Income and Benefits

These questions involve figures from the year prior to the base income. The processor is looking to see if you had a major change in income from 1995 to 1996.

PROFILE 44–46. 1995 Income tax information. If you filed tax returns for 1995, refer to your 1995 returns (most likely you filed these in early 1996). If you did not and will not file a tax return for 1995, leave these questions blank. Also U.S. taxes paid appeared on Line 46 of the 1995 IRS form 1040.

PROFILE 47. 1995 untaxed income and benefits. Include the same types of income and benefits requested in 55a–k. For your information, the IRS form 1040 line number for the earned income credit was different in 1995 compared to 1996.

Section K—Parents' 1996 Income and Benefits

PROFILE 48. Type of U.S. Income tax return. Same as FAFSA 65, however, the order of the response ovals is different. If you filled in oval 5 because you will not file a tax return in 1996, then you should skip PROFILE questions 49 through 52.

PROFILE 49. Total number of exemptions. Same as FAFSA 66.

PROFILE 50. Adjusted Gross Income. Same as FAFSA 67.

PROFILE 50a–f. Breakdown of AGI. These questions mimic some of the line numbers on the federal tax form so that the colleges can get a more precise picture of your income. If you've already done your taxes, or followed our advice and constructed a dummy version of your taxes, this question should be straightforward. The sum of 50a to 50e minus 50f must agree with FAFSA 67 as well as PROFILE 50.

PROFILE 51. U.S. Income tax paid. Same as FAFSA 68.

PROFILE 52. Itemized Deductions. If you have already completed your 1996 income taxes, refer to the last line on Schedule A of the IRS 1040 for the answer to this one. If you did not file a Schedule A and took the standard deduction, enter "0."

PROFILE 53 and 54. Income earned from work. Same as FAFSA 69 and 70 respectively.

PROFILE 55.   Untaxed Income. Question 55a is the same as FAFSA 72, question 55b is the same as FAFSA 73, and question 55c is the same as FAFSA 74. For questions 55 d, e, h, i, and j, you should refer to worksheet # 2 on page 11 of the FAFSA instructions. You will find that these questions correspond to certain lines on that worksheet. Question 55f refers to pre-tax deductions from your salary for dependent care or medical spending accounts; do not include deductions for health insurance premiums. Question 55g is the same as FAFSA 71. For question 55k, you should complete the PROFILE worksheet in the instructions. The sum of PROFILE questions 55d, e, h, i, j, and k should be the same number as your answer for FAFSA 75.

PROFILE Section L—Parents' 1997 Expected Income & Benefits

Since you are being asked about the future, there is no question of getting into trouble if your figures are off. In most cases, the colleges will be awarding aid using your base income year data rather than your projection for the coming year.

Unless You Are Recently Unemployed

If you have been terminated, laid off, have received notice that you will be laid off, or are self-employed but out-of-work due to harsh economic conditions or a natural disaster, then the questions in this section take on added importance.

Using "professional judgment," the FAOs may ignore the income you had in the base income year, and focus instead on the projections you have made here for the upcoming year. Since you are unemployed, your projections will be low. This can save you thousands of dollars.

Anyone who is out of work or even just feeling that her situation is unstable should read our section about "The Recently Unemployed Worker" in the "Special Topics" chapter.

Some Pointers For PROFILE Section L

- Everyone's impulse is simply to list the same figures he listed last year. Our advice is to be conservative. Don't talk about a raise you are supposed to get but haven't yet received. If you are out of work, give the FAOs the worst-case scenario so that they will be prepared if you haven't found work yet by next year.

- If you are self-employed, use your expected NET business income, not the gross.

- If you just took a job at a lower salary or you know you will have less overtime or a smaller bonus in the coming year, make sure the figures reflect this. It is difficult to say how much weight the colleges give the questions in this section if you are still gainfully employed. If you are already aware of any extreme changes in your situation for the coming year, you should probably write to the individual FAOs directly, rather than relying on them to take these projections into account.

PROFILE 56 and 57.   Income earned from work. These sound just like questions 53 and 54, but they are not quite the same; PROFILE questions 56 and 57 count as income questions this time. Be careful not to double-count your income. If you project that you will be contributing to deferred compensation provisions next year [such as 401(k) or 403(d) plans], you should include the contributions as regular income earned from work for that year and exclude them from **PROFILE question 59, untaxed income and benefits**. Do not count them twice.

For **PROFILE question 58**, make a rough projection of your other taxable income for next year (see pages 46–54 for our suggested strategies)—include interest, dividend, real estate income, etc.

PROFILE 59.   Untaxed income. Because social security benefits for your child will probably end sometime soon (when the child turns 18 or graduates from high school, whichever comes later), you shouldn't necessarily include the amount you received this past year in a projection for next year. Recalculate the amount based on the number of months you'll receive the benefits.

Despite what the instructions say, do not include deductible IRA and Keogh contributions as part of untaxed income for the coming year. Because you did not get to deduct your IRA and Keoghs in the preceding questions there is no need to list them here, as their inclusion would overstate your income. If 1996 income will be significantly less than 1995 income and you are applying to colleges that do not require the PROFILE form, we recommend that you write the FAO a separate letter explaining your change in circumstances. Be sure to give them a breakdown of your various income items utilizing the suggestions above.

PROFILE Section M—Family Member Listing

On the PROFILE form, there is no need to include the student who is currently applying to college because the form has already entered the student on line 1 of this question. Except for students who do not have to complete the green-shaded areas of the FAFSA but have to provide parental data on the PROFILE, the number of other people you list here must agree (after you add back in the student who is applying now) with the number of family members you entered in FAFSA question 46 or 51, but not necessarily with the number of exemptions you took in FAFSA question 54 or 66.

The question also asks you to indicate which of these family members will be attending college, on what basis (full-time, half-time), which schools (college or otherwise) they will be attending in the 1997–98 academic year, as well as information about the schools attended during the 1996–97 academic year. If a parent is in college, obviously the parent's contribution figure in the 1996–97 data section will be what came out of the parents' own pocket. Except for students who do not have to complete the green-shaded areas of the FAFSA but have to provide parental data on the PROFILE, the number of college students (attending at least half-time) for the next academic year must agree (once you add back in the student who is applying now) with the number you listed in FAFSA question 47 or 52. The status of the college students (full-time, half-time) can have an effect on state aid. The "parents'" contribution should include only their part of tuition, and room and board. This is not an expense question. Don't include the computer you bought her or the cash you gave him for spring break. Make sure that the age of the older parent or stepparent agrees with the age you listed on the FAFSA (question 84).

PROFILE Section N—Parents' Information

PROFILE 61 and 62. Information for these two questions should include only those parents or stepparents listed in PROFILE 60.

When it comes time to list the occupations of the parents, you should try to be humble. If you put down "CEO, General Motors," do not expect a lot of sympathy from the FAOs. For Item 61f and 62f, you should fill in all the ovals that apply. If you have previously contributed to 401(k)s, 403(b)s, TDA plan and other deferred compensation plans, you should fill in the oval that corresponds to IRA/Keogh/tax-deferred.

PROFILE Section 0

PROFILE 63.   Divorced, Separated, or Remarried Parents. Divorced or separated parents are always very anxious about this question. "Does this mean they're going to track down my ex-wife and ask her to pay for part of our son's college bills?" This is almost always not the case. We recommend that you read our section on divorced or separated parents in chapter 9.

PROFILE Section P— Explanations and Special Circumstances

You are required to explain the following items in this section: #27e if you list a number other than "0," #38 if your answer is "0," #41 and #42 if you own a business and/or a farm, and the amounts in Section L if 1997 total income differs by more than $3,000 from the 1996 total income. You should also explain the real estate in #43 if you own more than one piece of other real estate. Otherwise, we recommend that you leave this section blank. It is far more effective to send a separate letter to each college explaining any unusual circumstances.

Bottom of Page 4—Certification. Signatures are required of all individuals who give information on the form, including a stepparent. When you sign, you are affirming that to the best of your knowledge, the information you have supplied is true and complete. The place to sign this form is on the bottom of the last page of the core section. Be sure to enter the date and fill in the oval for the correct year.

That about does it for the core questions. Unfortunately, you may not be finished with the PROFILE form just yet. Depending on the colleges and the programs you designated when you registered with the CSS, there may be one or more additional questions that you have to answer. These will appear in:

PROFILE Section Q—Institutional Questions

At the time we went to press, the pool of available questions for this section had not been finalized. Nor had many individual colleges decided which additional questions, if any, they would be requiring of PROFILE applicants. As such, it is impossible for us to give you any specific advice regarding questions that may appear in this section of your PROFILE form.

It seems a safe bet to assume, however, that the majority of questions in Section Q will either be asking for further details regarding items previously listed on the PROFILE or about additional assets or resources not previously reported. After reading chapter 3 and this part of the book, by now you should have a very good idea of the strategy you should be applying in order to maximize your aid eligibility. If you also keep the following points in mind, any questions in this section should not pose too much of a problem for you:

- Read the questions carefully. Answer them honestly but do not disclose more information than required.

- Avoid overstating or double-counting assets or income (especially if you are estimating).

- Remember to include all allowable expenses or debts.

- Keep your responses consistent with other data previously listed on any form.

- If you are asked to explain any Section Q responses in Section P, be sure to do so.

Are You Done?

Congratulations! Put your work copy of the forms away for a day. You've earned a rest. Tomorrow, look the forms over very carefully. Are you happy with the numbers? If you filled out a PROFILE form, have you made sure all the answers agree with the answers you gave on the FAFSA? In addition, do the answers on the PROFILE form and the FAFSA agree with any supplemental aid forms required by the colleges? Check the newspaper today to see if your stock or bond investments have lost any value. If so, revise your figures downward and change the date. If they've gone up, remember, you filled out the form *yesterday*.

When you are convinced that everything is ready, carefully copy over all your figures onto the original forms. Date them, sign them, make photocopies for your records. If you did not give credit card information when you registered for the PROFILE, be sure to enclose a check or money order covering the processing fee. (A bill would have been included with your PROFILE packet if you didn't charge the fee.) Do not put the FAFSA and the PROFILE form in the same envelope since they will be processed at different locations. Send the originals via registered mail (return receipt requested) to the need analysis company. If you don't receive your return receipt within two weeks, start making inquiries immediately with the processor and the post office.

Your Student Aid Report (SAR) from the government should arrive within three to four weeks. If you also filed a PROFILE form, you will get an acknowledgment from the CSS about two weeks after you receive your SAR.

The SAR Report

After you send in your 1997–98 FAFSA, you will receive a green multipage form sent by the government called the Student Aid Report or SAR. It is vital that you keep it in a safe place, for you may need to give it to the college your child decides to attend. Again, check the information on this form carefully to make sure it agrees with the information you sent. Make sure that the SAR includes the correct names of the colleges to which you are applying for aid. If you are applying for aid at more than six colleges and/or you have decided to add some additional schools and/or the processor did not list a correct school, you will have to get the FAFSA data to those schools not listed in Section H of your SAR. You should call the FAOs at each of the schools not listed, explain the situation, and ask them how to proceed. Be sure to keep a record of the person you spoke with at each college as well as a summary of what was discussed. They will probably tell you one of two ways to get the data to them:

1. By sending them a copy of the green original SAR. While a number of schools will accept your data this way, you should be sure to mention that the school is not listed in Section H when you call the aid office. Since you should always have at least one original SAR for your records, you should call (319)337-5665 to request a duplicate 1997–98 SAR. You can request up to eight additional SARs at a time.

2. By revising the SAR and sending it back to the processor (via certified mail—return receipt requested). You will make all revisions in the "Correct answer should be" column on Part 2 of the SAR. If you have six schools already listed on the SAR, you will be substituting the unlisted school(s) for one or more of the schools previously listed. If you didn't have six schools listed on the original SAR, you should list (if at all possible) all the additional schools on the unused lines at the bottom of Section H, again using the "correct answer" column for your responses. Only the even-numbered questions can be used to list schools; the odd numbers are for the housing option. (If you have to substitute one school for the other because of the number of schools involved, you should first make sure that any school you are crossing out has received your FAFSA information.) Before mailing the SAR back to the processor, make a photocopy for your records. Within a few weeks after mailing, you will receive a new SAR which you should again review for accuracy. If you still have not been able to get all the schools listed after this first round of revising, keep repeating the process until every school gets the FAFSA data. Of course, if you have to do the process more than once, you should give preference on your first revision to those schools with the earliest deadlines.

Note: If you substitute one school for another, the originally listed school will no longer receive any revised data that you send back to the processor. Therefore, if you have to correct or change any items other than those in section H, you may need to put the original school(s) no longer listed back on the new SAR and send it back to the processor

If you haven't received a SAR within four weeks of filing, call (319) 337-5665 during business hours for a status report. Be sure to have the student's social security number handy when you call.

Two Moments of Truth

The SAR will tell you if you qualify for a Pell Grant. Don't panic if the SAR says you are ineligible. This is a federal grant for low-income families and most people do not qualify. Just because you didn't get a Pell Grant does not mean you won't qualify for any aid at all. The Pell is the toughest type of aid to get.

The SAR will also tell you your Expected Family Contribution. Below the date on the front page of part one of the SAR in small type are three letters followed by some numbers.

Here's a sample of what it might look like:

March 1, 1997
EFC: 08920

The EFC is your Expected Family Contribution under the federal methodology. There is no dollar sign, no explanatory paragraph, nothing to let you know how significant this number will be to you. In this example, the Expected Family Contribution for one year of college for one child was judged by the need analysis company to be $8,920.

Parents who don't know to look for these numbers will not know what their Expected Family Contribution under the federal guidelines is until they receive award letters in April.

Counting Chickens

Unfortunately, the federal EFC is not necessarily the number the colleges will elect to use. Schools that asked you to fill out the PROFILE form will most likely be using the institutional methodology to determine the family contribution. This figure could be lower, but most likely will be higher than the federal number.

The institutional EFC is never given to the parents by the CSS.

Revising Your Information

If the numbers on the SAR are different from the numbers you sent in, you will probably want to revise them immediately. The SAR gives you instructions on how to correct errors made either by the processor or by you. You will also want to revise immediately if you receive any notice stating that your FAFSA could not be processed, if there are comments on the SAR that there were problems with the processing, or if you need to change the list of schools.

How to Update Your Estimated Figures

While the instructions to the SAR tell you how to handle revisions, these instructions may conflict with the procedures many colleges would prefer you to follow. To find out the correct way to revise your SAR you must call the FAOs at all of the colleges still under consideration. In general, the FAOs will tell you to do one of three things:

1. Revise Part 2 of the SAR and send the revisions to the processor.

2. Revise Part 2 of the SAR and send all pages of the SAR directly to the FAO.

3. Send all pages of the unrevised SAR to the FAO; he or she will make the necessary revisions.

When you call the FAOs, ask when they expect you to send them the original SAR. See if you can hold off until you know for sure what college the student will be attending. If the college requires a physical copy of the SAR before the student is sure of his educational plans, you can request a duplicate SAR by calling (319) 337-5665. The duplicate SARs are free, so we suggest you call for several duplicate copies just in case.

The question numbers on the SAR should correspond exactly to the question numbers on the FAFSA. To help you in your revisions, you can refer to your photocopy of the FAFSA and your worksheets, as well as to the detailed instructions we gave for completing each line of the FAFSA form. Most likely, you will be revising only Section F of the SAR, which covers the 1996 Base Income Year information. The SAR processors prefer you to use a dark-ink ballpoint pen for the revisions. The asset information in Section G should be the values and debts at the time you completed the original FAFSA, not the values or debts on the day you are revising. You should therefore revise Section G only if a mistake was made when the FAFSA was originally filed.

A few weeks after you send your SAR Part 2 revisions to the processor, you'll get another complete SAR with the revised numbers. Look over the new SAR data to make sure it's accurate.

The Acknowledgment

If you filed an PROFILE form, then you will receive an acknowledgment from the CSS about two weeks after you receive your SAR. The acknowledgment will simply list the names of the colleges and (perhaps) the state agencies to which the PROFILE data was sent. No other student information is contained in the acknowledgment. Check to see that the acknowledgment correctly lists all the colleges you have designated to receive reports. The need analysis companies do make mistakes from time to time. Because of the tight deadlines, it is possible that if you don't catch a mistake now, you could miss out on any chance of financial aid at a particular school. If there are any errors, call the processor immediately. If you added any additional schools after you initially registered with the CSS, you may get more than one acknowledgment. You will also receive a Data Confirmation Report that summarizes your responses for certain sections of the PRO-FILE. Refer to your photocopy of the PROFILE and check to be sure your responses were correctly inputted.

Applying to More PROFILE Schools

If, after receiving the CSS acknowledgment, you decide to apply to additional schools that require the PROFILE form, you can have the data sent by calling or writing the CSS. Details on how to do this will be provided in the PROFILE materials. You will also have to get the FAFSA data to these schools by revising the SAR. (You should also call the FAOs at these additional schools to find out which institutional questions they require, if any, for Section Q of the PROFILE—see page 136 for more details on this.)

What to Do If You Get a Notice Saying Your Form Could Not Be Processed

Your need analysis form may get rejected for any number of reasons, but the most common are forgetting to answer one of the questions or not signing the form.

If your form is returned to you, the main thing is to get it back to the need analysis company as fast as possible. Even if the screwup was your fault, you will minimize the odds of missing out on aid if you snap into action immediately. The need analysis company will probably send an incomplete version of their report to all the colleges, so you will still be in the running. To be on the safe side, contact the individual schools to let them know what is happening.

In some cases, the need analysis companies or the government will question specific items because they are unusually low or high for a "typical family" with your income level. Don't feel you must change a number if it is really correct. For example, if you have a negative AGI due to property rental losses, but have positive income earned from work, the computers will automatically "flag" the AGI item by printing it in boldface. If the item is correct, you may need to place a check mark next to it when revising your SAR.

As always, photocopy any new information you send to the need analysis company or to the government, and send it certified mail (return receipt requested). And be sure that you follow all instructions to the letter.

If Your EFC Is Much Higher than You Expected

Somehow, no matter how prepared you are, seeing the federal EFC written down in ink is always a shock. Remember that the colleges do not expect you to be able to pay the entire amount out of current income. If they deem your resources sufficient, they expect you to liquidate assets each year that your child is in college and they expect you to have to borrow money on top of that. Your EFC is designed to include money that you have earned in the past (assets) and money that you will obtain in the future (loans) as well as the income you are currently earning.

Remember that your final contribution could be lower or higher than the EFC printed on the SAR. This will be especially true if the school uses the institutional methodology in awarding their own aid funds. Remember also that colleges have a broad latitude to change the EFC in either direction. This is where negotiation can come into play. Consult part four, "The Offer." We know of one case in which the EFC was judged to be $24,000. The school brought the actual family contribution down to $13,000.

In addition, some state aid formulas differ from the federal formula. We know of another case in which the EFC was judged to be $52,000, but the family managed to receive $4,000 a year in state aid because of quirks in the formula.

If you have used our worksheets to compute your federal Expected Family Contribution, you should not be surprised by the number on the SAR. If there is a large discrepancy between what you thought your EFC would be and what the SAR says it is, then *someone* may have made a mistake. Go through your worksheets carefully, and double-check to see that the income and assets figures on the need analysis form you sent in agree with the numbers you used in the worksheets and also be sure that these numbers agree with the numbers on the SAR. If an error was made on the FAFSA, start revising.

The Next Step: Supplying Completed Tax Returns

Some colleges will not give you a financial aid package until they've seen your taxes for the first base income year. Others will give you a "tentative" package, subject to change when they see the final numbers.

It is in your best interest to get your taxes done as fast as possible. Prod your accountant if he is dragging his heels. Better yet, if you are not reading this book at the eleventh hour, plan ahead. During the fall of senior year in high school, let your accountant know that you are going to need your taxes done as soon as possible this year.

Find out from the colleges that you are interested in whether they really do want to see your tax return. In most cases, the answer will be yes. In a few cases (such as New York University), they will not want your tax return unless you are randomly selected for verification. We recommend that you not send a return unless it is required. Why give them more information than they need?

The most effective time for negotiation with the FAOs is before May 1, the date by which many colleges require you to commit to attend. Obviously, you will have more bargaining power if you can still decide to go to another school. However, if your taxes are not done in time, you will lose your ability to negotiate a deal while you still have other options. The FAOs are much less likely to compromise once you are committed to their college.

The School's Own Forms

The standardized need analysis forms are probably not the only financial aid forms you will have to complete. Many selective colleges have their own forms as well with deadlines that may differ from those of both the standardized forms and the admissions applications to the schools themselves. The purpose of these forms is sometimes difficult to comprehend, since in many cases they ask many of the same questions you have already answered on the FAFSA or the PROFILE form all over again. Some counselors suspect this is done for the same reason police interrogate suspects several times: to look for discrepancies.

More Detailed Information

However, the individual forms do ask for some new information. In general, they are looking for more specific breakdowns of your income and assets. *Exactly* what kind of assets do you have? How liquid are they? In addition, you will often be asked about your other children's educational plans for the current year and the year to come.

While neither the FAFSA or the PROFILE form ask income and asset information about noncustodial parents, many of the individual schools will want to know all the financial details of a separated or divorced parent. Some may ask you to fill out the standardized Divorced/Separated Parents' Statement. If you own your own business, be prepared to fill out the standardized Business/Farm Supplement. We'll cover both of these situations in more detail in the "Special Topics" chapter of this book.

The forms may also ask questions to determine eligibility for specific restricted scholarships and grants. In general, these scholarships are left over from a different era when private citizens funded weird scholarships in their own name. The colleges hate administering these restricted scholarships—they would much rather be allowed to give money to whomever they feel like. However, if you are a direct blood descendant of a World War I veteran, the University of Chicago may have some money for you. If you can prove that one of your ancestors traveled on the Mayflower, Harvard may have some money for you. If you are of Huguenot ancestry, Bryn Mawr may have some money for you.

Be Careful

Take the time to be consistent. Your answers on this form may be compared to other information you've supplied elsewhere. Small differences, especially if you are estimating, are acceptable, but anything major will cause serious problems. Get out your photocopies of any previous aid forms you've completed and make sure you are not diverging.

Much as you may feel that your privacy is being invaded, do not skip any of the questions. This is the colleges' game and they get to make the rules. If you don't answer, they don't have to give you any money.

Send these forms to the schools themselves, registered mail, return receipt requested. If you are sending any supplementary information (such as tax returns) make sure that the *student's* name and social security number are prominently displayed on all pages. This is especially important if the student's last name is different from either of his parents'.

The Verification Process

"Verification" is the financial aid version of an audit, although the process is generally much more benign. You may be selected for verification by either an individual college or the federal government. If you are selected for verification, the college will ask for a copy of your federal taxes (if you have not already sent them). They may also ask for documentation of social security benefits if you receive them, or information about child support paid or received. You may also have to fill out a Verification Worksheet so that the colleges can double-check the number of members of your household and other income items.

While the IRS audits a minuscule percentage of taxpayers, financial aid verification is relatively commonplace. At some schools, 100% of the applicants are verified. Thus, if you receive a notice of verification, this does not mean that it is time to book plane tickets to a country that does not have an extradition treaty with the United States. It is all routine.

PART FOUR

The Offer

On the day that the offers from colleges arrive there will be many dilemmas for parents. One of the most vexing is deciding whether to steam open the letters from the colleges, or wait until the student gets home from school. We can set your mind at ease about this dilemma at least. You can usually tell an acceptance letter from a rejection letter even without opening it—acceptance letters weigh more. This is because as long as you met your deadlines, you should receive financial aid packages in the same envelopes the acceptance letters came in. Most colleges will need a commitment from you before May 1. This gives you only a few weeks to sift through the offers, compare them, and—if possible—negotiate with the FAOs to improve them.

The details of an aid package will be spelled out in the award letter. This letter will tell you the total cost of one year's attendance at the college, what the college decided you could afford to pay toward that cost, and what combination of grants, loans, and work-study the college has provided to meet your "need."

On the following page you will find a sample award letter from Anytown University located in Anytown, State:

ANYTOWN UNIVERSITY
OFFICE OF FINANCIAL AID

FIRST NOTICE

Academic Year
1996-97
Budget Assumptions
Resident Dependent Single
Identification Number
123-45-6789
Award Date
April 7, 1996

NOTIFICATION OF FINANCIAL AID

After careful consideration, the Financial Aid Committee has authorized this offer of financial assistance for the award period indicated at left. The decision was made after careful consideration of your application.

To accept this award, you must complete, sign and return the white copy of this form within four weeks of receipt. This award is subject to cancellation if you do not respond by the specified date.

If you choose to decline any part of this offer, please place a check mark in the "DECLINED" box for the corresponding part of the package.

Be sure to review the terms and conditions of the award as described in the Financial Aid booklet enclosed.

Joe Bloggs
123 Main Street
Sometown, ST 12345

DECLINED		FALL 96	SPRING 97
☐	Anytown University Scholarship	7,170.00	7,170.00
☐	Federal Education Opportunity Grant	1,000.00	1,000.00
☐	Estimated Federal Pell Grant	525.00	525.00
☐	Federal Perkins Loan	600.00	600.00
☐	Recommended Federal Stafford Loan	1,235.00	1,235.00
☐	Federal Work-Study	665.00	665.00
	TOTAL	11,195.00	11,195.00

FAMILY RESOURCES			SUMMARY	
Parent's Contribution	743.00		Total Estimated Budget	25,000.00
Student's Contribution	1,859.00		Less: Family Contribution	2,602.00
Other Resources	.00		Financial Need	22,398.00
TOTAL FAMILY CONTRIBUTION	2,602.00		TOTAL FINANCIAL AID	22,390.00

Jane Doe

Jane Doe, Director

Note that in this case, the family contribution was set at $2,602. The total cost of attendance at Anytown for that year was $25,000. Thus, this family had a remaining "need" of roughly $22,390 which was—in this case—met in full with a mixture of grants, loans, and work-study.

The Bloggs were evidently a high-need family, and received an excellent package: $17,390 in grants (outright gift aid, which did not need to be repaid), $1,330 in work-study, and $3,670 in loans for the year.

Not all colleges will meet the entire remaining "need" of every student, and there may have been a number of reasons why the package was so good in the case of the sample student in the report above. Perhaps Joe Bloggs was a particularly bright student or the impoverished grandchild of a distinguished alumnus.

The Different Types of Financial Aid in Detail

Let's examine the different types of financial aid that you may be offered in the award letter. An acceptance of the aid package does not commit you to attending the college, so be sure to respond by the reply date (registered mail, return receipt requested, as always). You are allowed to accept or reject any part of the package, but there are some types of aid that should never be rejected.

> **Grants and Scholarships:** These should never be rejected. This money is almost always tax-free and never has to be repaid. Grants and scholarships come in different forms.

> **The Federal Pell Grant:** This grant is administered by the federal government, and like all federal aid, is awarded only to U.S. citizens or eligible noncitizens. The Pell is primarily for low-income families. You automatically apply for the Pell Grant when you fill out the FAFSA. The size of the award is decided by the federal government and cannot be adjusted by the colleges. If you qualify, you will receive up to $2,470 per year, based on need.

> **The Federal Supplemental Educational Opportunity Grant or SEOG:** This is a federal grant that is administered by the colleges themselves. Each year, the schools get a lump sum that they are allowed to dispense to students at their own discretion. The size of the award runs from $100 to $4,000 per year per student.

> **Grants from the Schools Themselves:** The colleges themselves often award grants as well. Since this money comes out of their own pocketbook, these grants are in effect discounts off the sticker price.

And because this is not taxpayer money, there are no rules about how it must be dispensed. Some schools say they award money solely based on need. Many schools also give out merit-based awards. There is no limit on the size of a grant from an individual school. It could range from a few dollars to a full scholarship. Obviously, richer schools have more money to award to their students than poorer schools.

State Grants: If a student is attending college in his state of legal residence, or in a state that has a reciprocal agreement with his state of legal residence, then he may qualify for a state grant as well. These grants are administered by the states themselves. The grants are based on need, as well as on the size of tuition at a particular school. Thus the same student might find that his state grant at the local state university would be smaller than his state grant at a private college. These grants vary from state to state but can go as high as $5,000 per year.

Scholarships from the School: Some schools use the words *grants* and *scholarships* more or less interchangeably, and award scholarships just like grants—in other words, based on need. Other schools give scholarships in their more traditional sense, based on merit, either academic, athletic, or artistic. Some schools give scholarships based on a combination of need and merit.

The only real difference as far as you are concerned is whether the scholarship is used to meet need or whether it may be used to reduce your family contribution. If the school wants you badly enough, you may receive a merit-based scholarship over and above the amount of your need.

Outside Scholarships: If you have sought out and won a scholarship from a source not affiliated with the college—a foundation, say, or a community organization—you are required to tell the colleges about this money. Often the scholarship donor will notify the colleges you applied to directly. In most cases, the schools will thank you politely and then use the outside scholarship to reduce the amount of grant money they were going to give you. In other words, winning a scholarship does not mean you will pay less money for college; your family contribution often stays exactly the same.

By notifying the colleges about an outside scholarship before getting your award letter, you ensure that the outside scholarship will be included as part of your package. This is not very satisfactory because you have effectively given away an important bargaining chip.

If you have managed to find and win one of these scholarships, you may feel that you deserve something more than thanks from the school for your initiative. By telling the FAO about an outside scholarship for the first time when you are negotiating an improved package, you may be able to use the scholarship as a bargaining chip. Some schools have specific policies on this; others are prepared to be flexible. In some cases, we have seen FAOs let the parents use *part* of that money to reduce the family contribution. In other cases, FAOs have agreed to use the scholarship to replace loan or work-study components of the package instead of grants from the school.

Federal Work-Study: Under this program, students are given part-time jobs (usually on campus) to help meet the family's remaining need. Many parents' first inclination is to tell the student to reject the work-study portion of the aid package. They are concerned that the student won't have time to do well in class. As we've said earlier, several studies suggest that students who work during college have as high or higher grade point averages as students who don't work.

We counsel that you at least wait to see what sort of work is being offered. The award letter will probably not specify what kind of work the student will have to do for this money. You will get another letter later in the year giving you details. In many cases these jobs consist of sitting behind a desk at the library doing homework. Since students can normally back out of work-study jobs at any time, why not wait to see how onerous the job really is? (A minuscule number of colleges do have penalties for students who fail to meet their work-study obligations, so be sure to read the work-study agreement carefully.)

While work-study wages are usually low, they carry the important added benefit of being exempt from the aid formulas; work-study wages do not count as part of the student's income. Other earnings, by contrast, will be assessed at a rate of up to *50 cents on the dollar*. In addition, each dollar your child earns is a dollar you won't have to borrow.

Some colleges give you the choice of having the earnings paid in cash or credited toward the next semester's bill. If your child is a spendthrift, you might consider the second option.

Loans: There are many different kinds of college loans, but they fall into two main categories: need-based loans, which are designed to help meet part of a family's remaining need; and non-need-based loans, which are designed to help pay part of the family contribution when the family doesn't have the cash on hand. The loans that will be offered as part of your aid package in the award letter are primarily need-based loans.

The best need-based loans (the federally subsidized Perkins and Stafford loans) are such good deals that we feel families should always accept them if they are offered. (Both are far below prevailing interest rates.) In most cases, no interest is charged while the student is in school, and repayment does not begin on Perkins or Stafford loans until the student graduates, leaves college, or dips below half-time status. Even if you have the money in the bank, we would still counsel your taking the loans. Let your money earn interest in the bank. When the loans come due, you can pay them off immediately, in full if you like, without penalty. Most college loans with the exception of the Perkins loans have some kind of an origination fee (a one-time-only cost that averages about 3% of the value of the loan) and perhaps an insurance fee as well. These fees are deducted from the value of the loan itself; you will never have to pay them out of your pocket.

Here are the different types of loans in order of attractiveness.

Federal Perkins Loans: Formerly known as National Direct Student Loans (NDSL), these are the best of the federally subsidized loans. The current interest rate is 5%. The loans are made only to the student, with no need for the parent to cosign. Payment begins only after the student graduates, leaves college, or drops below half-time status. No interest accrues during the college years, and students have up to ten years to repay. Although the money comes from the government, these loans are administered through the college aid office.

The federal government gives the college a lump sum each year, but the FAO gets to decide which students receive these loans and how much they receive, based on need. Undergraduates can borrow up to $3,000 per year, with a cap of $15,000. The amount of money each school has available to lend out each year depends to some extent on the vicissitudes of Congress, but also on the default rate of the school's former students. If the school's students have a low default rate on paying back these loans, there will be more money available to recycle to new student borrowers. The government also tends to reward these schools with larger infusions of new loan capital.

In order to receive the funds, the student will have to sign a promissory note later in the spring or summer.

Federal Stafford Loans: There are two kinds of Stafford loans. The better kind is the *subsidized* Stafford loan. To get this, a student must be judged to have need by the college. The federal government then subsidizes the loan by not charging any interest until six months after the student graduates, leaves college, or goes below half-time attendance status.

The second kind of Stafford loan is known as *unsubsidized* and is not based on need. From the moment a student takes out an unsubsidized Stafford loan, he or she will be charged interest. Students are given the option of paying the interest while in school, or deferring the interest payments (which will continue to accrue) until repayment of principle begins. Virtually all students who fill out a FAFSA are eligible for these unsubsidized Stafford loans.

In both cases, the federal government guarantees the loan, and makes up any difference between the student's low interest rate and the prevailing market rate once repayment has begun. The dependent student may be eligible to borrow up to $2,625 for the freshman year, up to $3,500 for the sophomore year, and up to $5,500 per year for the remaining undergraduate years.

What happens if a student is awarded a subsidized Stafford loan, but the amount is less than the annual borrowing limit? In this case, the student can borrow up to the amount of her need as a subsidized Stafford loan and, if she wants, she can also take out an unsubsidized Stafford loan for the remainder of the annual borrowing limit. The interest rate for Stafford loans is currently a variable rate pegged to the 91-day Treasury bill rate in June of each year plus 3.1 percent, with a lifetime cap of 8.25%. For the 1996–97 year, the rate will be 8.25% for new borrowers who are in repayment and 7.66% for new borrowers with unsubsidized loans who are in school, the post-school grace period, or an authorized period of deferment.

An independent undergraduate can borrow up to $6,625 for the freshman year (of which at least $4,000 must be unsubsidized), up to $7,500 for the sophomore year (of which at least $4,000 must be unsubsidized), and up to $10,500 per year for the remaining undergraduate years (of which at least $5,000 per year must be unsubsidized).

Because the government guarantees the loans, the banks don't care about the credit history of the student and parents are never required to cosign the loan.

The banks, of course, love Stafford loans. Where else are they going to find an opportunity to make loans that are not only profitable but virtually risk-free as well?

Starting in the 1994–95 academic year, under a law proposed by President Clinton, some of the Stafford loans will be funded directly by the government and administered by the schools—thus eliminating the role of banks. This program, referred to as the Federal Direct Stafford/Ford Loan Program, is designed to assess the feasibility of lowering administrative costs of the program. If successful, the banks may eventually be cut out of the picture entirely. The banking lobby is fighting this pilot program fiercely.

However, for all intents and purposes, the effect on students will be minor, if any. If you are selected for the Direct Loan Program, you will borrow from the government. If not, you will borrow from a bank. The terms of the loans will be identical.

Once you have decided on a college and accepted the aid package, the FAO will tell you how to go about obtaining the funds. You will have to fill out a promissory note, and because the process can take as long as six weeks, it is necessary to apply for the loan by mid-June for the fall term.

If you are not selected for the Direct Loan program, you should be sure to read chapter 10 in this book before you sign the promissory note, as the choice of lender can have a significant impact on the total amount of interest charged during the course of the loan.

State Loans: Some states offer alternative loan programs as well. The terms vary from state to state; some are available only to students, others only to parents; many are below market rate. Unlike state grants, state loans are often available to nonresidents attending approved colleges in that state.

The College's Own Loans: These loans vary widely in attractiveness. Some are absolutely wonderful: Princeton University offers special loans for parents at very low rates. Some are on the edge of sleazy: Numerous colleges have loan programs that require almost immediate repayment at rates that rival VISA and MasterCard. While these types of loans do not normally appear as part of an aid package, a few colleges try to pass them off as need-based aid to unsuspecting parents. Remember that you are allowed to reject any portion of the aid package. It is a good idea to examine the terms of loans from the individual colleges extremely carefully before you accept them.

Financial Sleight of Hand

As we've already said, there are two general types of college loans: the need-based loans (such as the Perkins and the subsidized Stafford loans we've just been discussing), are meant to meet a family's "remaining need"; the other kind of loan is meant to help when families don't have the cash to pay the family contribution itself.

By its very nature this second type of loan should not appear as part of your aid package. As far as the colleges are concerned, your family contribution is your business, and they don't have to help you to pay it. However, a number of schools do rather unfairly include several types of non-need-based loan in their aid package, including the unsubsidized Stafford loan we just discussed, and the PLUS (Parent Loans for Undergraduate Students) which is intended to help those who are having trouble paying their family contribution. Subsidized by the government, the PLUS loan is made to parents of college children. Virtually any parent can get a PLUS loan of up to the total cost of attendance minus any financial aid received—provided the lender thinks the parent is a good credit risk.

The two real downsides of PLUS loans are that repayment generally begins within 60 days of the date the loan was made, and that you may eventually run out of credit. At some point, it is possible that the lender will tell you that you are overextended and refuse to make further PLUS loans to you.

Thus when a college tries to meet your need with a PLUS loan or an *unsubsidized* Stafford loan, the college is engaging in financial aid sleight of hand, ostensibly meeting your need with a loan that was not designed for that purpose and which you could have gotten anyway, as long as your credit held up. If you are offered either of these loans as part of your need-based aid, you should realize that the college has really *not* met your need in full. An aid package that includes a PLUS or an unsubsidized Stafford loan is not as valuable as a package that truly meets a family's remaining need.

Non-Need-Based Loans

While the other types of college loans won't be part of your aid package, this seems like a good place to describe a few of them, and they are certainly relevant to this discussion, for as you look at the various offers from the colleges you will probably be wondering how you are going to pay your family contribution over the next four years. Most families end up borrowing. There are so many different loans offered by banks and organizations that it would be impossible to describe them all. College bulletins usually include information about the types of loans available at the specific schools, and applications can usually be picked up at the colleges' financial aid offices. Here's a sampling of some of the more mainstream alternatives (we'll talk about a few of the more offbeat loans in the next chapter):

> **PLUS Loans:** We've already discussed some details of PLUS loans above. As credit-based loans go, the PLUS is the best. Parents can borrow up to the annual total cost of attendance at the college minus any financial aid received. The variable interest rate is set at 3.10 percentage points above the T-bill rate, with a cap of 9%. The current rate for the 1996–97 academic year is 8.72% for new borrowers. Repayment begins 60 days after you receive the loan and may extend up to ten years. If the college your child is attending is a school that participates in the Direct Loan Program, you can apply for the PLUS loan through the financial aid office. Otherwise, you can apply for a PLUS loan at most banks.
>
> When we suggest the PLUS loans to some of our clients, their immediate response is, "There's no way we'll qualify; we don't have a good credit rating!" Before you automatically assume you won't qualify, you should realize that the credit test for the PLUS is not as stringent as it is for most other loans. You don't have to have excellent credit to qualify. You just can't have an adverse credit rating (i.e., outstanding judgments, liens, extremely slow payments). Even if you fail the credit test, you may still be able to secure a PLUS loan provided you are able to demonstrate extenuating circumstances (determined on a case-by-case basis by the lender) or you are able to find someone (a friend or relative) who can pass the credit test, who agrees to co-sign the loan, and who promises to pay it back if you are unable to do so. Since some lenders may not permit you to use a co-signer, you should be sure to ask the lender about this before you complete the loan application.
>
> If you are rejected for the PLUS loan and are unable to get a creditworthy co-signer, there is still another option available to you.

In this case, dependent students can borrow extra Stafford loan funds over the normal borrowing limits. First-and second-year students can get an additional $4,000 per year, while those in the third year and beyond can get an additional $5,000 per year. In all cases, these additional Stafford loan funds must be unsubsidized. Obviously, this approach is going to put the student deeper in debt. However, if you need to borrow a few thousand dollars to cover the family contribution and are unable to get credit in your name, this strategy may be your only option.

Lines of Credit: Some banks offer revolving credit loans that do not start accruing interest until you write a check on the line of credit.

SHARE Loans [(800)634-9308]: Thirty-two selective colleges got together with Nellie Mae to set up this program, which offers credit-based supplemental loans to the parents of children who attend the member schools. Parents can borrow from $2,000 up to the cost of attendance minus any financial aid offered per year (subject to creditworthiness) and have up to 20 years to repay at a variable interest rate. Here is a list of the colleges that offer the SHARE loan:

Amherst	Princeton
Barnard	Radcliffe
Brown	Rice
Bryn Mawr	Smith
Carleton	Stanford
Columbia	Swarthmore
Cornell	Trinity
Dartmouth	University of Chicago
Duke	University of Pennsylvania
Georgetown	University of Rochester
Harvard	Washington University
Johns Hopkins	(in St. Louis)
MIT	Wellesley
Mount Holyoke	Wesleyan
Northwestern	Williams
Oberlin	Yale
Pomona	

TERI Loans [(800) 255-TERI]: Run by a not-for-profit organization called the Education Resources Institute, the TERI program offers undergraduate and graduate student loans from $2,000 up to the cost of attendance minus any financial aid offered. Students unable to pass the credit test on their own will be required to have a creditworthy cosigner. The interest rate charged will depend on the TERI lender selected by the student and the prime rate.

EXCEL Loans [(800) 634-9308]: Also offered by Nellie Mae, these loans can range from $2,000 up to the cost of attendance minus any financial aid offered, with repayment varying from 4 to 20 years. Parents can choose a monthly variable rate or a yearly variable rate set up to 2 or 3 points above the prime rate respectively.

P.L.A.T.O. Loans [(800) 467-5286]: This is a "nonprofit private sector initiative" that offers non-need-based loans for college at a variable interest rate currently based on the commercial paper rate plus 4 to 6 percentage points. The student can be the borrower, but the parents and/or another individual usually must cosign.

This is only a partial listing of the different loans available. When choosing which type of loan to take out, you should consider all of the following questions:

- Is the interest rate fixed or variable, and if variable, is there a cap?

- What are the repayment options? How many years will it take to pay off the loan? Can you make interest-only payments while the child is in school? Can you repay the loan early?

- Who is the borrower—the parent or the student?

- Is the loan secured or unsecured? The rates on a loan secured by the home or by securities are generally lower, but you are putting your assets on the line.

- Is the interest on the loan tax deductible?

On balance, the PLUS loan is probably the best of all these options. The only reason to consider the other types of non-need-based loans is if you wish to defer principle repayment, if you can lock in a very low fixed rate, or if you are better off having the loans in the student's name.

Should You Turn Down Individual Parts of an Aid Package?

Some parents worry that by turning down part of the financial aid package they are endangering future aid. Clearly, by refusing a work-study job or a need-based loan, you are telling the FAOs that you can find the money elsewhere, and this *could* have an impact on the package you are offered next year. In our experience we can't remember many times when we thought it was a good idea for a family to turn down grants, scholarships, need-based loans, or work-study.

Certainly Not Before You Compare All the Packages

Before you turn down any part of a single financial aid package, you should compare the packages as a group to see what all your options are.

The Size of the Package Is Not Important

Families often get swept up by the total value of the aid packages. We've heard parents say, "This school gave us $12,000 in aid, which is much better than the school that gave us only $7,000." The real measure of an aid package is how much YOU will have to end up paying, and how much debt the student will have to take on. Let's look at three examples:

School A:
total cost—$20,000
family contribution—$6,000
grants and scholarships—$9,000
need-based loans—$3,000
work-study—$1,000
unmet need (what the parents will have to pay in addition to the family
    contribution)—$1,000
value of the aid package—$13,000
money the family will have to spend—$7,000
need-based debt—$3,000

School B:
total cost—$19,000
family contribution—$6,000
grants and scholarships—$12,000
need-based loans—$500

work-study—$500
unmet need—$0
value of the aid package—$13,000
money the family will have to spend—$6,000
need-based debt—$500

School C:
total cost—$15,000
family contribution—$5,500
grants and scholarships—$5,750
need-based loans—$3,250
work-study—$500
unmet need—$0
value of the aid package—$9,500
money the family will have to spend—$5,500
need-based debt—$3,250

School A and school B gave identical total dollar amounts in aid, but the two packages were very different. School B gave $12,000 in grants (which do not have to be repaid), while A gave only $9,000. School B would actually cost this family $6,000 with only $500 in student loans. School A would cost the family $7,000 with $3,000 in student loans. Leaving aside for the moment subjective matters such as the academic caliber of the two schools, school B was a better buy.

School C would cost this family $5,500 in cash. On the other hand, this school also asked the student to take on the largest amount of debt: $3,250.

You've probably noticed that the sticker prices of the three colleges were almost totally irrelevant to our discussion. After you've looked at the bottom line for each of the colleges that have accepted the student, you should also factor in the academic quality of the schools; perhaps it is worth a slightly higher price to send your child to a more prestigious school. You should also look at factors like location, reputation of the department your child is interested in, and the student's own idea of which school would make her happiest. In the end, you'll have to choose what price you're willing to pay for what level of quality.

Is the Package Renewable?

An excellent question, but unfortunately this is a very difficult question to get a straight answer about. Of course there are some conditions attached to continuing to receive a good financial aid package. Students must maintain a minimum grade point average, and generally behave themselves.

It also makes sense to avoid colleges that are on the brink of bankruptcy, since poor schools may not be able to continue subsidizing students at the same level.

Bait and Switch?

Most reputable colleges don't indulge in bait-and-switch tactics, whereby students are lured to the school with a sensational financial aid package that promptly disappears the next year.

We have found that when parents feel they have been victims of bait and switch, there has often been a misunderstanding of some kind. This might occur when parents have two children in school at the same time. If one of the children graduates, the parents are often surprised when the EFC for the child who remains in college goes up dramatically. This is not bait and switch. The family now has more available income and assets to pay for the child who is now in college alone.

Sometimes, schools minimize work-study hours during the first year so that students have a chance to get accustomed to college life. Parents are often shocked when the number of work-study hours is increased the next year, but again this is not bait and switch. It is reasonable to expect students to work more hours in their junior and senior years.

Negotiating with the FAOs

Once you've compared financial aid packages and the relative merits of the schools that have said yes, you may want to go back to one or more of the colleges to try to improve your package.

We are not saying that every family should try to better their deal. If you can comfortably afford the amount the college says you must pay, then there is little chance that the college is going to sweeten the deal—it must be pretty good already. College FAOs know just how fair the package they have put together for you is. If you are trying to be piggish, you will not get much sympathy. It is also a good idea to remember that the average FAO is not making a great deal of money. Parents who whine about how tough it is to survive on $100,000 a year will get even less sympathy.

However, if you are facing the real prospect of not being able to send your child to the school she really wants to attend because of money, or if two similarly ranked colleges have offered radically different packages and your son really wants to go to the school with the low package, then you should sit down and map out your strategy.

Negotiate While You Still Have Leverage

After you've accepted the college's offer of admission, the college won't have much incentive to sweeten your deal, so you should plan to speak to the FAO while it is clear that you could still choose to go to another school. Similarly, you will not have much leverage if you show the FAO a rival offer from a much inferior college.

Try to make an objective assessment of how badly the college wants you. Believe us, the FAOs know exactly where each student fits into their scheme of things. We know of one college that keeps an actual list of prospective students in order of their desirability, which they refer to when parents call to negotiate. If a student just barely squeaked into the school, the family will not be likely to improve the package by negotiating. If a student is a shining star in one area or another, the FAOs will be much more willing to talk.

In the past few years, colleges—especially the selective ones—have become more flexible about their initial offer. Now that FAOs from the different colleges are limited in their ability to sit down together to compare offers to students, the "fudge factor" by which they are willing to improve an offer has increased. We heard one FAO urge a group of students to get in touch with her if they were considering another school. "Perhaps we overlooked something in your circumstances," she said. What she meant of course was, "Perhaps we want you so much we will be willing to increase our offer." This FAO represented one of the most selective schools in the country.

Prepare Your Ammunition

Before you call, you should have gathered all the supporting ammunition you can in front of you. If you've received a better offer from a comparable school, have it in front of you when you call and be prepared to send a copy of the rival award letter to the school you are negotiating with. (They will probably ask to see it, which brings up another point: don't lie.)

If you feel that the school has not understood your financial circumstances, be ready to explain clearly what those special circumstances are (such as high margin debts or any other expenses that are not taken into account by the aid formula, support of an elderly relative, or unusually high unreimbursed business expenses). Any documentation you can supply will bolster your claim.

If your circumstances have changed since you filled out your need analysis form (for example, you have recently separated, divorced, been widowed, or lost your job), you should be frank and let the FAOs know. They will almost certainly make changes in your aid package.

The Call

Unless you live within driving distance of the school, your best negotiating tool is the telephone. The FAOs will find it hard to believe that you need more money if you can afford to fly to their college just to complain to them.

If possible, try to speak with the head FAO or one of the head FAO's assistants. Make sure you write down the name of whoever speaks to you. It is unlikely that he will make a concession on the telephone, so don't be disappointed if he says he will have to get back to you or if he asks you to send him something in writing.

Some telephone tips:

- Be cordial and frank. Like everyone, FAOs do not want to be yelled at and are much more likely to help you if you are friendly, businesslike, and organized.

- Have a number in your head. What would you like to get out of this conversation? If the FAO asks you, "All right, how much can you afford?" you do not want to hem and haw.

- Be reasonable. If the family contribution you propose has no relation to your EFC, you will lose most of your credibility with the FAO.

- Avoid confrontational language. Rather than start off with, "Match my other offer or else," just ask if there is anything they can do to improve the package.

- If you are near a deadline, ask for an extension and be doubly sure you know the name of the person you are speaking to. Follow up the phone call with a letter (registered mail, return receipt requested) reminding the FAO of what was agreed to in the conversation.

- Parents, not students, should negotiate with the FAOs. Some colleges actually have a question on their own financial aid forms in which the parents are asked if they will allow the colleges to speak to the student rather than the parents. Colleges prefer to speak to students because they are easier to browbeat.

- Read through this book again before you speak to the FAO. You'll never know as much about financial aid as she does, but at least you'll stand a good chance of knowing if she says something that isn't true.

- If you applied "early decision" to a college and that college accepts you, you are committed to attend, and you won't have much bargaining power to improve your aid package. If you applied and are accepted "early action," you are not required to attend that school, and it is in your interest to apply to several other schools in order to improve your bargaining position. We discuss both of these options in more detail in the "Special Topics" chapter.

The Worst They Can Say Is No

You risk nothing by trying to negotiate a better package. No matter how objectionable you are, the school cannot take back their offer of admission, and the FAOs cannot take back their aid package unless you have lied about your financial details.

Appealing

If you still feel that your package is not fair, you can make a formal appeal to the college. There may be special forms from the school to fill out. Time is of the essence here, so decide quickly. Making an appeal will not jeopardize your chances for future aid.

Accepting an Award

Accepting an award does not commit a student to attending that school. It merely locks in the award package in the event the student decides to attend that school. If you haven't decided between two schools, accept both packages. This will keep your options open for a little longer. Be careful not to miss the deadline to respond. Send your acceptance registered mail, return receipt requested, as always. Above all, don't reject any award until you have definitely decided which school the student is going to attend. If a school's aid package has not arrived yet, call the college to find out why it's late.

If you have been awarded state aid as part of the aid package at the school of your choice, but the award notice you received from the state agency lists the wrong college, you will have to file a form with the state agency to have the funds applied to the school you chose.

Now That You Have Chosen a School

By the time you have chosen a college, you will already be halfway through the second base income year. Now that you understand the ins and outs of financial aid, you will be able to plan ahead to minimize the apparent size of your income and assets, and be in an even better position to fill out next year's need analysis forms. The first application for financial aid is the hardest, in part because you're dealing with a number of different schools, in part because it is a new experience. From now on, that first application will serve as a kind of template.

CHAPTER EIGHT

Innovative Payment Options

Innovative Options

We've already discussed the mainstream borrowing options and methods for paying for college. Over the years, colleges, private companies, public organizations, and smart individuals have come up with some alternative ways to pay for college. These ideas range from the common sense to the high-tech, from good deals for the family to self-serving moneymakers for the colleges and institutions that came up with them. Here is a sampling.

Transfer in Later

Every year a few parents make an unfortunate decision: they send the student off to a college that didn't give them enough aid. After two years of tuition bills, they've spent their life savings, and the banks won't lend them any more money. The student is forced to transfer to a public university. The result? A diploma from a state school that could end up costing the family as much as $75,000. The parents paid private school prices for a state school diploma.

What if they had done it the other way around? The student starts out at a state school, paying low prices. She does extremely well, compiling an outstanding academic record and soliciting recommendations from her professors. In junior year she transfers to a prestigious private college. Even if the cost were exactly the same as in the previous example, she now has a diploma from the prestigious private school, at a savings of as much as $35,000 over the regular price.

This scenario won't work without the part about the "outstanding academic record." Prestigious private colleges will almost certainly not be interested in a transfer student with a B average or less. The other thing to bear in mind is that aid packages to transfer students are generally not as generous as those given to incoming freshmen.

Both of these points must be factored into a decision to start with a public college and transfer into a select private college. However, if a student really wants a diploma from that selective private college, and the family can't afford to send her for all four years, then this is a way for her to realize her dream. Anyone interested in this tactic should be sure to consult the individual schools to see how many transfer students are accepted per year, what kind of financial aid is available to them, and how many of the credits earned at the old college will be accepted by the new college.

Cooperative Education

Over 900 colleges let students combine a college education with a job in their field. Generally, the students spend alternate terms attending classes full-time and then working full-time at off-campus jobs with private companies or the federal government, although some students work and study at the same time. The students earn money for tuition while getting practical on-the-job experience in their areas of interest. This program differs from the Federal Work-Study Program in which the subsidized campus-based jobs are probably not within the student's area of interest, and take up only a small number of hours per week. After graduating, a high percentage of cooperative education students get hired permanently by the employers they worked for during school. Companies from every conceivable field participate in this program. The federal government is the largest employer of cooperative education students.

Getting a degree through the cooperative education program generally takes about five years, but the students who emerge from this program have a huge head start over their classmates; they already have valuable experience and a prospective employer in their field. They owe less money in student loans, and they are often paid more than a new hiree.

If you are eligible for financial aid, you should contact the financial aid office at any college you are considering to determine the effect of cooperative earnings on your financial aid package. At most schools, you will find that as long as you are in the cooperative education program for need-based reasons, the money you earn in the program will not affect your aid eligibility. To find out more about cooperative education write to:

The National Commission for Cooperative Education
360 Huntington Avenue
Boston, MA 02115

Short-Term Prepayment

Recently, some colleges have been touting tuition prepayment as the answer to all the ills of higher education. In the short-term version of tuition prepayment, the parent pays the college the entire four years' worth of tuition (room and board are generally excluded) sometime shortly before the student begins freshman year. The college "locks in" the tuition rate for the entire four years. Regardless of how much tuition rises during the four years, the parent will not owe any more toward tuition.

Since most parents don't have four years of tuition in one lump sum, the colleges lend it to them. The parents pay back the loan with interest over a time period set in advance. The colleges love this arrangement, because it allows them to make a nice profit. If you pay the entire amount without borrowing, the colleges invest your money in taxable investments, which (because of their tax-exempt status) they don't have to pay taxes on. If you borrow the money from the college, they charge you interest on the money you borrow. Whatever course you pursue, the revenue the colleges earn from these prepayment plans more than makes up for any tuition increases.

Is Prepayment a Good Idea for the Parent?

While the colleges may tell you that you will save money by avoiding tuition increases each year, your savings, if any, really depend on what interest rates are doing. If you would have to borrow the money to make the prepayment, the question to ask yourself is whether your after-tax cost of borrowing will be less than the tuition increases over the four years. If so, prepayment may make sense.

If you can afford to write a check for the entire amount of the prepayment, the question to ask yourself is whether the after-tax rate of return on your investments is higher than the rate at which tuition is increasing. If so, then prepayment makes no sense.

Any prepayment plan should be examined carefully. What happens if the student drops out after one year? What happens if the program is canceled after only two years? What is the interest rate on the loan you take out? Is the loan rate fixed or variable, and, if variable, what is the cap? These are a few of the questions you should ask before you agree to prepayment.

However, unless the interest rates are extremely low—*and will remain low over the four years your child is in college*—prepayment may end up costing you more money than paying as you go.

ROTC and the Service Academies

The Reserve Officer Training Corps has branches at many colleges. To qualify for ROTC scholarships you generally need to apply to the program early in the senior year of high school. Competition for these awards is keen, but if a student is selected he or she will receive a full or partial scholarship plus a $100-per-month allowance. The catch, of course, is that the student has to join the military for four years of active duty plus two more years on reserve. While on active duty, many students are allowed to go to graduate school on full scholarship. A student can join an ROTC program once he's entered college, but will not necessarily get a scholarship.

To qualify for the program, students (male and female) must have good grades, SAT combined scores generally above 1200 (with an emphasis on math), they must pass a physical, and they must also impress an interviewer.

The service academies (the U.S. Military Academy at West Point and the U.S. Naval Academy at Annapolis are probably the best known) are extremely difficult to get into. Good grades are essential, as is a recommendation from a senator or a member of Congress. However, all this trouble may be worth it, for the service academies have a great reputation for the quality of their programs and they are absolutely free. Again, in exchange for this education, a student must agree to serve as an officer in the armed forces for several years.

Outside Scholarships

Opinions are divided about outside scholarships. The companies that sell scholarship data bases say there are thousands of unclaimed scholarships sponsored by foundations, corporations, and other outside organizations just waiting to be found. Critics charge that very few scholarships actually go unclaimed each year, and that the data base search companies are providing lists that families could get from government agencies or the local library free.

Certainly it must be said that many scholarships in the search services' data bases are administered by the colleges themselves. There is almost never a need to "find" this type of scholarship. The colleges know they have this money available, and will match up the awards with candidates who meet the requirements attached to the awards. It is in the colleges' interest to award these "restricted" scholarships since this frees up unrestricted funds for other students. Every year, colleges award virtually *all* the scholarship money they have at their disposal.

It must also be pointed out that when you notify a college that you have won an outside scholarship (and if you are on financial aid you are required to tell the school how much you won), the college will often say thank you very much and deduct that amount from the aid package they have put together for you. As far as the colleges are concerned, your "need" just got smaller. Thus if you hunt down an obscure scholarship for red-haired flutists, it will often not really do you any monetary good. Your family contribution (what the colleges think you can afford to pay) will stay exactly the same. The FAOs will use the outside scholarship money to reduce your grant money.

This is not to say that there aren't circumstances when outside scholarships can help pay for college, but you must be prepared to fight. If you have found outside scholarships worth any significant amount, you should talk to the FAO in person or on the phone and point out that without your initiative, the college would have had to pay far more. Negotiate with the FAO. He may be willing to let you use part of the scholarship toward your family contribution, or at least he may improve your aid package's percentage of grants versus loans.

We've talked to people who've had terrible experiences with the scholarship search companies and we've talked to other people who swear by them. Just keep in mind that this type of aid accounts for less than 1% of the financial aid in the United States. Of course, 1% of the financial aid available in the United States is still a lot of money.

Innovative Loans

The very best type of loans, as we've said before, are the government-subsidized student loans. We've also already discussed home equity loans and margin loans (both of which reduce the appearance of your assets) as well as some of the more popular parent loan programs.

There is one other type of loan that can help you write the checks:

Borrow from Your 401(k) Plan or a Pension Plan

If you are totally without resources, the IRS may allow you to make an early withdrawal of money without penalty from a 401(k) plan to pay for education. However, rather than get to this desperate situation (which will increase your income taxes and raise your income for financial aid purposes), it would make a lot more sense for you to take out a loan from your 401(k) plan or from your pension plan.

Not all plans will allow this, but some will let you borrow *tax-free* as much as half of the money in your account, up to $50,000. There are no penalties, and this way you are not irrevocably depleting your retirement fund. You're merely borrowing from yourself; in many cases, the interest you pay on the loan actually goes back into your own account. Generally, the loan must be repaid within five years. This kind of borrowing will not decrease your assets as far as the FAOs are concerned because assets in retirement provisions are not assessed anyway. However, if you've come to this point, your non-retirement assets are probably already fairly depleted.

A self-employed individual can borrow from a Keogh plan, but there will almost certainly be penalties, and the loan will be treated as a taxable distribution. Loans against IRAs are not currently permitted.

Loans Forgiven

A few colleges have programs under which some of your student loans may be forgiven if you meet certain conditions. At Cornell, for example, Tradition Fellows, who hold jobs while they are in college, are given awards that reduce their student loans by up to $2,500 per year in acknowledgment of their work ethic. Even federal loans can be forgiven under certain circumstances. Head Start, Peace Corps, or VISTA volunteers may not have to repay all of their federal loans.

Moral Obligation Loans

Here's a novel idea: the college makes a loan to the student, and the student agrees to pay back the loan. That's it. There is no *legal* obligation to pay back the money. The student has a moral obligation to repay. Several schools have decided to try this, and the results, of course, won't be in for some time. At the moment, when a student repays the loan, the repayment is considered a tax-deductible charitable contribution. The IRS will probably have closed that loophole by the time your child is ready to take advantage of it. Nevertheless, this is a wonderful deal because it allows the student flexibility in deciding when to pay the loan back, and does not affect the child's credit rating. If your college is offering this option, grab it.

Payment Plans and Financing Plans

If a family is having difficulty paying the entire semester's bill at once, they can go to a bank or other lender who will make the entire payment. The family then makes monthly payments to the lender (plus interest.) Obviously, you end up paying more money in the end, so this makes sense only if you cannot meet the due date any other way. The one attractive feature about these plans is that they often include an insurance package to cover college costs in the event of the death or disability of the parents. However, you can get this kind of coverage quite cheaply from any insurance company.

Some colleges are getting into the act, offering their own payment plans. At a few colleges, the plans carry no financing charge; however, at other schools, the interest rates can be deadly. Be sure to read the fine print regarding repayment terms and interest rates.

Junior Fellowships

Students apply for this program while still in high school. If accepted, they will be given jobs in federal agencies during the summer vacation and breaks between semesters. Like all earnings, the students' wages are taxable, and will be assessed by the colleges at the usual high rates. These jobs do provide valuable work experience and future job contacts, as well as the chance to earn a good amount of money. To apply for this program, students need to be in the top 10% of their graduating class, and be able to demonstrate financial need. You can get more information from high school guidance counselors.

Come to CRAZY COLLEGE!
Our Prices Are INSANE!

Some colleges have begun incentives that owe more to the world of retailing than to the world of the ivory tower. Among the offers you may find:

- discounts for bringing in a friend
- rebates for several family members attending at the same time
- discounts for older students
- reduced prices for the first semester so you can see if you like it
- option of charging your tuition on a credit card

CHAPTER NINE

Special Topics

DIVORCED OR SEPARATED PARENTS

The breakup of a marriage is always painful, and some parents are understandably reluctant to share their pain with strangers. We know of one set of parents who went through four years of need analysis forms without ever telling the college that they were divorced. Unfortunately, by not telling the schools about the divorce, those parents lost out on a great deal of financial aid, and put themselves through unnecessary hardships in paying for college.

No matter how painful or bizarre your personal situation is, the FAOs have heard worse, and you will find that being up-front about such problems as refusal by a former spouse to pay alimony or to supply needed financial aid data to the schools, will make the financial aid process easier. While the FAOs are quite expert at understanding the convoluted and intricate family relationships that arise out of divorce or separation, you will find that the aid formula itself tries to fit these complex relationships into a few simple categories. The result is completely baffling to most parents.

Who Are the Custodial Parents?

The formula doesn't really care who the biological parents of a student are. Ultimately, the formula wants to know only whom the student lived with most during the first base income year. This parent, called the "custodial parent," gets the honor of completing the standardized need analysis form. And according to federal guidelines, it is this parent whose financial information will be used to determine the parents' contribution to college.

Soap Opera Digest

Let's say that Mr. and Mrs. Jergins separated two years ago. Their only daughter Jill lives now with Mr. Jergins, and will be attending college next year. While some standardized aid forms may ask a few vague questions about Mrs. Jergins, as far as the federal financial aid formula is concerned, Mr. Jergins is the sole custodial parent and the only parent whose income and assets can be requested and analyzed by the processor. This counts as a family of two under the aid formula.

Let's say that Mr. Jergins gets a divorce from Mrs. Jergins and then marries another woman, Francine. The aid formula will now want to look at the assets and income of Mr. Jergins *and* the assets and income of his new wife as well. The instructions to the need analysis form will tell Mr. Jergins to check the box marked "married" and to consider Francine as the "mother" of his 18-year-old, even if he just married her last week. Francine's income and assets will be assessed just as heavily as Mr. Jergin's, even if she didn't meet Jill until the day of the wedding, and even if they signed a prenuptial agreement stating that she would not be responsible for Jill's college expenses. This is now a family of three in the eyes of the FAOs.

What if Mr. Jergins's new wife has a child of her own, Emily, from a previous marriage, who will also come to live with Mr. Jergins? Now there is a family of four. Neither of the *previous* spouses will be considered for assessment by the federal formula. When it comes time for Emily's college education, Mr. Jergins's assets and income will be assessed just as heavily as Francine's.

Let's suppose that Mr. Jergins also had a son, Michael, from a much earlier marriage. The son has never lived with him, but Mr. Jergins provides more than half support. Even though the son has never lived with him, Michael is considered part of Mr. Jergins's "household" by the federal guidelines as long as he receives half support. We now have a family of five for aid purposes.

If Michael were attending college at least half-time in a degree or certificate program, he would also be included as part of the number of "household" members attending "college, graduate/professional school, or other post-secondary school." This would help to reduce the Jergins's family contribution for Jill's college expenses.

By the way, when Michael (who lives with his mother, Mr. Jergins's long-ago ex) goes to college, his mother will be considered the custodial parent on *his* aid application. In effect, Michael can be claimed as a member of both of his natural parents' households, depending on whose aid application is being completed.

By now you may be asking why Emily (you remember Emily—Mr. Jergins's stepchild) was automatically included as part of his household without regard to who provides the majority of her support. Since Emily lives with her mother and Mr. Jergins, the question of support is irrelevant: they are her *custodial* parents under the federal aid guidelines. Even if Emily's natural father were providing all of Emily's support, Emily would still be considered a part of the Jergins's household. Of course, any child support received by Francine would have to be included as untaxed income on Jill's aid applications.

Number of Exemptions

As you know from reading the rest of this book, the more family members you can list on the need analysis form, the lower your family contribution will be. This number will not necessarily coincide with the number of tax exemptions you claim. Let's say you have a son who lives with you, but who receives more than half support from your ex. This other parent is entitled to take the son's income tax exemption, and you are not. You will have one more member of your family than you have exemptions. The colleges are used to this situation. You may have to explain, and possibly provide documentation, but they will understand. The same situation might occur if, as part of a divorce agreement, your ex is allowed to claim the son as a tax deduction, even though the son lives with you.

In either case, when it is time for college, you'll list your son as part of your household, and your ex will not be assessed by the federal financial aid formula.

A Quick Summary

Because parents find all this so confusing, and because the information they receive over the telephone from the college aid offices is often contradictory or misleading, we're going to summarize the key points:

1. The parent with whom the child resided most during the 12 months prior to completing the aid application is considered the "custodial parent." The custodial parent is not necessarily the parent who was initially awarded custody in the divorce agreement.

2. Siblings (including stepsiblings and half-siblings) can be considered part of the custodial parents' household provided they
   a. get more than half support from the custodial parent *or*
   b. lived with the custodial parent for the majority of the time during the 12 months prior to completing the aid forms, and cannot be considered independent students under federal aid guidelines.

3. A stepparent who resides with the custodial parent will be treated by the aid formula as if he/she were the natural parent.

4. It doesn't matter who claims a child as a tax exemption; the number of family members is based on the rules in the previous items.

Read the instructions carefully when you complete the aid forms. If a college challenges your application by trying to disallow some members of your household, don't automatically assume that they are right and you are wrong. When you speak to the FAO, refer to the section in the instructions to the aid form on which you based your decision.

Will an Ex-Husband or Ex-Wife's Assets and Income Ever Be Used to Determine the Family Contribution?

Parents are always concerned that the colleges will look at ex-spouses' income and assets and decide that the student is ineligible for aid, even if the ex-spouse refuses to help pay for college.

The vast majority of colleges will never even ask to see income or asset information from a noncustodial parent. The FAFSA has no questions about the noncustodial parent at all. While the PROFILE form asks a few questions about the noncustodial parent, the processor does not take this information into account in providing the Expected Family Contribution, and most colleges will not take the matter any further. (Of course, if you received alimony or child support from your ex, this will appear as part of *your* income.)

However, a few colleges do require that you fill out their own supplemental forms, and that the noncustodial parent fill out a form called the Divorced/Separated Parent's Statement. The colleges that ask for this information tend to be the most selective, including all the Ivy League schools. If your child applies to one of these schools, you may find that your ex-wife's or ex-husband's income and assets will indeed have a bearing on how much a college ultimately decides your family contribution ought to be.

Even if this is the case, you should not lose heart. Some types of aid must, by law, be awarded without reference to the noncustodial parent. These include the Pell Grant, the Stafford loan, and some forms of state aid.

To find out if you need to fill out any of these supplemental forms, consult the college's own financial aid instructions. Since the Divorced/Separated Parent's Statement is not analyzed by a central processor, you can send signed photocopies of the completed form to any schools that request it.

What If the Ex-Husband or Ex-Wife Refuses to Fill Out the Form?

The schools that require financial information about former spouses will not process your application for aid until you have supplied *all* the information they requested. If your ex refuses to supply the information you need to apply for aid, you have two options.

First, try to use reason. Your ex may be worried that merely by filling out the form, he/she is accepting legal responsibility for paying for college. Point out to your former spouse that on the Divorced/Separated Parent's Statement, there is a question that asks, "How much are you willing to pay?" By writing down "0" the parent expresses a clear desire to be left out of this responsibility.

It is also worth noting that even if a college decides to assess a noncustodial parent's income or assets, this does not mean that the noncustodial parent will ever get a bill from the college. Yes, the family contribution will probably be larger, but the bill for tuition will go, as always, to the student's custodial parent. There is no legal obligation for the ex-husband or ex-wife to help pay for college unless an agreement was signed beforehand.

The second option, if the ex-spouse refuses to cooperate, is to get a waiver from the colleges. The FAOs can decide at *their* discretion not to assess an ex-spouse if it is really clear that the ex-spouse can never be persuaded to help. You are going to have to make a strong case to get colleges to give you that waiver. This is the time to pull out all the dirty laundry—alcoholism, physical or mental abuse, chemical dependency, abandonment, chronic unemployment, and so on. Send the FAO a letter presenting your case, and include any documentation from agencies or third parties (such as an attorney, guidance counselor, or member of the clergy) that supports your case. Follow up with a phone call, and do this as soon as possible after you've decided to apply. Any information you supply will be confidential and will not go farther than the financial aid office. This will *not* jeopardize your child's chances for admission. It may, however, get you the aid you need to send your child to the school.

Is There an Agreement Specifying a Contribution from an Ex?

You may find this question included on your need analysis form. Be very careful how you answer it. If there is an agreement, and you have every reason to expect that your ex will honor that agreement, then say yes and give the figure. However, if there is a *disagreement* as to what your ex originally agreed to provide, then it would be calamitous to say yes. The colleges will assess your ability to pay based in part on this figure. If your ex then refused to pay, you would be in bad shape. If you are not sure you can count on your ex-spouse to provide the promised money, then write "no" on the form and write a letter explaining the situation to the various colleges.

The Divorced/Separated Parent's Statement

This form should be sent directly to the colleges that request it. However, you should NEVER send this form to schools unless they require it. Read the individual college's financial aid instructions carefully. Some always require the form, while others want it only if you've recently divorced or separated, or if your ex has claimed the child as a tax deduction in the past few years. The information on this form should agree with that on any other forms that have already been sent in—the need analysis form and tax returns. If you and your ex still have assets held in common, make sure that your proportionate shares of these assets as reported on your need analysis forms add up to the whole. Alimony and child support figures should also agree.

Remarriage

A stepparent's income and assets will be assessed by the FAOs just as severely as if he/she were the natural parent—even if there is a prenuptial agreement to the contrary. This being the case, it may make sense to postpone marriage plans until after your child is out of the base income years. A couple that decided just to live together while their children were in college might easily save enough money to take a round-the-world honeymoon cruise when it was all over.

Note: a few colleges give you the option of using the financial information of either your former spouse or your new spouse to determine eligibility for the school's own grant money.

The Difference Between Being Divorced, Legally Separated, or Just Separated

For financial aid purposes, there is absolutely no difference. If you are not legally separated, you may be asked to provide documentation to show that you no longer live together.

If You Are in the Process of Separating or Getting a Divorce

We have actually known of cases in which a couple separated or divorced in order to get more financial aid. This is taking the pursuit of free money way too far. We know of another couple that pretended to separate to qualify for more aid. Aside from the moral implications (you have to wonder what kind of warped view of life the children will bring away from that experience), this is also illegal.

However, if your situation has become impossible, and there is absolutely no choice but to separate, then you should try to take financial aid into account as you consider your legal options. An agreement by the soon-to-be-ex-spouse to provide for your child's education could be an expensive mistake.

Let's say that a father formally agrees to pay $10,000 per college year for his daughter's education. Many colleges will say thank you very much and decrease their aid packages by $10,000. If this is an amicable separation, it might be better if no agreement were made on paper. The father could then voluntarily write the mother a check when the money came due, thus preventing any loss of aid eligibility. If the separation is not amicable, and the mother is afraid she will never see the money unless there is an agreement in writing, it would be infinitely better if the father made one lump-sum payment to the mother toward college. In this way, the money becomes part of her overall assets, which can be assessed at up to only 5.65% a year.

Avoid Acrimony

A couple in the midst of splitting up is not always in the most rational frame of mind. It is essential, however, that you try to keep your heads clear, and prevent the education of your children from becoming one more brickbat to hurl back and forth.

Cooperation is the most important part of the process. We have seen parents childishly miss financial aid deadlines just to spite their former spouse. The person who really loses out when this happens, of course, is the child.

TRANSFER STUDENTS AND GRADUATE STUDENTS

The process of applying for financial aid as a transfer student or a graduate student is very similar to applying for aid as a freshman in college. However, there are a few differences that should be discussed:

- Deadlines for transfer and graduate students are often different from the deadlines for regular undergrads. Check your applications carefully for the specific deadlines.

- If you have previously attended any colleges, you will need a financial aid transcript sent from each one of them to the schools you are applying to. A financial aid transcript is not the same thing as a transcript of your academic record (which you will probably need as well). You will have to send financial aid transcripts even if you received no financial aid from the previous schools.

The colleges want to look at these records in part to see what kind of a deal you were getting at your previous school, and in part to see how much you've already borrowed, for there are aggregate limits to certain types of aid. For example, an undergraduate can receive a total of only $15,000 in Perkins loans.

The best way to go about getting financial aid transcripts is to pick up blank copies from the school to which you are applying, which come already addressed, ready to be sent back to the school. You can then mail these forms to the schools you previously attended. You'll have to keep on top of the process to make sure the transcripts are sent. The records offices at colleges are often worse than the motor vehicle bureau.

- Some colleges have separate aid policies for transfer students. Often, priority is given to students who began as freshmen. This is particularly true if a student transfers in the middle of the year; the FAOs will have already committed the bulk of their funds for that school year.

- It may help if you have some kind of bargaining chip—for example, if there is another school that is also interested in you. Your *previous* school won't be much of a bargaining chip since you have probably already given them a compelling reason for why you wanted to leave.

- It will certainly help if you've maintained a high grade point average. In particular, students who are transferring to a "designer label" college from a less well-known school will need good grades and good recommendations.

Graduate and Professional School Financial Aid Tips

Graduate and professional school aid is parceled out in much the same way as college aid but the ratio of grants to loans to work-study is unfortunately very different. Grant money has dried up in the past ten years.

Student loans, on the other hand, are somewhat easier to come by in graduate school. (For example, if you are attending law school, you can borrow up to the full cost of attendance without much trouble—which is pretty scary when you think about it.) The cap on subsidized Stafford loans rises to $18,500 per year in graduate school (of which at least $10,000 must be unsubsidized).

The paperwork you will be asked to fill out varies widely. All schools require the FAFSA, but many schools will also require the PROFILE form and possibly a Graduate/ Professional Student Information Supplement. Other schools may require the Need Access computer diskette, which asks questions similar to the PROFILE form and Graduate/Professional Student Supplement.

Fortunately, all graduate school students will find they now meet the federal government's independent student test. If you are a graduate student, you are independent by definition for federal aid purposes—even if your parents still claim you as a dependent on their tax returns, and you still live at home.

However, a few of the very selective schools will insist on seeing parent information anyway. The Harvard Law School FAOs, for example, require parents' financial data even if the student is 40 years old and the parents have long since retired to Miami Beach. Though the schools may refuse to give you any of their own money, you can still qualify for Stafford loans since you meet the federal regulations for independent status.

If the school requires parental information on the PROFILE form, you will have to find out if they want parental information on the PROFILE form only or on the PROFILE form and the FAFSA. If any one of them requires parental information on the FAFSA, you will have to complete the grey, green, and white sections of the 1997–98 FAFSA.

If you are planning on law school, medical school, or business school, taking on large amounts of debt is, although unpleasant, at least feasible. However, if you are planning on, say, a Ph.D. in philosophy, you should be very cautious about borrowing large amounts of money. An alternative to borrowing is to find grant money that is not administered by the financial aid office—in graduate school, some fellowships are administered by department heads instead. In addition, students sometimes find opportunities to teach or work on professors' grant projects.

THE COLLEGES' SPECIAL NEEDS: ACADEMICALLY GIFTED, MINORITIES, ATHLETES, LEGACIES

While financial aid is based on *your* need, it is always wise to remember that it is also based to some extent on what *the colleges* need. If you fit a category a particular college is looking for, your package is going to be much better than if you don't.

Preferential packaging comes in many forms. Perhaps the FAO will decide that your expected family contribution, as computed by the need analysis computer, is a bit high. Perhaps you will be offered an athletic scholarship or a non-need-based grant.

Whatever the school chooses to call it, you are being offered a preferential package—more grant or scholarship money, less loans and work-study.

No Time for Modesty

In many cases, these are not scholarships or grants for which you can apply. The schools themselves select the recipients, with a keen eye toward enticing high-caliber students to their programs. It is therefore crucial that the student sell herself in her application. This is no time for modesty. For example, a promising student violinist should make sure that one of her application essays is about the challenge of mastering a difficult instrument. This should be backed up by recommendations from music teachers, reviews of her performances that have appeared in newspapers, and a listing of any awards she has won. If a student is offered one or more of these merit-based grants or scholarships, it is important to find out if these awards are one-time only or whether they are renewable, based on performance. If renewable, just how good does the student's performance have to be in order to get the same package next year?

Bargaining

Colleges are particularly likely to increase their offer if they really wanted you in the first place. Students with excellent academic records are in an especially strong position to bargain. See part four, "The Offer," for more details.

Financial Aid for the Academically Gifted

Some awards come directly as a result of test scores. The National Merit Scholarship Program gives out about 1,800 nonrenewable scholarships and 2,800 renewable college-sponsored scholarships to students who score extremely well on the PSAT/NMSQT. Based on their performance on the SAT or the ACT, 120 students are designated Presidential Scholars.

At schools where all aid is based on need, a National Merit finalist will not necessarily get one penny of aid unless "need" is demonstrated. Other schools, however, automatically give National Merit finalists a four-year free ride—a full scholarship.

Some awards come as a result of the student's performance in college. These kick in during the sophomore year—an example is the Harry S. Truman Scholarship.

Merit grants based on academic performance in high school are becoming more widespread as time goes on. We believe this trend will continue as colleges begin to compete in earnest for the best students. However, most of the money awarded to students with high academic performance is less easy to see. It comes in the form of preferential packaging.

Athletes

In general, it is up to the student to tell the colleges why the student is special through his or her application.

Athletes, however, should get in touch with the athletic department directly. When you go to visit the school, make it a point to meet the coach of the team you are interested in. Do not assume that a school is not interested in you merely because you have not been approached by a scout during the year. Get your coach to write letters to the schools you are interested in. Don't sell yourself short either—an average football player might not get a scholarship at Notre Dame, but the same applicant at Columbia might get a preferential package. Even if the school does not award athletic scholarships per se (Columbia, like the rest of the Ivy League, does not), many FAOs bend the numbers to come up with a lower family contribution for an athlete the school particularly wants.

Remember, too, that football is not the only sport in college. Schools also need swimmers, tennis players, long-distance runners, and the like.

Minorities

While there is currently some controversy about scholarships directed specifically at attracting minority students, colleges in 19 states continue to make these awards. Critics of these scholarships should remember that the money spent on these programs represents only a tiny fraction of the total money available for financial aid, and helps to make the college environment a more interesting place for everyone. Minority students should contact the schools directly to find out about the availability of these programs.

Again, even if there are no specific scholarships for minority students, FAOs often use preferential packaging to help make college affordable for top applicants. A strong academic record in high school and excellent recommendations are vital.

Legacies

Many colleges will go out of their way for the children of alumni. If the student's parents' circumstances are such that they cannot pay the entire cost of college, they should not be embarrassed to ask for help. At many schools it will be forthcoming.

RUNNING YOUR OWN BUSINESS OR FARM

As we have already mentioned, the tax benefits of running your own business or farm are considerable: you are allowed to write off legitimate expenses, put relatives on your payroll, and possibly claim a percentage of your home for business use. The financial aid benefits are even better: your business or farm assets are assessed at a much lower rate than personal assets. This is because the colleges recognize a business's need for working capital. Thus a business's net worth (assets minus liabilities) of $50,000 will draw roughly the same assessment as a $20,000 personal asset.

If you have been planning to start your own business, now might be a good time to begin.

The Four Types of Business—C Corporation, S Corporation, General Partnership, Sole Proprietor

A **C corporation**'s profits are taxed at the corporate rate. C corporations must file an IRS 1120 corporate income tax return. The profits from a C corporation owned by a parent should not be included on the standardized financial aid forms, but the assets and liabilities must be listed. The owner of an **S corporation** (short for subchapter S) files a 1120S corporate income tax return, but also reports profits and losses on his own personal income tax return on schedule E. On the aid forms, the owner will thus have to report assets and liabilities as well as profits (or losses). A parent who is part of a **general partnership** reports profits and losses to the IRS on schedule E of the 1040. For aid purposes, she reports net profits (or losses) as well as assets and liabilities on the need analysis form.

A **sole proprietor** reports profits and losses to the IRS on schedule C of the 1040. Again, profits (or losses) and assets and liabilities must also be reported on the need analysis form. A **farmer** is treated like a sole proprietor but reports profits and losses to the IRS on schedule F of the 1040. On the FAFSA form, farmers who live on their farm and who can claim on Schedule F of their 1040 that they "materially participated in the farm's operation" (defined as a "family farm") should not include the value of the family farm under assets and liabilities.

Keep in mind that whatever business arrangement you have, you should never report your gross revenues on the standardized aid forms. Your net income (or net loss) is what counts—gross receipts less your deductible business expenses.

Financial Aid Strategies for Business and Farm Owners

Before the first base income year begins, it would make sense to accelerate billings, and take in as much cash as possible in advance. Try to defer expenses into the base income year. The idea, of course, is to minimize your income and maximize your expenses for the snapshot the college financial offices will be taking of your business. During the base income year itself, you might decide finally to do that remodeling or expansion you've been thinking about. In the last base income year, you will want to reverse the process you began before the first base income year: accelerate expenses and defer income, until after the colleges have taken their last snapshot.

Starting a Business or Farm

The beginning years of a business are very often slow. Many businesses lose money in their first couple of years, until they develop their niche and find a market. Parents who dream of starting their own company often feel that they should wait until after the kids are done with college before they take on the risk of an entrepreneurial enterprise. If you always dreamed of starting your own business, but have decided to wait until after the children are done with college, think again.

The perfect time to start a business is just before your child starts college. Consider: you'll have high start-up costs (which will reduce your assets) and low sales (which will reduce your income) for the first couple of years. If you time it right, these years will coincide exactly with the base income years, which means you will be eligible for substantially increased amounts of financial aid. Any business assets will also be assessed at a lower rate than personal assets. Like many businesses, yours may well start to be profitable within four years—just as your child is finishing college.

In effect, the college will be subsidizing the start-up costs of your business. This strategy is obviously not for everyone. A business must show a profit three out of five years (even if profits are small) or risk running afoul of the IRS. If you are merely indulging in a hobby, your farm or business losses may be disallowed. In addition, many schools that use the institutional methodology will disallow losses when determining eligibility for the school's own funds.

Any new business contains an element of risk, which should be carefully considered before you start. On the other hand, if you wait until your children are done with college, you may not have enough money left to start up a lemonade stand.

Estimating Your Company's Assets and Liabilities on the Aid Form

Owners of businesses sometimes overstate the value of their assets by including intangibles such as goodwill and location. These are important elements if you were to sell the company, but irrelevant to the need analysis formula. You are being asked to list only the total value of cash, receivables, inventory, investments, and your fixed assets (such as machinery, land, and buildings).

If your net worth is negative, that's what you should write down, but you will find that most colleges will not subtract a negative net worth from your total assets.

The Business/Farm Supplement

Many schools require the owner of a business or farm to fill out the Business/Farm Supplement, created by the College Scholarship Service (CSS). The form more or less mimics the IRS forms you will probably be sending the colleges anyway. If you are not the sole owner, be careful to distinguish between questions that ask for the business's total income, assets, and liabilities, and questions that ask for your proportionate share of the business's income, assets, and liabilities.

High expenses during the base income years will help to maximize financial aid. However, large business purchases cannot be deducted all at once under IRS rules. There are several different methods to depreciate your fixed assets. During the college years, accelerated depreciation probably makes the most sense, especially during the critical *first* base income year. As always, however, you should consult with your accountant, and perhaps a financial aid consultant as well.

If You Own a Significant Percentage of the Stock of a Small Company

A parent who owns more than 5% of the stock in a small company could report this asset on the standardized need analysis form under "other investment," but it would be much more beneficial to report it under "business and farm." If you own a significant part of a small company, accountants argue that you can be said to be a part-owner of the company. Most colleges will go along with this. The advantage, of course, is that the value of the stock will be assessed less heavily as a business asset than it would have been as a personal asset.

Selling Your Business or Farm

A huge capital gain from the sale of your business or farm will probably wipe out any chance for financial aid. On the other hand, if you are receiving a huge capital gain, you don't need aid. If possible, delay the sale until you are out of the base income years, but if the offer is good enough, take it and enjoy the feeling of never having to look at a need analysis form ever again. Oh, yes, and expect a call almost immediately from the fund raisers at your child's college. It's amazing how fast good news travels.

Putting Your Child on the Payroll

This is a good tax move, since it shifts income to the child, who may pay tax at a reduced rate. From a financial aid standpoint, however, increasing your child's income can backfire. Each year up to 50% of the child's income gets assessed by the FAOs. If the income is of any size, it may disqualify your family from receiving aid, or at least reduce the amount you receive.

If you are not eligible for aid, by all means consider putting your child on the payroll. A self-employed parent who hires a son or daughter does not even have to pay social security taxes on the child's earnings until the child turns 18.

THE RECENTLY UNEMPLOYED WORKER

If you have been terminated, or laid off, or if you have received notice that you will be terminated, or laid off, or if you are a self-employed person who cannot make a living due to harsh economic conditions, then you should be sure to point this out to the FAO.

Many schools can use what is called "professional judgment" to increase aid for the child of a recently unemployed worker. Instead of using the base income year (when you may have been gainfully employed) they can elect to look at your projected income for next year. Since you are now unemployed, your projection will be understandably bleak. Your child's college will probably want to see some sort of documentation (i.e., termination letter from your employer, unemployment benefits certification, etc.). Taking these extra steps could be worth thousands of dollars to you in aid.

How Do You Let the Colleges Know Your Projection for Next Year?

You will be asked on the PROFILE form to project your income for the coming year. Project conservatively. You may be out of work for a while, so assume the worst-case scenario. Do not project based on a tentative job offer; if it doesn't come through, you will be making much less than the colleges will think based on your over-optimistic projections.

If all the schools to which you are applying require the PROFILE form, then the schools will get your projected income from the CSS analysis. Just remember to mention your work status in the "Explanations/Special Circumstances" section of the form.

Contrary to what the PROFILE instructions say, you should not list any deferred compensation—401(k), or 403(b)—or contributions to IRAs or Keoghs as part of your untaxed income in Section L. Do, however, list your gross wages, including any deferred compensation as part of your projected income from work.

The reason you should not include these items as untaxed income is that by doing so you would be overstating your income. For example, let's take married parents with projected gross wages of $30,000 (and no other income) who made a $4,000 deductible IRA contribution. If this couple followed the instructions, they would be listing a total income of $34,000 ($30,000 income earned from work, plus $4,000 untaxed income). Obviously, they should only be reporting their total income—$30,000.

If your child is applying to schools that do *not* require the PROFILE form, then you should send them a separate letter detailing your changed employment status and a projection of next year's income. When listing your projections, you should break them down into separate categories: father's income from work (if any), mother's income from work (if any), income from unemployment benefits, and all other taxable and untaxable income.

In fact, it wouldn't be such a bad idea to send copies of this letter even to the schools that require the PROFILE form, since the FAOs at these schools sometimes miss comments written in the "Explanations/Special Circumstances" section of the form.

If You Lose Your Job While Your Child Is in College

Write a letter to the FAO explaining what happened as soon as possible, and include some form of documentation. It will probably be impossible for the FAO to revise your aid package for the current semester, but this will give them warning that you will be needing more aid next semester.

Other Disasters

If you are a nonworking parent who has been financially abandoned by a spouse, if you've had an accident that cost you a lot of money in unreimbursed medical expenses, if you lost your second job, if you received a pay cut or reduction in overtime, if you recently separated from your spouse, if your business lost its major client, if you become disabled, or had a major casualty or theft loss, you should be sure to notify the FAO immediately—even if the school year has already begun. Many schools have emergency aid funds for just these situations.

INDEPENDENT STUDENTS

If a student is judged to be independent, the need analysis companies assess only *the student's* income and assets. The income and assets of the parents do not even have to be listed on the form. Obviously, this can have a tremendous impact on financial aid. Most students have limited resources, and so the aid packages from the colleges have to increase dramatically if they are to meet the student's entire "need."

Parents often erroneously believe that by not claiming the student as a dependent on taxes, or by having the student declared "emancipated," their child will be considered independent for aid purposes, but this is not the case.

It is in the school's interest to decide that a student is not independent, since independent students need so much more aid. In fact, a student is presumed to be dependent unless he meets certain criteria. The rules change from year to year (in general going from stringent to more stringent). For the 1997–98 academic year, you are considered independent for federal aid purposes if:

A. You were born before January 1, 1974.

B. You are a veteran of the U.S. Armed Services.

C. You are an orphan or a ward of the court, or you were a ward of the court until age 18.

D. You have legal dependents (other than a spouse).

E. You are a graduate or professional school student.

F. You are married.

With the exception of certain health profession students whom we discuss in part 3 (Filling Out the Forms), meeting any one of these conditions makes you an independent student for federal aid purposes. However, the schools themselves may have their own, even tougher rules. A few schools (these tend to be the most expensive private colleges) state flat out that if the student is under 22 years old, he is automatically dependent unless both parents are dead.

These schools and others may insist that the parents fill out the parents' information section of the PROFILE form and/or the FAFSA, even if the student meets the federal rules for independence. To find out if this is the case at the schools you are interested in, consult the individual school bulletins. This will also give you an early clue as to whether a school uses the federal definition of independence, or a more rigid definition of their own.

If you don't meet the rules for independence, but have special circumstances, the FAOs have the authority to grant independent status on a case-by-case basis. To convince schools to do this requires extensive documentation. If the student has been abandoned by his parents, letters from a social service agency, court papers, or letters from a guidance counselor or member of the clergy acquainted with the situation may tip the scales.

If You Meet the Federal Requirements, but Not the School's Requirements

A student can meet the federal requirements for independence without meeting the school's own requirements. In this case, an undergraduate student may qualify for Pell Grants, Stafford loans, and possibly some state aid based on his status as an independent student. The school's own grant money, however, will be awarded based on his status as a dependent student, taking his parents' income and assets into account.

Independence and Graduate School

Graduate schools generally have more flexible rules about independence, and anyway, graduate students are usually no longer minors. Some graduate schools (in particular law schools and medical schools) will continue to ask for parents' financial information in awarding their own money. Even if the school will not grant independent status, virtually all students will meet the federal guidelines and be eligible for federal aid. The borrowing limits on the Stafford loans rise dramatically in graduate school, making this very worthwhile. Currently, graduate students can borrow up to $18,500 per year, of which at least $10,000 must be unsubsidized. The same limits and restrictions hold if the school is participating in the Direct Loan Program.

ESTABLISHING RESIDENCY IN A STATE

Establishing residency in another state is probably worthwhile only if the school you want to attend is a public university with lower in-state rates. The difference between in-state and out-of-state rates can be as much as $10,000. It is true that in-state residents also may qualify for additional state grant aid available for students who attend public or private colleges, but this will generally be less than $4,000 a year—sometimes a lot less. In addition, most private colleges that meet a student's entire need will replace any money you might have gotten from the state anyway with their own funds. In this case, changing your state of residence is not worth the trouble.

Whether you will be able to pull this off at all is another story. Each state has its own residency requirements and, within those requirements, different rules that govern your eligibility for state grants and your eligibility for in-state tuition rates at a public university. These days, the requirements are usually very tough and they are getting tougher. There are some states, Michigan for example, where a student cannot be considered an in-state resident unless her parents pay taxes and maintain a primary residence in that state. Period. To find out about residency requirements for a school in a particular state, consult the financial aid office at that school.

Planning Ahead

If you decide you need to do this, you should begin investigating residency requirements even before you apply to schools. Write to the individual state universities to ask about their rules, and set about fulfilling them before the student arrives at college. If the parents live in different states, it might be worth considering with which parent the child should spend the base income year.

EARLY DECISION, EARLY ACTION, EARLY NOTIFICATION, EARLY READ

Some colleges allow students to apply early and find out early whether or not they have been accepted. You are allowed to apply **early decision** to only one school, because your application binds both you and the school. If they decide to admit you, you are committed to attend. The schools like early decision because it helps them to increase their "yield"—the percentage of students they accept who ultimately decide to attend. An early decision candidate must apply by as early as mid-October and will find out if he has been accepted, rejected, or deferred as early as mid-December.

Early decision applicants may also need to apply early for aid. You should be sure to consult the college's admissions literature for early decision financial aid filing requirements. Provided that you meet your deadlines, you should receive an aid package in the same envelope with your acceptance letter.

Early action is an admissions option offered by Harvard, M.I.T., and Brown, in which you are notified early of your acceptance but are not bound to attend the school. You have until the normal deadline in May to decide whether to attend. The financial aid package, however, will usually not arrive in your mailbox until April and you usually file for aid as if you were a regular applicant.

Early notification is offered by many colleges that use rolling admissions. As the admissions committee makes its decisions, it mails out acceptance letters. Generally, you still have until the normal deadline to let the colleges know if you are accepting their offer. You apply for aid as if you were a regular applicant. Financial aid packages may arrive with acceptances or they may come later.

Some of these schools may try to put pressure on you by giving you an early deadline to decide if you are coming. If they are just asking you to accept the financial aid package, that's fine. An acceptance of the aid package does not commit you to attend the school. However, if they are trying to force you to accept their offer of admission before you've heard from your other schools, stall. Call the school and ask for an extension. Make sure you get the name and title of the person you speak to on the phone, and send a "we spoke and you agreed" letter via registered mail to confirm.

What Are the Financial Aid Implications of These Programs?

Early decision: For a high-need or moderate-need family, early decision is a big gamble, because you are effectively giving up your bargaining position. By committing to the school before you know what kind of aid package you will receive, you lose control of the process. It is a bit like agreeing to buy a house without knowing how much it costs. If the school has a good reputation for meeting a family's need in full, then this may be acceptable. However, even if the aid package they offer meets your need completely, you may not like the proportion of loans to grants. The school will have little incentive to improve the aid package since the child is already committed to attending.

If the aid you are offered is insufficient, there is a way to get out of the agreement, but this will leave you with little time to apply to other schools. We recommend that any student who applies to one school early decision should have completely filled out the applications to several other schools in the meantime. If the student is rejected or deferred by the early decision school—or if the aid package is insufficient—then there will still be time to apply to other colleges.

Early action: Even if a student is accepted early action, the student should probably still apply to several comparable schools. If one of these schools accepts the student as well, this will provide bargaining leverage with the FAOs, particularly if the second school's aid package is superior.

Early notification: The only financial aid implications of early notification occur if you are being squeezed. If a college is putting pressure on you to accept an offer of admission before you have heard from other schools, the college is also taking away your potential to negotiate an improved aid package. Fight back by asking for an extension.

The Early Read

Some schools say that, as a courtesy, they will figure out your Expected Family Contribution for you early in the fall if you submit your financial data to them—even if you aren't applying to their school. On the face of it, this seems like an offer too good to pass up.

However, you should understand that by letting them perform this early read, you are giving up complete control over the aid process. Your financial data are now set in stone, and if your child applies to that school, there won't be much you can do to change it (in any of the ways we have set forth in this book). We think you are better off figuring out your EFC for yourself using our worksheets, or hiring a financial aid consultant to do it for you. Letting the colleges figure out your EFC is a bit like letting the IRS figure your taxes.

AID FOR THE OLDER STUDENT

People who go back to school later in life often say they get more out of the experience the second time. We've found that from a financial aid standpoint, things are actually just about the same. Returnees still have to apply for aid and demonstrate need just like any incoming freshman. They are awarded aid in the same fashion.

The major difference is that they were probably employed at a full-time job during the base income year. If an older student is returning to school full-time, he should point out to the FAOs that there is no way he can earn as much money while he is in school. The first base income year is just not very representative in this case. Older students are probably independent by now, but they should not be surprised if some schools ask for their parents' financial information. Old habits die hard.

Two strategies for older students that should not be overlooked:

1. Let your company pay for it. Many companies have programs that pick up the cost of adult education.
2. Life credits! Some colleges will give you free credits for your life experience. We can't think of a better form of financial aid than that.

INTERNATIONAL STUDENTS

For students who are not U.S. citizens or eligible noncitizens (see instructions in the standardized need analysis forms), financial aid possibilities are severely limited. No federal aid is given to nonresident aliens. However, the schools themselves are free to give their own grants and scholarships.

You should check with the individual schools to find out their filing requirements. Many colleges require that you complete special aid forms designed solely for international students. Some of these colleges will also require a certificate of finance (which is issued by the family's bank certifying how much money the family has) and proof of earnings.

Because you are dealing with the vagaries of *two* separate postal systems, you should begin the application process as early as possible.

FOREIGN TAX RETURNS

The standardized need analysis form is not equipped to deal with foreign currency, so you will have to convert to U.S. dollars, using the exchange rate in effect on the day you fill out the form. There are special instructions in the forms that apply if you fit this category. Some colleges will ask to see your actual tax return, and they will insist that it be translated into English. Believe it or not, there is someone in your country's tax service whose job it is to do this, though it may take a while for you to find him.

STUDY ABROAD

There are two general types of study abroad programs:

1. Programs run by your own college
2. Programs run by someone else

In the former case, there is usually no problem getting your school to give you the same aid package you would normally receive. While some of these programs are a bit more expensive than a year on campus, the cost is usually not that much greater.

In the latter case, you may have more difficulty. At some schools you may be eligible only for federal aid. To avoid an unpleasant surprise, call on your FAO to find out what the aid consequences of a year abroad in another school's program would be.

TO THE PROFESSIONAL

A word to the guidance counselors, financial planners, stockbrokers, accountants, tax advisers, and tax preparers who may read this book:

We spoke recently to a broker from one of the big firms who said, "We don't take financial aid into account in our investment advice because . . . well, frankly, we assume that none of our clients are eligible."

This is dangerous thinking. These days lots of people are eligible for financial aid, including (we happen to know) two of his clients. While no one can be an expert at everything, we think it would be a good thing if brokers, accountants, tax advisers, tax lawyers, and counselors knew a bit more about financial aid strategy, or were willing to admit to their client when they didn't know.

Our intent here was to give *the parent and child* an understanding of the aid process and some idea of the possibilities for controlling that process. If you can use this as a resource tool as well, we are just as happy. We would caution you, however, that this book is by no means encyclopedic, and the rules change almost constantly. To be truly on top of the situation you would have to subscribe to industry newsletters, read the *Federal Register,* attend the conventions, develop your own contacts at the colleges, and then take what those contacts tell you with a large measure of salt.

Or you could just hire a financial aid consultant.

CHAPTER TEN

Managing Your Debt

For most people, there is really no choice; if you or your child want a college education, you have to go into debt. But it turns out that there are a number of choices to make about *how* you go into debt and how you eventually pay it off. Most parents and students assume they have no control over the loan process—this assumption may cost them thousands of dollars.

In previous chapters we've discussed the different kinds of loans that are available. Of course, the most common types of loans are Stafford and PLUS loans.

In this chapter, we'll talk about how to get the best deals on Stafford and PLUS loans while the child is still in school—and how to pay off these loans once the child is out of school.

As usual, this advice comes with our standard caveat: We can't recommend any specific course of action since we don't know your specific situation. These strategies are only meant to steer you in the right direction. Please consult with your accountant or a financial aid planner.

If you're taking part in the Direct Lending program (in which the government loans you money directly) then you can skip the following section on how to pick a lender—the choice has been made. (Go straight to the section on paying off your loans on page 232.) However, most families don't have this option. They must find a lender to give them the money.

How to Pick a Lender:

The rates for government-subsidized loans (such as the Stafford and the PLUS) are set by the government, so why, you might ask, would it matter which lender you choose? Why not just go to the bank your family has always used?

The answer is that some lenders are better than others.

By State: In some cases, the banks of an entire state may be better than others. Under federal regulations, you can borrow only from a lender in the state you're living in or the state in which the student will be attending college.

Normally, it makes sense to borrow from a bank in your home state—for one thing, it's convenient; for another, it can be difficult to switch lenders later. However, some lenders in some states—Rhode Island and Maine come to mind—offer rate reductions for a student who attends school in their states—even if the student doesn't live there. Some lenders in these states (the state itself chooses one or more lenders) will take up to one full percentage point off the regular interest rate of government-sponsored loans. Thus, you should check to see if you can qualify for one of these rate reduction programs *before* you apply to your local bank. You can get this information from the school's financial aid office or by contacting the higher education loan authority in your state. You can find these listings in chapter 6.

By Special Incentives: A number of banks offer special deals. For example, some banks reward eligible borrowers who make their first 48 monthly loan payments on time with a 2% reduction on all Stafford interest for the rest of the life of the loan.

If you make the first 24 monthly payments on time for loans taken out after July 1995, some banks will subtract the 3% origination fee you were originally charged on the loan from your outstanding loan balance (minus the first $250).

Many banks offer direct repay plans for Stafford and Plus loans, which enable them to cut down on costs. To entice customers like you, these banks will reduce the interest rate one quarter of one percent (.25%) if you authorize automatic deductions from your checking or savings account—Over the 10-year lifetime of a $10,000 loan, these three incentives could save you over $800.

By Method of Capitalization: No matter what bank you go to, if you will be taking out an unsubsidized Stafford loan, always ask how the lender will capitalize your loan. Banks can do this in a number of ways: quarterly (this is the worst—and most expensive—for you), semiannually, annually, or at repayment (this is the best—and least expensive—for you).

Remember, if the student chooses not to pay the interest while in school, the unpaid interest will be added on to the principle amount borrowed. This is called *interest capitalization*. Once the student is out of school, she must begin paying it all back. If the loan is capitalized at repayment as opposed to one of the other methods, there will be much less accrued interest to pay back. A $20,000 unsubsidized Stafford debt capitalized at repayment will save almost $500 in interest over a similar loan capitalized quarterly.

These amounts may not seem like much to you, but added together, they can become pretty significant—and they become even more significant the more you borrow.

Look Before You Leap

It's also important to understand that the rules make it hard to switch lenders once you've started the educational loan process. Once you have a bank, you're effectively stuck with it. So take the time to research the points we've made above. This is particularly important if a student is going on to graduate school.

Sample loan applications are printed in the back of this book on pages 276–277. To apply for a Stafford or PLUS loan you will need to secure an actual loan application.

How to Pay Off Your Loans:

As soon as a student graduates, the clock starts ticking. The government gives you a six-month grace period to find a job and catch your breath—and then the bills start arriving. You might think that at least this part of the process would be straightforward: they send you a bill, you pay. But in fact, there are a bewildering number of repayment options, as well as opportunities to postpone and defer payment.

Overriding all of this is one simple maxim: The longer you take to pay, the more it costs you. Putting it in practical terms, choosing to lower your monthly payments will stretch out the amount of time you'll be making these payments, and ultimately add thousands of dollars in interest to your bill. Sometimes this is worth it, as we'll see.

It's impossible for us to predict exactly what your monthly payments will be, since everyone owes different amounts, and borrowed on different terms. Just to give you a ballpark figure, someone who owes $15,000, at an average rate of 8% would have 120 monthly payments of about $182. Someone who owes $50,000 would have 120 monthly payments of about $607.

The only way to defer these loan payments long-term is to stay in school. As long as you are at least a half-time student at an approved post-secondary school, you can keep those bills at bay forever. If you get a job and then later decide to go on to graduate school, your loan payments may be deferred while you are in graduate school, and resume as soon as you get out.

Above All, Avoid Default

When all the loans come due, and a few personal crises loom as well, there's a very human urge to shove the bills in a drawer and hope for the best. This is absolutely the worst possible thing you can do.

The default rate on government guaranteed student loans is almost 22% at the moment. This might give you the erroneous impression that a default is no big deal. You should realize that a large portion of that 22% comes not from college loans, but from loans made to students of trade schools with three initials and two faces. These trade schools are often scam operations designed to fleece the federal government by preying on immigrants and poor people. A new arrival to this country may not care about, or understand the importance of his credit rating, but you certainly do.

When people get into economic trouble, they tend to get very reticent, and often don't ask for help. Even though you may feel embarrassed, it is much better to call your lender and explain the situation than to miss a payment with no explanation.

As you will see, there are so many different payment options, that there is really no need for anyone ever to go into default. If you lose a job, or "encounter economic hardship," you can get a temporary deferment (suspension of principal and interest payments for a specified time) or something called *forbearance,* which can include temporary suspension of payments, a time extension to make payment—even a temporary reduction in the amount of monthly installments. Many banks will draw up new repayment plans, or accept a missed payment as long as you inform them ahead of time.

Work *with* the lender. Or rather, lenders. If you have loans from more than one lender (the Perkins loans are administered separately from the Stafford loans), one lender isn't necessarily going to know what's happening with the other, unless you tell them.

It can take years to build up a good credit rating again once you've loused it up. Meantime, you may not be able to get credit cards, a mortgage, or a car loan. And if you're in default, getting additional loans for graduate school can be difficult if not impossible.

The Different Payment Plans

If you are repaying Stafford loans, Supplemental Loans for Students (SLS), or PLUS loans, there are five main repayment options at present. When you pick an option, it is not for life. You can switch payment plans at any time. Here is a brief summary of the options. For more details, contact your lender(s).

Standard repayment: The loans must be repaid in equal installments spread out over up to ten years. This is a good plan for people who have relatively little debt, or have enough income to afford the relatively high payments.

Long-term, equal-installment repayment: The loans must be repaid in equal installments over a period that can extend up to 30 years. The increased time period reduces monthly payments, but long-term interest expenses go up dramatically.

Graduated repayment: Loan payments start out low and increase over time. The payments must always at least equal the monthly interest that's accruing. This is a good plan for young people whose earnings are low, but are expected to increase over time. Over the lifetime of the loan, interest expenses are much higher.

Income-sensitive repayment: This relatively new option allows payments that are initially low, but increase as income rises. The lender works with the borrower to establish a payment schedule that reflects the borrower's current income and prospects for future earnings. The payments are adjusted annually to accommodate changes in the borrower's income. This option is available only to borrowers who took out Stafford or PLUS loans from private lenders.

Income contingent repayment: This option is available only to borrowers with direct government loans, but does not cover PLUS loans. In this plan, the payments are based on a combination of the borrower's level of debt and current income. This is the only plan with payments that can be lower than the monthly interest accruing (this is called *negative amortization*). Of course, this can add substantially to the final cost of long-term interest expenses. To counter this, at the end of 25 years, the government will forgive any unpaid balance. But don't start jumping for joy: the IRS will tax you on this unpaid balance. Thus, if the government were to forgive a $10,000 remaining debt, a person in the 28 percent tax bracket would have to come up with $2,800 in additional taxes that year.

Loan Consolidation

Government regulations allow you to consolidate all your education loans from different sources into one big loan—often with lower monthly payments than you were making before. As usual, the catch is that the repayment period is extended, meaning that you end up paying a lot more in interest over the increased life of the loan.

The loans that can be consolidated are: the Stafford, SLS, Perkins, PLUS loans, and loans issued by the government's programs for health-care professionals. You can't consolidate SHARE, TERI, or private loans from colleges or other sources.

If you have direct Stafford and direct PLUS loans, they can be consolidated only under the direct consolidation plan. Nondirect loans may be consolidated only as a direct loan if the borrower meets one of the following four criteria: the borrower has at least one direct loan; the borrower attends a school participating in direct lending and arranges for direct consolidation while in school; the borrower was unable to consolidate through a private lender; the borrower was able to get a consolidation loan from a private lender but was unable to get income-sensitive repayment terms acceptable to the borrower.

If you don't meet one of these four criteria, you'll have to consolidate through a private lender. If your original private lender won't consolidate your loans, you can go to another bank. That bank will essentially buy the loan from your original lender.

How It Works

A consolidation loan can be paid back using one of the plans outlined above. In some cases, loan consolidation doesn't make sense—for example, if a student is planning on going back to graduate school. For the most part, student loans can be consolidated only once, and it would be better to wait to do this until a student is completely finished with school.

You also don't have to consolidate all your loans. The rules on how your new interest rate will be calculated change constantly, so you'll need to get up-to-date information from your lender. In general, under private consolidation, the new rate will be some kind of weighted average of the various old rates. If you have one loan set at a particularly high rate, you might want to leave that loan out of the package to get a lower overall rate on your consolidated debt. In the long run, this will reduce your total interest payments on all of your loans.

You also may want to time your consolidation to lock in lower rates. For example, older Stafford loans (made prior to 1992) charged 8% for the first four years, then jumped to 10% for the remaining six years. If you consolidate right before the rate changes, you would save quite a bit of money.

If, like most people, you did not borrow directly from the government, and you have any thought of returning to school, it would be a mistake to consolidate subsidized and unsubsidized loans together. If you go back to school, the government will pay the interest on your subsidized loans, but not on your unsubsidized loans. If you consolidate the two types of loans together, you permanently lose that subsidy.

The Smartest Loan Strategy: Prepayment

All federally guaranteed education loans can be prepaid without any penalty. This means that by paying just a little more than your monthly payment each month, you can pay down the loan much faster than you might have thought possible, and save yourself a bundle in interest.

Obviously, if you're going to do this, try to prepay the loans with the highest interest rates first. It wouldn't make sense to prepay your 8% Stafford loan if you're paying 14% on an unsecured bank loan, or 19.9% on some huge credit card bill.

In some cases, it might make sense to pay off student loans with a home equity loan, depending on interest rates. As we've said earlier, home equity loans may be tax deductible. Student loans are not.

CHAPTER ELEVEN

Future Trends in Financial Aid

Future Trends in Financial Aid

The world of financial aid is always in flux. Making any predictions whatsoever is dangerous. However, it is safe to say that college tuition will continue to rise and will rise at a rate faster than that of inflation. While we don't believe that there will be any truly earth-shaking changes in the next few years, there are some events unfolding that may be important to watch.

National Service

One of the more recent developments in educational financing has been the Clinton Administration's efforts involving the AmeriCorps program. This is a national service program created in order to encourage young people to serve in educational, environmental, or police programs or in programs to assist the elderly or the homeless. In return for taking part in national service, a participant receives training, a living allowance at the minimum wage, health insurance, child care, and $4,725 per year in educational grants.

While we think this is a generally great idea, the program in its current form has a few problems from a financial aid standpoint. First, if a student joins this program after he or she has graduated, the student will not be able to use money from this program to pay college bills directly. Students would have to come up with the money in the first place. Only later could AmeriCorps grants be used to pay back loans that the student had taken out along the way. Second, with a provision for only $4,725 per year in grant money, national service may not be the most economically efficient way for a student to pay back student loans. Unless national service appeals to you for altruistic reasons, you may be able to repay loans faster by taking a conventional job and putting yourself on a minimum wage allowance. Finally, for students who participate in the program prior to college and who demonstrate need when they apply for financial aid, the AmeriCorps grants would simply reduce those students' "need" in the aid formulas and not the family contribution. This is why many higher education organizations have criticized Clinton's references to national service as a student aid program.

At present, the future of the AmeriCorps program is in doubt. The House of Representatives has proposed eliminating all funding for the program. The Senate has proposed continued funding at the same level. While current participants will be fully funded for now, after September 1997 it is anyone's guess what will happen to this program.

Stafford Loan Interest Subsidies

There is often talk in the media regarding the possible elimination of the in-school interest subsidies that students receive on subsidized Stafford loans. For now, it seems safe to say that the interest subsidies for eligible students have survived the Congressional budget cutters' ax. However, because of uncertainty regarding this matter, we recommend that all students ask their lender or FAO about the current status of the interest subsidies before they submit any Stafford Loan applications to the lender or the school. This is especially true for loans for the 1997–98 academic year and beyond.

Taxes

Since the maximum personal U.S. income tax rate rose to 39.6% in the Clinton era, the benefits of putting money into the child's name have increased because of the spread between the parents' (higher) tax rates and the child's (lower) tax rate. This has led to more stories in the media and recommendations by accountants and financial planners that you should invest or save money in your child's name. As we said in earlier chapters, if you have *any* hope of financial aid, keep the money in your child's name to a minimum.

Two Rays of Hope

One of the more positive recent developments regarding college financing has been the fact that some of the more expensive colleges finally seem to be realizing that they are pricing themselves out of the market. Of particular note was Bennington College's announcement that they would cut tuition costs over the next few years by eliminating some faculty positions and major fields of study. Many private colleges (such as the University of Rochester and Lehigh University) have also expanded their merit-based aid in order to stem the "middle-class flight" to the public institutions.

Critics have been charging for years that the price of tuition at many private colleges reflected not so much the actual cost of educating a student as what the college administrators thought the market would bear. It may be that colleges are finally realizing that their pool of applicants is beginning to question whether the benefits of a private college education are worth the expense of an artificially inflated sticker price. To survive in today's leaner times, many college administrators are realizing that they will have to become more efficient if they are to survive. This trend is good news for students.

Another positive sign for college-bound students are the recent discussions by a number of colleges (Oberlin, Stanford, and the State University of New York for example) regarding the possibility of offering a three-year bachelor's degree.

The Importance of Planning Ahead

If financial aid history has taught us anything, it is that it is never too early to start planning ahead. At whatever stage you are reading this book, there are some tangible strategies that you can use to help take control over the financial aid process. The purpose of this book has been to show you those strategies. We hope they will make the dream of a college education a reality.

Good luck.

PART FIVE

Worksheets and Forms

Calculating Your Expected
Family Contribution

We realize that the pages of worksheets and tables that follow may seem a little intimidating. There are some books out there that claim you can calculate your EFC by consulting a single table that has been prepared by the book's author. Unfortunately, these tables ask for such vague information from the parent that they do not provide an accurate estimation in the end. There is no way to get an accurate reading of your EFC without going through the calculations on the pages that follow.

When you fill out your need analysis form, you provide the processor with very specific information, but you will not be required to complete a worksheet such as this. The processor simply plugs your information into a computer that automatically does all the calculations we are about to show you.

So Why Should You Bother to
Go Through These Worksheets at All?

There are two excellent reasons.

First, by making the calculations yourself, you will be able to see how the process works; it is amazing how small changes in the way you list your financial information can produce big changes in the final result.

Second, by having an *accurate* idea of what your Expected Family Contribution will be, you can make informed decisions about which schools to apply to, how to answer questions on the individual school aid forms like, "How much do you think you can afford to pay for college?" and what early steps you can take for next year.

Ughhhh

If these worksheets fill you with dread, you can always hire an independent financial aid consultant to do these calculations for you. Details on how to find one are in chapter 7.

The Standard Disclaimer

While we believe that these worksheets and tables are accurate, they have not been approved by the U.S. Department of Education. In addition, the worksheets and tables regarding calculation of income have not been approved by the IRS and should not be used to calculate your tax liability for your income tax return.

Worksheet for Calculating the Expected Family Contribution for a Dependent Student

Please note that by TAXABLE INCOME, we mean income that the IRS considers subject to possible taxation, even if the IRS does not require that a tax return be filed because the income is below a minimum level determined by them. As such, it is possible to pay no tax on a small amount of taxable income. UNTAXED INCOME or NONTAXABLE INCOME refers to income that is never subject to income tax. Some income items, such as social security benefits, can be considered either taxable income or untaxed income, depending on the taxpayer's total income.

Unless otherwise indicated, all references in this worksheet to specific IRS line numbers relate to those lines of the 1996 IRS 1040 form (the long form). To avoid confusion, we suggest that you refer to chapter 3 for more detailed descriptions of these various items. If the student's natural parents are not married and living together, please consult pages 208–213 if you are unsure whose income should be listed on this worksheet.

In the main worksheets there will be two columns for making your calculations: the left column titled "FM" is for the Federal Methodology. If none of the colleges that interest you are using the Institutional Methodology, then you can skip the calculations under the "IM" column.

The worksheets and tables that follow are based on the formula for calculating the EFC for the 1997–98 academic year. For those students who file the PROFILE form as well as the FAFSA, the state and local tax expense item, the income protection allowance, the asset protection allowance, and the employment allowance will be only slightly different for the Institutional Methodology vs. the Federal Methodology. For simplicity, we are only providing you with the necessary information to calculate these expense and allowance items under the federal formula. You should therefore write down the same number in the FM and IM columns for these items on the worksheets.

Even if you are only calculating your EFC under the Federal Methodology, we still recommend that you complete Table 8 which will help you determine if you have enough unreimbursed medical expenses to warrant a letter of explanation to the FAOs at those schools which use only the federal formula.

If you meet all of the criteria for the Simplified Needs Test (see pages 39–43), you can calculate your EFC under the simplified formula by listing zero in the "FM" column on Line Q of the Parents' Worksheet and on Line GG of the Student's Worksheet. However, we recommend that you also calculate your EFC using asset information since some schools do not use the simplified formula when awarding their own aid funds. If you are performing calculations for the Institutional Methodology, assets are always considered in the formula even if you meet the criteria for the Simplified Needs Test.

Some helpful tips for completing the worksheets:

1. Round off all figures to the nearest dollar.

2. All income/expense items relate to yearly amounts. Do not use monthly or weekly figures. All asset/liability items relate to current amounts.

3. For those individuals who have not yet completed their 1996 tax returns: If *all* of the parents' income and expense items are basically the same from year to year, you can use figures from your 1995 IRS form and minimize some of the calculations involved in Table 3 and Table 6. For these tables, you can simply proceed to the last line of the table and enter the appropriate amount from your tax return. (Regarding Table 15, the same is true if the student's income is basically similar from year to year.) Please note that if a 1040A or a 1040EZ tax return was filed instead of the 1040 long form, the IRS line references on the tables and worksheets will not be the same numbers, in most cases, as the lines on your tax return(s).

    If, however, you anticipate significant changes in *any* income or expense figures from your 1995 figures, you will get a more accurate assessment of your Family Contribution if you project these amounts using your best estimates. In this case, you should complete all the lines on the appropriate tables. You may, however, find it helpful to use your 1995 tax return(s) as a point of comparison. The references to various IRS line numbers in the tables will assist you when making your projections. Please note however, that the 1995 and 1996 line numbers on the tax returns may differ for some items.

4. Tables 1 through 9 and Table 11 (if applicable) must be completed (in order) *before* you can begin work on the Parents' Expected Contribution worksheet. The bottom lines from Tables 5 through 9 and Table 11 will be entered on the appropriate section of that worksheet. Table 10 and Tables 12 through 14 should be utilized *as* you are completing that worksheet. Table 15 should be completed *before* you begin work on the Student's Expected Contribution worksheet.

5. When completing Tables 1 and 2, be sure to enter the appropriate amounts under the proper column. Do not combine the amounts into one column, as this will give you an incorrect estimate of your Family Contribution.

6. Any number listed in parentheses should be subtracted from the number in the same column above it.

7. The columns "FM" and "IM" are separate columns; do not combine the amounts in the different columns. In addition, if there is an XXXXX preprinted on a particular line of the worksheet, it means that you should not list any number for that particular item in that column only.

8. If you are doing calculations for the institutional methodology, you should pay particular attention to the help "notes" on the worksheets if your situation involves one or more of the following: 1) You have losses that would appear on the 1996 1040 long form (Lines 12, 13, 14, 17, 18, or 21); 2) You paid elementary or secondary school tuition for the student's sibling(s) during the base income year; 3) You own a home and you wish to calculate your contribution for a college that caps home value at three times income; 4) One or more of the student's custodial parents (or custodial stepparent) will attend college on at least a half-time basis during the same academic year the student will attend college; 5) You have amounts withheld from wages for dependent care and medical spending accounts. You may also find it helpful to refer to the summaries of the differences in the two methodologies listed on pages 67, 88, and 93 before you start on the worksheets.

9. And last, but not least, we suggest that you check your math. Even better, you should consider having another family member review your completed tables and worksheets for accuracy. Even if your family contribution figures are higher that the cost of attendance, you should still consider applying for aid since the FAOs may take other factors into account, you may be eligible for state aid benefits not based on these formulas, and/or you may have made an error in your calculations when doing these worksheets.

TABLE 1
Parents' Income Earned From Work

		Father (Stepfather)	Mother (Stepmother)

For lines B, C, and D list losses as zero.

A. Wages, tips, salary, and other compensation subject to income tax (IRS 1040 Line 7) — $ _____ $ _____

B. Business income: self-employment (IRS Line 12) — + $ _____   + $ _____

C. Partnership income from the operation of a business (Part 2—Schedule E IRS 1040) — + $ _____   + $ _____

[Do not include subchapter S corporations or income from limited partnerships not subject to self-employment taxes.]

D. Farm income (IRS Line 18) — + $ _____   + $ _____

E. Untaxed income

[Include contributions to deferred compensation plans such as 401(k), 403(b), tax-deferred annuities, etc. This does not include IRA or Keogh contributions. Do not include amounts withheld from wages for dependent care and medical spending accounts.] — + $ _____   + $ _____

TOTAL INCOME EARNED FROM WORK
(Sum of lines A through E) — $ _____ $ _____

TABLE 2
Student's (and Spouse's) Income Earned from Work

	Student	Spouse

For lines B, C, and D list losses as zero.

A. Wages, tips, salary, and other compensation subject to income tax (IRS Line 7) $ _____ $ _____

B. Business income: Self-employment (IRS Line 12)   + $ _____   + $ _____

C. Partnership income from the operation of a business   + $ _____   + $ _____

(Part 2—Schedule E IRS 1040) [Do not include subchapter S corporations or income from limited partnerships not subject to self-employment taxes.]

D. Farm income (IRS Line 18)   + $ _____   + $ _____

E. Untaxed income

[Include contributions to deferred compensation plans such as 401(k), 403(b), tax-deferred annuities, etc. This does not include IRA or Keogh contributions. Do not include amounts withheld from wages for dependent care and medical spending accounts.]   + $ _____   + $ _____

Gross Income Earned From Work $ $
(Sum of lines A through E)

MINUS: Any need-based work study earnings or taxable grants/scholarships (in excess of tuition, fees, books, and required supplies) included in lines A through E above   ($ _____)   ($ _____)

TOTAL INCOME EARNED FROM WORK $ ===== $ =====

TABLE 3
Adjusted Gross Income

Helpful hint: Losses, if any, should be listed in parentheses and should be subtracted in your calculations.

Sum of:

Father's wages, tips, salary, and other
compensation subject to tax $ _____
(From Line A for Father [Stepfather] on Table 1)

Mother's wages, tips, salary, and
other compensation subject to tax + $ _____
(From Line A for Mother [Stepmother] on Table 1)

Taxable interest (IRS Line 8a) + $ _____

Dividend income (IRS Line 9) + $ _____

Taxable refunds of state and
local income taxes, if any (IRS Line 10) + $ _____

Alimony received (IRS Line 11) + $ _____

Father and/or mother's income or (loss)
from self-employment (IRS Line 12) + $ _____

Capital gain or (loss) (IRS Lines 13) + $ _____

Other gains or (losses) (IRS Line 14) + $ _____

Taxable IRA distributions (IRS Line 15b) + $ _____

Taxable pensions and annuities (IRS Line 16b) + $ _____

Rents, royalties, estates, partnerships,
and trusts, etc. (IRS Line 17) + $ _____

Farm income or (loss) (IRS Line 18) + $ _____

Unemployment compensation (IRS Line 19) + $ _____

Taxable social security benefits (IRS Line 20b) + $ _____

Other taxable income (IRS Line 21) + $ _____

A. Gross Income (same as IRS Line 22) $ _____

Adjustments to Income

Sum of:

Deductible portion of IRA contributions $ _____
(IRS Line 23a plus b)

Moving expenses (IRS Line 24) + $ _____

One half of self-employment tax (IRS Line 25) + $ _____

Self-employed health insurance deduction
(IRS Line 26) + $ _____

Keogh and SEP deductions (IRS Line 27) + $ _____

Penalty on early withdrawal of savings
(IRS Line 28) + $ _____

Alimony paid (IRS Line 29) + $ _____

B. Total Adjustments (IRS Line 30) ($ _____)

C. ADJUSTED GROSS INCOME (IRS Line 31) $ _____
(Gross Income [Line A] minus Total Adjustments [Line B])

TABLE 4
Parents' Untaxed Income

Sum of:

Untaxed social security benefits	$ _____
[Include any benefits paid to the parent for the children]	
(Total social security benefits minus taxable benefits [from IRS Line 20b], if any)	
Aid to Families with Dependent Children (AFDC or ADC)	+ $ _____
Child Support received for all children	+ $ _____
Deductible IRA and/or Keogh payments (from IRS 1040, total lines 23a, 23b, and 27)	+ $ _____
Earned income credit (from IRS 1040, line 54)	+ $ _____
Untaxed portions of pensions (from IRS 1040, line 15a minus 15b, and line 16a minus 16b [excluding rollovers])	+ $ _____
Credit for federal tax on special fuels (from IRS 4136—Part III: Total Income Tax credit)	+ $ _____
Foreign income exclusion (from IRS 2555, line 43)	+ $ _____
Tax-exempt interest income from IRS 1040, line 8b	+ $ _____
Payments to tax-deferred pension and savings plans (paid directly or withheld from earnings). Include untaxed portions of 401(k) and 403(b) plans.	+ $ _____
Welfare benefits (except AFDC/ADC, which were listed above)	+ $ _____
Workers compensation	+ $ _____
Veterans' noneducational benefits such as death pension, and dependency and indemnity compensation (DIC), etc.	+ $ _____
Housing, food, and other living allowances (excluding rent subsidies for low-income housing) paid to members of the military, clergy, and others (including cash payments and cash value of benefits)	+ $ _____
Any other untaxed income and benefits, such as Black Lung Benefits, Refugee Assistance, untaxed portions of Railroad Retirement benefits, or Job Training Partnership Act noneducational benefits	+ $ _____

D. TOTAL UNTAXED INCOME $ ══════════

TABLE 5
Parents' Total Income

C.   Parents' Adjusted Gross Income
     (From Table 3—Line C) $ _____

D.   Parents' Total Untaxed Income
     (From Table 4—Line D)   + $ _____
                                                       _____

E.   **Subtotal** $ _____

F.   Title IV Income Exclusions   ($ _____)
     (From Table 5A below.
     If no Exclusions, enter -0-.)   _____

G.   **PARENTS' TOTAL INCOME** $ _____
     (Line E minus F)
     (This figure will be listed at the top
     of the Parents' Expected Contribution
     Worksheet [Line G].)

• •

TABLE 5A
Title IV Income Exclusions

Sum of:
     Child Support PAID $ _____

     Living allowances received
     under National and Community
     Service Act of 1990 included in
     Line D in Table 5 above.   + $ _____

     Parents need-based work study
     earnings and taxable grant/scholarship
     aid in excess of tuition, fees, books, and
     required supplies.   + $ _____
                                                       _____

Total Exclusions $ _____
     *(This figure will be listed
     on Line F in Table 5 above)*

TABLE 6
U.S. Income Taxes Paid

Adjusted Gross Income (from Table 3—Line C) $ _____

Minus: Total Itemized Deductions (same as the   ($ _____)
bottom line on Schedule A of IRS 1040)   _____
(If you do not/will not itemize deductions,
use the following numbers based on $ _____
your tax filing status:
   Single—$4,000
   Head of Household—$5,900
   Married filing jointly or qualifying
   widow(er)—$6,700
   Married filing separately—$3,350)

Minus: Number of exemptions you can claim
multiplied by $2,550   ($ _____)

                                                            _____
Taxable Income (If zero or less, skip charts
below and enter zero at the end of the four tables.) $ _____

Use the Taxable Income figure listed above with the appropriate table below
based on your tax filing status to calculate your U.S. Income Taxes paid.
Enter the result at the end of the four tax tables. Tax tables are based on 1996
tax rates.

Use if your filing status is **Single**

If your taxable income is: Over—	But not over—	Income taxes paid is—	of the amount over—
$0	$24,000	15%	$0
$24,000	$58,150	$3,600.00 + 28%	$24,000
$58,150	$121,300	$13,162.00 + 31%	$58,150
$121,300	$263,750	$32,738.50 + 36%	$121,300
$263,750	—	$84,020.50 + 39.6%	$263,750

Use if your filing status if **Married filing jointly or Qualifying widow(er)**

If your taxable income is: Over—	But not over—	Income taxes paid is—	of the amount over—
$0	$40,100	15%	$0
$40,100	$96,900	$6,015.00 + 28%	$40,100
$96,900	$147,700	$21,919.00 + 31%	$96,900
$147,700	$263,750	$37,667.00 + 36%	$147,700
$263,750	—	$79,445.00 + 39.6%	$263,750

Use if your filing status is **Married filing separately,**

If your taxable income is: Over—	But not over—	Income taxes paid is—	of the amount over—
$0	$20,050	15%	$0
$20,050	$48,450	$3,007.50 + 28%	$20,050
$48,450	$73,850	$10,959.50 + 31%	$48,450
$73,850	$131,875	$18,833.50 + 36%	$73,850
$131,875	—	$39,722.50 + 39.6%	$131,875

If the parents (or the custodial parent and a stepparent) are married and living together yet file separately, calculate a separate number for each parent (stepparent) and add the numbers together to determine a figure for U.S. taxes paid.

Use if your filing status is **Head of the household**

If your taxable income is: Over—	But not over—	Income taxes paid is—	of the amount over—
$0	$32,150	15%	$0
$32,150	$83,050	$4,822.50 + 28%	$32,150
$83,050	$134,500	$19,074.50 + 31%	$83,050
$134,500	$263,750	$35,024.00 + 36%	$134,500
$263,750	—	$81,554.00 + 39.6%	$263,750

U.S. TAXES PAID BY PARENTS $ _____

(1996 IRS 1040—Line 44*;
1996 IRS 1040A—Line 25;
1996 IRS 1040EZ—Line 10)

*This was Line 46 on the 1995 IRS 1040.

(This figure will be listed on the Parent's Expected Contribution Worksheet [Deductions Against Income section].)

TABLE 7
Social Security Taxes Paid

Make separate calculations for each parent (stepparent) as well as for the student (and spouse, if applicable).

(Refer to the bottom line of Table 1 for father [stepfather] and mother [stepmother]; refer to the bottom line of Table 2 for student [and spouse].)

If income earned from work is: Then social security taxes paid for
                                      that individual are:

Less than $62,700   (Income earned from work × .0765)

Between $62,701 or more   (The amount of income earned from work over
                                      $62,701 × .0145) + $4,797

	Social security taxes paid by father (stepfather):	$ _____
Plus:	Social security taxes paid by mother (stepmother):	+ $ _____
		_____

Equals: SOCIAL SECURITY TAXES PAID BY PARENTS $ _____

(This figure will be listed on the Parents' Expected Contribution Worksheet [Expenses & Allowances section].)

• •

	Social security taxes paid by the student	$ _____
Plus:	Social security taxes paid by student's spouse (if unmarried, enter 0 for this line)	+ $ _____
		_____

Equals: SOCIAL SECURITY TAXES PAID
BY STUDENT (AND SPOUSE) $ _____

(This figure will be listed on the Student's Expected Contribution
Worksheet [Deductions Against Income section].)

TABLE 8
Medical and Dental Expenses

Total of all medical and dental expenses
that you paid during the year for all
members of your household. Include
amounts paid for doctors, dentists, nurses,
hospitals, therapists, prescription drugs
and medications, insulin, eyeglasses,
contact lenses, hearing aids, dentures, etc.
Be sure to list only amounts actually paid
or charged to your credit cards during
the year. $ _____

Plus: Health insurance premiums paid by you
and/or deducted from your paycheck during
the year minus the self-employed health
insurance deduction (if any) from Table 3,
adjustments to income section   + $ _____

Plus: Medical-related transportation expenses
and/or lodging expenses   + $ _____
                                                   _____

SUBTOTAL $ _____

Minus: Any expenses covered by insurance or
your company medical reimbursement
account   ($ _____)
                                                   _____

TOTAL OF UNREIMBURSED EXPENSES $ _____

Minus: 4% of Parents' Total Income
(amount from line G on Table 5
$_____ × .04)   ($ _____)
                                                   _____

MEDICAL AND DENTAL EXPENSES $ _____
(If negative, enter 0)

*(This figure will be listed on the Parents' Expected Contribution Worksheet
[Expenses & Allowances section for the Institutional Methodology only].)*

TABLE 9
Employment Allowance

To complete Table 9, refer to the bottom line on Table 1 to obtain the appropriate "Income Earned From Work" figure.

IF A ONE-PARENT FAMILY

Total income earned from work × .35 = $ _____

The maximum employment allowance is $2,700. If the above number is greater than $2,700, then $2,700 should be entered on the Parents' Expected Contribution Worksheet (Expenses & Allowances section).

IF A TWO-PARENT FAMILY

Father's (stepfather's) total income earned from
work × .35 = $ _____
(*Refer to left column, bottom line TABLE 1*)

Mother's (stepmother's) total income earned from
work × .35 = $ _____
(*Refer to right column, bottom line TABLE 1*)

Take the smaller of the two numbers above. If both numbers are greater than $2,700, then $2,700 should be entered on the Parents' Expected Contribution Worksheet (Expenses & Allowances section). There is no allowance for a two-parent family in which only one parent works.

• •

TABLE 10
Income Protection Allowance

NUMBER OF FAMILY MEMBERS (Including Student)	NUMBER IN COLLEGE				
	1	2	3	4	5
2	$11,750	$ 9,740	....	....	....
3	14,630	12,630	$ 10,620	....	....
4	18,070	16,060	14,060	$12,050	....
5	21,320	19,310	17,310	15,300	$13,300
6	24,940	22,930	20,930	18,920	16,920

(For each additional family member above 6, add $2,810. For each additional college student above 5, subtract $2,000.)

TABLE 11
Business/Farm Net Worth Adjustment

Business and farm net worth is somewhat sheltered in the aid formula. To determine the proper amount to list on Line M of the Parents' Expected Contribution Worksheet, first determine the net worth of the business/farm and then use the conversion rates below. For the Federal Methodology, do not include assets or liabilities for a "family farm" in your calculations. If you are a part owner, use only your share of the net worth for the calculations.

Net Worth (NW) = Assets minus Liabilities

If you do not have a current balance sheet available for the business and/or farm, you can use the following guidelines:

Business and/or farm assets $ _____
(Include cash, investments, receivables,
 inventories, land and buildings, machinery
 and equipment net of accumulated depreciation,
 and other assets. Do not include the value of
 intangible assets such as goodwill.)

Minus: Business liabilities   ($ _____)
          (Accounts payable, mortgages on land and   _____
          buildings, other debts)

        Net Worth (NW) (if negative, list 0) $ _____

Now that you have a net worth figure, use the adjustment table below to calculate the adjusted business/farm net worth.

Helpful hint: The ADJUSTED NET WORTH FIGURE that you calculate
             should be smaller than the Net Worth figure.

BUSINESS OR FARM ADJUSTMENTS	
If Net Worth (NW)	**Adjusted Amount Is**
Less than $1	$ 0
$ 1 to 85,000	$ 0 + 40% of NW
$ 85,001 to 250,000	$ 34,000 + 50% of NW over $ 85,000
$ 250,001 to 420,000	$ 116,500 + 60% of NW over $ 250,000
$ 420,001 or more	$ 218,500 +100% of NW over $ 420,000

ADJUSTED BUSINESS/FARM NET WORTH
(This figure will be listed on Line M of the $ _____
Parents' Expected Contribution Worksheet under
the Federal Methodology (FM) column.)

If you are calculating an EFC under the Institutional Methodology (IM) and you do not own a "family farm," this figure can also be listed on Line M under the IM column. If you do own a "family farm," add back the assets and liabilities for the "family farm," recalculate the adjusted business/farm net worth, and enter this figure on Line M under the IM column.

TABLE 12

ASSET PROTECTION ALLOWANCE (LINE O)		
Age of Older Parent in Household	Two-Parent Family	One-Parent Family
39 or less	$33,100	23,200
40-44	37,300	26,000
45-49	42,400	29,000
50-54	48,300	32,700
55-59	55,900	36,900
60-64	65,400	42,300
65 or more	72,400	46,100

TABLE 13

For Institutional Methodology (IM) only

INCOME SUPPLEMENT FROM ASSETS	
Use when line P is negative. When Line P is $0 or more, use 12%. (Line Q)	
If available income (Line I) is:	**Use:**
$ 0 or less	6%
$ 0 to 5,800	5%
$ 5,801 to 11,600	4%
$ 11,601 to 17,400	3%
$ 17,401 to 23,200	2%
$ 23,201 to 29,000	1%
$ 29,001 or more	0%

TABLE 14

PARENT'S EXPECTED CONTRIBUTION (Line S)	
Adjusted Available Income [AAI] (Line R)	**Total Parents' Contribution (Line S)**
Less than $ -3,409	$-750
$ -3,409 to 10,500	22% of AAI
$ 10,501 to 13,200	$2,310 + 25% of AAI over $ 10,500
$ 13,201 to 15,900	$2,985 + 29% of AAI over $ 13,200
$ 15,901 to 18,500	$3,768 + 34% of AAI over $ 15,900
$ 18,501 to 21,200	$4,652 + 40% of AAI over $ 18,500
$ 21,201 or more	$5,732 + 47% of AAI over $ 21,200

PARENTS' EXPECTED CONTRIBUTION WORKSHEET
Use Left Column for Federal Methodology (FM);
Right Column for Institutional Methodology (IM)

	FM	**IM**

Note: For line G in the IM column only: add back any losses that reduce your income; these losses correspond to the 1996 IRS 1040 Lines 12, 13, 14, 17, 18, and/or 21. Refer to the top part of Table 3 (above Line A) and add back any of those items which appear in parentheses on that table. As a check, if you have any of these loss items, the figure for the IM column for Line G of the worksheet should be higher that the figure you wrote in the FM column. You should also add any amounts withheld from wages for dependent care and medical spending accounts.

G.   PARENTS' TOTAL INCOME $ _____ $ _____
       (From Table 5—Line G)

(For FM, if Line G is negative, enter –0–.)

Expenses & Allowances
(For explanations consult pages 57–66)

Sum of:

	FM	IM
U.S. income taxes paid *(From Table 6)*	$ _____	$ _____
Social security taxes paid *(From Table 7)*	+ $ _____	+ $ _____
State and other taxes *(Line G × .07)*	+ $ _____	+ $ _____
Employment allowance *(From Table 9)*	+ $ _____	+ $ _____
Income protection allowance (From Table 10)	+ $ _____	+ $ _____
Medical and dental expense *(From Table 8)*	XXXXXXXXXX	+ $ _____
Elementary and secondary school tuition for siblings and other dependents*	XXXXXXXXXX	+ $ _____

(Total amount paid up to a maximum of $5,770 per sibling/other dependent. Do not include tuition paid for student applicant.)

H.   TOTAL EXPENSES AND ALLOWANCES   ($ ═══════)   ($ ═══════)

I.   AVAILABLE INCOME (Line G minus H) $ ═══════ $ ═══════

*Note: Elementary/secondary school tuition paid for siblings is an institutional option under the institutional methodology. Colleges using the IM may choose to ignore this expense, deduct the full amount of the tuition paid, or elect to cap it at a certain amount per child. You may wish to perform multiple calculations using the different options, should this expense item apply to your situation.

Assets & Liabilities

(For explanations consult pages 68-88)
List only your share of assets and liabilities for this section
Do not include value of home or debt on home in FM column.

		FM	IM

ASSETS
Sum of:

Cash, savings and checking accounts $ _____ $ _____

Other investments   + $ _____   + $ _____

Market value of home*   XXXXXXXXXX   + $ _____

Market value of other real estate   + $ _____   + $ _____

J.   TOTAL PERSONAL ASSETS $ _____ $ _____

DEBTS
Sum of:

Debts owed on home   XXXXXXXXXX $ _____

Debts owed on other real estate $ _____   + $ _____
(For real estate debt add principal balance(s) outstanding on mortgages plus home equity line(s) of credit outstanding plus other debts against real estate)

Other debts against assets listed above
(margin debt, passbook loan, etc.)   + $ _____   + $ _____

K.   TOTAL PERSONAL DEBTS   ($ _____)   ($ _____)

L.   PERSONAL NET ASSETS $ _____ $ _____
(Line J minus K)

*Note: If you wish to calculate the Parents Contribution under the IM for a college that elects to cap the home value based on income, you should do the following: Multiply Parent's Total Income (from Table 5 – Line G) by 3. Compare this number to the actual market value of the home and list the smaller of the two numbers as your entry for the "Market value of the home" line in the IM column of the worksheet. Then for the "Debts on the home" line in the IM column, list the smaller of the actual debts owed on the home or the "Market value of the home" figure that you entered in the IM column.

		FM	IM
L.	PERSONAL NET ASSETS (From last line on prior page)	$ _____	+ $ _____
Plus: M.	ADJUSTED BUSINESS/FARM NET WORTH (From Table 11)	+ $ _____ _____	+ $ _____ _____
N.	**TOTAL NET ASSETS** (Line L plus M)	$ _____	$ _____
Minus: O.	ASSET PROTECTION ALLOWANCE (From Table 12)	($ _____)	($ _____)
P.	**REMAINING ASSETS** (Line N minus O)	$ _____	$ _____
Q.	INCOME SUPPLEMENT FROM ASSETS (For each column, if Line P is a positive number, multiply Line P by .12 for that column. If Line P is a negative number in the FM column, enter -0- in FM column. If Line P is a negative number in the IM column, multiply Line P by the conversion factor listed on Table 13. List the result in parentheses in the IM column.)	$ _____	$ _____
R.	ADJUSTED AVAILABLE INCOME (Line I plus Line Q [For IM if Q is negative subtract Q from I instead])	$ _____	$ _____
S.	PARENTS' EXPECTED CONTRIBUTION (Refer to Table 14; multiply the amount on Line R by the appropriate assessment rate.)	$ _____	$ _____
T.	**PARENTS' EXPECTED CONTRIBUTION PER STUDENT** *(if more than one member of the household is in college during the same academic year)* (For FM, divide the amount on Line S by the number of household members in college or other postsecondary schools on at least a half-time basis, i.e., 6 credits or more a semester or the equivalent. For IM, exclude any parents in college when dividing Line S by the number in college.)	$ _____	$ _____

TABLE 15
Student's U.S. Income Taxes Paid

Note: We assume that most students are claimed as a dependent on the parent(s)' tax return. If this is not the case, you can use Table 6 as a guideline for calculating this item.

Standard Deduction Worksheet

Sum of:

    Student's wages, tips, salary, and other compensation subject to tax (similar to IRS 1040—Line 7) Exclude only earnings from a need based work-study job. $ _____

Plus:

    Student's earned income from self-employment or farming (similar to IRS 1040— Lines 12 and 18)   + $ _____

        SUBTOTAL $_____

Minus:

    1/2 Self-employment tax paid (if any)   ($ _____)

    A.   Student's earned income $_____

    B.   Minimum amount $ ___650___

    C.   Enter the larger of Line A or B $ _____

    D.   **STANDARD DEDUCTION** $ _____
        (enter the smaller of Line C or $4,000)

• •

Student's wages, tips, salary, and other compensation subject to tax (IRS 1040—Line 7) Exclude any earnings from need-based work study. $ _____

Plus:

    Student's other taxable income (IRS 1040—Lines 8a to 21)   + $ _____

Minus:

    Adjustments to income (if any) (IRS 1040—Lines 23a to 29)   ($ _____)

    ADJUSTED GROSS INCOME $ _____
    (IRS 1040—Line 31)

Continued on Next Page

ADJUSTED GROSS INCOME $_____
from prior page

Minus:

Standard deduction (From Line D above)   ($ _____)

_____

E.   TAXABLE INCOME $_____

Use the Taxable Income figure listed above with the table below to calculate the student's U.S. Income Taxes.

If your taxable income is: Over—	But not over—	Income taxes paid is—	of the amount over—
$0	$24,000	15%	$0
$24,000	$58,150	$3,600.00 + 28%	$24,000
$58,150	$121,300	$13,162.00 + 31%	$58,150
$121,300	$263,750	$32,738.50 + 36%	$121,300
$263,750	—	$84,020.50 + 39.6%	$263,750

U.S. TAXES PAID BY STUDENT $ _____
(1996 IRS 1040—Line 44*;
1996 IRS 1040A—Line 25;
1996 IRS 1040EZ—Line 10)

This was Line 46 on the 1995 IRS 1040.

(This figure will be listed on the Student's Expected Contribution Worksheet [Deductions Against Income section].)

DEPENDENT STUDENT'S EXPECTED CONTRIBUTION WORKSHEET

Student's (and Spouse's) Income

(Do not include any earnings from need-based work-study jobs or taxable grants/scholarships in excess of tuition, fees, books, and required supplies.)

	FM	IM
Sum of:		
Student's wages, tips, salary and other compensation subject to tax	$ _____	$ _____
Student's spouse's (if applicable) wages, tips, salary, and other compensation subject to tax	+ $ _____	+ $ _____
All other income of student and spouse (This item represents all other taxable and untaxed items such as interest, dividends, income from self-employment, capital gains, etc. DO NOT INCLUDE SOCIAL SECURITY BENEFITS THAT ARE PAID TO THE PARENT FOR THE STUDENT, WHICH HAVE PREVIOUSLY BEEN LISTED AS PART OF TABLE 4 — PARENTS' UNTAXED INCOME.)	+ $ _____	+ $ _____
AA. TOTAL INCOME	$ _____	$ _____

Deductions Against Income

	FM	IM
Sum of:		
U.S Income tax student will be expected to pay on taxable income (from Table 15 or Table 6)	$ _____	$ _____
Allowance for state and local taxes (amount on line AA above × .04)	+ $ _____	+ $ _____
SOCIAL SECURITY TAX *(from Table 7)* (If student is married add the tax for the student and the spouse together)	+ $ _____	+ $ _____
INCOME PROTECTION ALLOWANCE	+ $ __1,750__	XXXXXXXXXX
BB. **TOTAL DEDUCTIONS AGAINST INCOME**	($ _____)	($ _____)
CC. AVAILABLE INCOME (Total Income *[Line AA]* minus Total Deductions *[Line BB]*) (*For FM, if Line CC is negative enter –0–.*)	$ _____	$ _____

Student's (and Spouse's) Assets and Liabilities

(For FM column, exclude value of student's home and debts on that home, as
well as net worth of student's "family farm." If the student owns a business or
farm calculate the adjusted net worth use Table 11 and list this figure on the
appropriate line below. Don't include the business or farm debts again as part
of Line EE below.)

	FM	IM
Sum of:		
Cash, savings and checking accounts	$ _____	$ _____
Uniform Gifts to Minors Act and custodial accounts	+ $ _____	+ $ _____
Other investments	+ $ _____	+ $ _____
Market value of any real estate	+ $ _____	+ $ _____
Adjusted business/farm net worth	+ $ _____	+ $ _____
DD. TOTAL ASSETS	$ _____	$ _____

Minus:

EE. TOTAL DEBTS
(Any debts against assets listed above)　　($ _____)　　($ _____)

FF. **TOTAL NET ASSETS**
(Line DD minus EE)　　$ _____　　$ _____

Student's Contribution

Sum of:

GG. CONTRIBUTION FROM ASSETS
(Line FF × .35)　　+ $ _____　　+ $ _____

HH. CONTRIBUTION FROM INCOME
(For FM, [LINE CC] × .50;　　+ $ _____　　+ $ _____

For IM, list the
greater of [Line CC] × .50
　　　-or-
$900 if the student is an incoming
freshman; $1,100 if the student
will be an upperclassman)

II. OTHER GIFTS AND SCHOLARSHIPS
RECEIVED OR AWARDED　　+ $ _____　　+ $ _____

JJ. **STUDENT'S CONTRIBUTION**　　$ _____　　$ _____

Sample Forms

Free Application for Federal Student Aid
1997–98 School Year

WARNING: If you purposely give false or misleading information on this form, you may be fined $10,000, sent to prison, or both.

"You" and "your" on this form always mean the student who wants aid.

Form Approved
OMB No. 1840-0110
App. Exp.

U.S. Department of Education
Student Financial
Assistance Programs

Use dark ink. Make capital letters and numbers clear and legible.

`E X M 2 4`

Fill in ovals completely. Only one oval per question. Correct ● **Incorrect marks will be ignored.** Incorrect ⊗ ✓

Section A: You (the student)

1–3. Your name

1. Last name   2. First name   3. M.I.

Your title (optional)   Mr. ○ 1   Miss, Mrs., or Ms. ○ 2

4–7. Your permanent mailing address *(All mail will be sent to this address. See Instructions, page 2 for state/country abbreviations.)*

4. Number and street (Include apt. no.)

5. City   6. State   7. ZIP code

8. Your social security number (SSN) *(Don't leave blank. See Instructions, page 2.)*

15–16. Are you a U.S. citizen? *(See Instructions, pages 2–3.)*

Yes, I am a U.S. citizen. ○ 1
No, but I am an eligible noncitizen. ○ 2

A [_____]

No, neither of the above. ○ 3

9. Your date of birth   Month Day Year   1 9

10. Your permanent home telephone number   Area code

17. As of today, are you married? *(Fill in only one oval.)*

I am not married. (I am single, widowed, or divorced.) ○ 1
I am married. ○ 2
I am separated from my spouse. ○ 3

11. Your state of legal residence   State

12. Date you became a legal resident of the state in question 11 *(See Instructions, page 2.)*   Month Day Year   1 9

18. Date you were married, separated, divorced, or widowed. If divorced, use date of divorce or separation, whichever is earlier. *(If never married, leave blank.)*   Month   Year   1 9

13–14. Your driver's license number *(Include the state abbreviation. If you don't have a license, write in "None.")*
State   License number

19. Will you have your first bachelor's degree before July 1, 1997?   Yes ○ 1   No ○ 2

Section B: Education Background

20–21. Date that you (the student) received, or will receive, your high school diploma, either—

(Enter one date. Leave blank if the question does not apply to you.)

- by graduating from high school   **20.**   Month Year   1 9

OR

- by earning a GED   **21.**   Month Year   1 9

22–23. Highest educational level or grade level your father and your mother completed. *(Fill in one oval for each parent. See Instructions, page 3.)*

	22. Father	23. Mother
elementary school (K–8)	○ 1	○ 1
high school (9–12)	○ 2	○ 2
college or beyond	○ 3	○ 3
unknown	○ 4	○ 4

If you (and your family) have **unusual circumstances**, complete this form and then check with your financial aid administrator. Examples:

- tuition expenses at an elementary or secondary school,
- unusual medical or dental expenses not covered by insurance,
- a family member who recently became unemployed, or
- other unusual circumstances such as changes in income or assets that might affect your eligibility for student financial aid.

These forms have been reprinted with permission. They are for information purposes only. Do not send in. This is a draft version of the form; the final version may have some changes.

Section C: Your Plans *Answer these questions about your college plans.*

24–28. Your expected enrollment status for the 1997–98 school year
(See Instructions, page 3.)

School term	Full time	3/4 time	1/2 time	Less than 1/2 time	Not enrolled
24. Summer term '97	○ 1	○ 2	○ 3	○ 4	○ 5
25. Fall semester/qtr. '97	○ 1	○ 2	○ 3	○ 4	○ 5
26. Winter quarter '97-98	○ 1	○ 2	○ 3	○ 4	○ 5
27. Spring semester/qtr. '98	○ 1	○ 2	○ 3	○ 4	○ 5
28. Summer term '98	○ 1	○ 2	○ 3	○ 4	○ 5

29. Your course of study *(See Instructions for code, page 3.)* ▢ Code

30. College degree/certificate you expect to receive ▢
(See Instructions for code, page 3.)

31. Date you expect to receive your degree/certificate [Month | Day | Year]

32. Your grade level during the 1997–98 school year *(Fill in only one.)*

1st yr./never attended college ○ 1	5th year/other undergraduate ○ 6	
1st yr./attended college before ○ 2	1st year graduate/professional ○ 7	
2nd year/sophomore ○ 3	2nd year graduate/professional ○ 8	
3rd year/junior ○ 4	3rd year graduate/professional ○ 9	
4th year/senior ○ 5	Beyond 3rd year graduate/professional ○ 0	

33–35. In addition to grants, what other types of financial aid are you (and your parents) interested in? *(See Instructions, page 3.)*

33. Student employment   Yes ○ 1   No ○ 2
34. Student loans   Yes ○ 1   No ○ 2
35. Parent loans for students   Yes ○ 1   No ○ 2

36. If you are (or were) in college, do you plan to attend **that same college** in 1997–98? *(If this doesn't apply to you, leave blank.)*   Yes ○ 1   No ○ 2

37. For how many dependents will you (the student) pay child care or elder care expenses in 1997–98? ▢▢

38–39. Veterans education benefits you expect to receive from July 1, 1997 through June 30, 1998

38. Amount per month $ [▢▢▢].00

39. Number of months ▢▢

DRAFT 6/17

Section D: Student Status

40. Were you born **before** January 1, 1974? .... Yes ○ 1   No ○ 2
41. Are you a veteran of the U.S. Armed Forces? .... Yes ○ 1   No ○ 2
42. Will you be enrolled in a graduate or professional program (beyond a bachelor's degree) in 1997-98? ... Yes ○ 1   No ○ 2
43. Are you married? .... Yes ○ 1   No ○ 2
44. Are you an orphan or a ward of the court, or were you a ward of the court until age 18? .... Yes ○ 1   No ○ 2
45. Do you have legal dependents (other than a spouse) that fit the definition in Instructions, page 4? .... Yes ○ 1   No ○ 2

If you answered **"Yes"** to any question in Section D, go to Section E and fill out **both the GRAY and the WHITE** areas on the rest of this form.

If you answered **"No"** to **every** question in Section D, go to Section E and fill out **both the GREEN and the WHITE** areas on the rest of this form.

Section E: Household Information

Remember:
At least one "Yes" answer in Section D means fill out the **GRAY** and **WHITE** areas.

All "No" answers in Section D means fill out the **GREEN** and **WHITE** areas.

STUDENT (& SPOUSE)

46. Number in your household in 1997–98
(Include yourself and your spouse. Do not include your children and other people unless they meet the definition in Instructions, page 4.) ▢▢

47. Number of college students in household in 1997–98
(Of the number in 46, how many will be in college at least half-time in at least one term in an eligible program? Include yourself. See Instructions, page 4.) ▢

PARENT(S)

48. Your parent(s)' **current** marital status:

single ○ 1   separated ○ 3   widowed ○ 5
married ○ 2   divorced ○ 4

49. Your parent(s)' state of legal residence ▢ State

50. Date your parent(s) became legal resident(s) of the state in question 49 *(See Instructions, page 5.)* [Month | Day | Year   1 9]

51. Number in your parent(s)' household in 1997–98
(Include yourself and your parents. Do not include your parents' other children and other people unless they meet the definition in Instructions, page 5.) ▢

52. Number of college students in household in 1997–98
(Of the number in 51, how many will be in college at least half-time in at least one term in an eligible program? Include yourself. See Instructions, page 5.) ▢

Section F: 1996 Income, Earnings, and Benefits
You must see Instructions, pages 5 and 6, for information about tax forms and tax filing status, especially if you are estimating taxes or filing electronically or by telephone. These instructions will tell you what income and benefits should be reported in this section.

Page 3

STUDENT (& SPOUSE)
Everyone must fill out this column.
53. *(Fill in one oval.)*

PARENT(S)
65. *(Fill in one oval.)*

The following 1996 U.S. income tax figures are from:

A—a completed 1996 IRS Form 1040A, 1040EZ, or 1040TEL .... ○ 1   A .... ○ 1

B—a completed 1996 IRS Form 1040 .... ○ 2   B .... ○ 2

C—an estimated 1996 IRS Form 1040A, 1040EZ, or 1040TEL .... ○ 3   C .... ○ 3

D—an estimated 1996 IRS Form 1040 .... ○ 4   D .... ○ 4

E—will not file a 1996 U.S. income tax return ......*(Skip to question 57.)* ○ 5   E ......*(Skip to 69.)* ○ 5

1996 Total number of exemptions (Form 1040–line 6e, or 1040A–line 6e; 1040EZ filers— *see Instructions, page 6.*)   **54.** [ ]   **66.** [ ]

1996 Adjusted Gross Income (AGI: Form 1040–line 31, 1040A–line 16, or 1040EZ–line 4—*see Instructions, page 6.*)   **55.** $ [ ] .00   **67.** $ [ ] .00

1996 U.S. income tax **paid** (Form 1040–line 46, 1040A–line 25, or 1040EZ–line 10   **56.** $ [ ] .00   **68.** $ [ ] .00

1996 Income earned from work   (Student) **57.** $ [ ] .00   (Father) **69.** $ [ ] .00

1996 Income earned from work   (Spouse) **58.** $ [ ] .00   (Mother) **70.** $ [ ] .00

TAX FILERS ONLY

1996 Untaxed income and benefits (yearly totals only):

Earned Income Credit (Form 1040–line 57, Form 1040A–line 29c, or Form 1040EZ–line 8)   **59.** $ [ ] .00   **71.** $ [ ] .00

Untaxed Social Security Benefits   **60.** $ [ ] .00   **72.** $ [ ] .00

Aid to Families with Dependent Children (AFDC/ADC)   **61.** $ [ ] .00   **73.** $ [ ] .00

Child support received for all children   **62.** $ [ ] .00   **74.** $ [ ] .00

Other untaxed income and benefits from Worksheet #2, page 11   **63.** $ [ ] .00   **75.** $ [ ] .00

1996 Amount from Line 5, Worksheet #3, page 12 *(See Instructions.)*   **64.** $ [ ] .00   **76.** $ [ ] .00

Section G: Asset Information   ATTENTION!

Fill out Worksheet A or Worksheet B in Instructions, page 7. If you meet the tax filing and income conditions on Worksheets A and B, you do not have to complete Section G to apply for Federal student aid. Some states and colleges, however, require Section G information for their own aid programs. Check with your financial aid administrator and State Agency.

Age of your older parent **84.** [ ]

STUDENT (& SPOUSE)   **PARENT(S)**

Cash, savings, and checking accounts   **77.** $ [ ] .00   **85.** $ [ ] .00

Other real estate and investments value *(Don't include the home.)*   **78.** $ [ ] .00   **86.** $ [ ] .00

Other real estate and investments debt *(Don't include the home.)*   **79.** $ [ ] .00   **87.** $ [ ] .00

Business value   **80.** $ [ ] .00   **88.** $ [ ] .00

Business debt   **81.** $ [ ] .00   **89.** $ [ ] .00

Investment farm value *(See Instructions, page 8.)* *(Don't include a family farm.)*   **82.** $ [ ] .00   **90.** $ [ ] .00

Investment farm debt *(See Instructions, page 8.)* *(Don't include a family farm.)*   **83.** $ [ ] .00   **91.** $ [ ] .00

These forms have been reprinted with permission. They are for information purposes only. Do not send in. This is a draft version of the form; the final version may have some changes.

Section H: Releases and Signatures

92–103. What college(s) do you plan to attend in 1997–98?
(Note: The colleges you list below will have access to your application information. See Instructions, page 8.)

Housing codes	1—on-campus	3—with parent(s)
	2—off-campus	4—with relative(s) other than parent(s)

	Title IV School Code	College Name	College Street Address and City	State		Housing Code
XX.	0 5 4 3 2 1	EXAMPLE UNIVERSITY	14930 NORTH SOMEWHERE BLVD. ANYWHERE CITY	S T	XX.	2
92.					93.	
94.					95.	
96.					97.	
98.					99.	
100.					101.	
102.					103.	

104. The U.S. Department of Education will send information from this form to your state financial aid agency and the state agencies of the colleges listed above so they can consider you for state aid. Answer **"No"** if you **don't** want information released to the state. *(See "Deadlines for State Student Aid" in Instructions, page 10.)* ....104. No ○ 2

105. Males not yet registered for Selective Service (SS): Do you want SS to register you? *(See Instructions, page 9.)* ....105. Yes ○ 1

106–107. Read, Sign, and Date Below

All of the information provided by me or any other person on this form is true and complete to the best of my knowledge. I understand that this application is being filed jointly by all signatories. If asked by an authorized official, I agree to give proof of the information that I have given on this form. I realize that this proof may include a copy of my U.S. or state income tax return. I realize that if I do not give proof when asked, the student may be denied aid.

Statement of Educational Purpose. I certify that I will use any Federal Title IV, HEA funds I receive during the award year covered by this application solely for expenses related to my attendance at the institution of higher education that determined or certified my eligibility for those funds.

Certification Statement on Overpayments and Defaults. I understand that I may not receive any Federal Title IV, HEA funds if I owe an overpayment on any Title IV educational grant or loan or am in default on a Title IV educational loan unless I have made satisfactory arrangements to repay or otherwise resolve the overpayment or default. I also understand that I must notify my school if I do owe an overpayment or am in default.

Everyone whose information is given on this form should sign below. The student (and at least one parent, if parental information is given) must sign below or this form will be returned unprocessed.

106. Signatures *(Sign in the boxes below.)*

1 Student

2 Student's Spouse

3 Father/Stepfather

4 Mother/Stepmother

107. Date completed

Month	Day	Year

1997 ○
1998 ○

Section I: Preparer's Use Only

For preparers other than student, spouse, and parent(s). Student, spouse, and parent(s), sign above.

Preparer's name (last, first, MI)

Firm name

Firm or preparer's address (street, city, state, ZIP)

108. Employer identification number (EIN)

OR

109. Preparer's social security number

Certification: All of the information on this form is true and complete to the best of my knowledge.

110. Preparer's signature   Date

School Use Only

D/O ○

Title IV Code

FAA Signature _____

MDE Use Only
Do not write in this box

Spec. handle □

MAKE SURE THAT YOU HAVE COMPLETED, DATED, AND SIGNED THIS APPLICATION.
Mail the original application (NOT A PHOTOCOPY) to: Federal Student Aid Programs, P.O. Box xxxxx

These forms have been reprinted with permission. They are for information purposes only. Do not send in. This is a draft version of the form; the final version may have some changes.

CSS/FINANCIAL AID PROFILE™ 1997-98

SAMPLE DO NOT USE

Application

Section A - Student's Information

1. How many family members will the student (and spouse) support in 1997-98? _Always include the student and spouse._ List their names and give information about them in Section M. See instructions.

2. Of the number in 1, how many will be in college at least half-time for at least one term in 1997-98? Include yourself.

3. What is the student's state of legal residence?

4. What is the student's citizenship status?

   a.
   - 1 ○ U.S. citizen (Skip to Question 5.)
   - 2 ○ Permanent resident (Skip to Question 5.)
   - 3 ○ Neither of the above (Answer 'b' and 'c' below.)

   b. Country of citizenship?

   c. Visa classification?
   - 1 ○ F1
   - 2 ○ F2
   - 3 ○ J1
   - 4 ○ J2
   - 5 ○ G
   - 6 ○ Other

Section B - Student's 1996 Income & Benefits

If married, include spouse's information in Sections B, C, D, and E.

Tax Filers Only

5. The following 1996 U.S. income tax return figures are (Fill in only one oval.)
   - 1 ○ estimated. Will file IRS Form 1040EZ, 1040A, or 1040TEL. Go to 6.
   - 2 ○ estimated. Will file IRS Form 1040. Go to 6.
   - 3 ○ from a completed IRS Form 1040EZ, 1040A, or 1040TEL. Go to 6.
   - 4 ○ from a completed IRS Form 1040. Go to 6.
   - 5 ○ a tax return will not be filed. Skip to 10.

6. 1996 total number of exemptions (IRS Form 1040, line 6d or 1040A, line 6d or 1040EZ - see instructions.)

7. 1996 Adjusted Gross Income from IRS Form 1040, line 31 or 1040A, line 16 or 1040EZ, line 4 (Use the worksheet in the instructions.) $ .00

8. 1996 U.S. income tax paid (IRS Form 1040, line 44 or 1040A, line 25 or 1040EZ, line 10) $ .00

9. 1996 Itemized deductions (IRS Form 1040, Schedule A, line 28. Write in "0" if deductions were not itemized.) $ .00

10. 1996 income earned from work by student (See instructions.) $ .00

11. 1996 income earned from work by student's spouse $ .00

12. 1996 dividend and interest income $ .00

13. 1996 untaxed income and benefits (Give total amount for year.)

    a. Social security benefits (See instructions.) $ .00

    b. Aid to Families with Dependent Children $ .00

    c. Child support received for all children $ .00

    d. Earned Income Credit (IRS Form 1040, line 54 or 1040A, line 29c or 1040EZ, line 8) $ .00

    e. Other - write total from worksheet, page 4. $ .00

14. 1996 earnings from Federal Work-Study or other need-based work programs plus any grant and scholarship aid required to be reported on your U.S. income tax return. $ .00

Section C - Student's Assets

Include trust accounts only in Section D.

15. Cash, savings, and checking accounts $ .00

16. Total value of IRA, Keogh, 401k, 403b, etc. accounts as of December 31, 1996. $ .00

17. Investments (Including Uniform Gifts to Minors. See instructions.)

What is it worth today?	What is owed on it?
$ .00	$ .00

18. Home (Renters write in "0".) $ .00 | $ .00

19. Other real estate $ .00 | $ .00

20. Business and farm $ .00 | $ .00

21. If a farm is included in 20, is the student living on the farm? Yes ○ 1 No ○ 2

22. If student owns home, give

    a. year purchased 1 9

    b. purchase price $ .00

Section D - Student's Trust Information

23. a. Total value of all trust(s) $ .00

    b. Is any income or part of the principal currently available? Yes ○ 1 No ○ 2

    c. Who established the trust(s)? 1 ○ Student's parents 2 ○ Other

Section E - Student's 1996 Expenses

24. 1996 child support paid by student $ .00

25. 1996 medical and dental expenses not covered by insurance (See instructions.) $ .00

These forms have been reprinted with permission. They are for information purposes only. Do not send in. This is a draft version of the form; the final version may have some changes.

Section F - Student's Expected Summer/School-Year Resources for 1997-1998

	Amount per month	Number of months
26. Student's veterans benefits (July 1, 1997 - June 30, 1998.)	$_____.00	□□

27. Student's (and spouse's) resources
(Don't enter monthly amounts.)

	Summer 1997 (3 months)	School Year 1997-98 (9 months)
a. Student's wages, salaries, tips, etc.	$_____.00	$_____.00
b. Spouse's wages, salaries, tips, etc.	$_____.00	$_____.00
c. Other taxable income	$_____.00	$_____.00
d. Untaxed income and benefits	$_____.00	$_____.00
e. Grants, scholarships, fellowships, etc. from other than the colleges or universities to which the student is applying (List sources in Section P.)		$_____.00
f. Tuition benefits from the parents' and/or the student's or spouse's employer		$_____.00
g. Contributions from the student's parent(s) for 1997-98 college or university expenses		$_____.00
h. Contributions from other relatives, spouse's parents, and all other sources (List sources in Section P.)		$_____.00

Section G - Parents' Household Information - See page 5 of the instruction booklet.

28. How many family members will your parents support in 1997-98? □□
Always include the student and parents.
List their names and give information about them in Section M.

29. Of the number in 28, how many will be in college at least half-time for at least one term in 1997-98? Include the student. □□

30. How many parents will be in college at least half-time in 1997-1998? (Fill in only one oval.)

₁ ○ Neither parent   ₂ ○ One parent   ₃ ○ Both parents

31. What is the current marital status of your parents?
(Fill in only one oval.)

₁ ○ single   ₃ ○ separated   ₅ ○ widowed

₂ ○ married   ₄ ○ divorced

32. What is your parents' state of legal residence? □□

Section H - Parents' Expenses

	1996	Expected 1997
33. Child support paid by the parent(s) completing this form	33. $_____.00	$_____.00
34. Repayment of parents' educational loans (See instructions.)	34. $_____.00	$_____.00
35. Medical and dental expenses not covered by insurance (See instructions.)	35. $_____.00	$_____.00
36. Total elementary, junior high school, and high school tuition paid for dependent children		
a. Amount paid (Don't include tuition paid for the student.)	36. $_____.00	$_____.00
b. For how many dependent children? (Don't include the student.)	□	□

Section I - Parents' Assets - If parents own all or part of a business or farm, write in its name and the percent of ownership in Section P.

	What is it worth today?	What is owed on it?
37. Cash, savings, and checking accounts	$_____.00	
41. Business	$_____.00	$_____.00
38. Monthly home mortgage or rental payment (If none, explain in Section P.)	$_____.00	
42. a. Farm	$_____.00	$_____.00

b. Does family live on the farm?

Yes ○₁   No ○₂

	What is it worth today?	What is owed on it?
39. Investments	$_____.00	$_____.00
40. a. Home (Renters write in "0".)	$_____.00	$_____.00
b. year purchased |1|9|_|_|	c. purchase price $_____.00

43. a. Other real estate $_____.00 $_____.00

b. year purchased |1|9|_|_| c. purchase price $_____.00

These forms have been reprinted with permission. They are for information purposes only. Do not send in. This is a draft version of the form; the final version may have some changes.

Section J - Parents' 1995 Income & Benefits

44. 1995 Adjusted Gross Income (IRS Form 1040, line 31 or 1040A, line 16 or 1040EZ, line 4) $_____.00

45. 1995 U.S. income tax paid (IRS Form 1040, line 46, 1040A, line 25 or 1040EZ, line 10) $_____.00

46. 1995 itemized deductions (IRS Form 1040, Schedule A, line 28. Write "0" if deductions were not itemized.) $_____.00

47. 1995 untaxed income and benefits (Include the same types of income & benefits that are listed in 55 a-k.) $_____.00

Section K - Parents' 1996 Income & Benefits

48. The following 1996 U.S. income tax return figures are (Fill in only one oval.)

1. ◯ estimated. Will file IRS Form 1040EZ, 1040A, or 1040TEL. Go to 49.
2. ◯ estimated. Will file IRS Form 1040. Go to 49.
3. ◯ from a completed IRS Form 1040EZ, 1040A, or 1040TEL. Go to 49.
4. ◯ from a completed IRS Form 1040. Go to 49.
5. ◯ a tax return will not be filed. Skip to 53.

Tax Filers Only

49. 1996 total number of exemptions (IRS Form 1040, line 6d or 1040A, line 6d or 1040EZ - see instructions)   **49.** ☐

50. 1996 Adjusted Gross Income (IRS Form 1040, line 31 or 1040A, line 16 or 1040EZ, line 4)   **50.** $_____.00

Breakdown of income in 50

   a. Wages, salaries, tips (IRS Form 1040, line 7 or 1040A, line 7 or 1040EZ, line 1)   **50. a.** $_____.00

   b. Interest income (IRS Form 1040, line 8a or 1040A, line 8a or 1040EZ, line 2)   **b.** $_____.00

   c. Dividend income (IRS Form 1040, line 9 or 1040A, line 9)   **c.** $_____.00

   d. Net income (or loss) from business, farm, rents, royalties, partnerships, estates, trusts, etc. (IRS Form 1040, lines 12, 17, and 18). If a loss, enter the amount in (parentheses).   **d.** $_____.00

   e. Other taxable income such as alimony received, capital gains (or losses), pensions, annuities, etc. (IRS Form 1040, lines 10, 11, 13, 14, 15b, 16b, 19, 20b and 21 or 1040A, lines 10b, 11b, 12, and 13b or 1040EZ, line 3)   **e.** $_____.00

   f. Adjustments to income (IRS Form 1040, line 30 or 1040A, line 15c)   **f.** $_____.00

51. 1996 U.S. income tax paid (IRS Form 1040, line 44, 1040A, line 25 or 1040EZ, line 10)   **51.** $_____.00

52. 1996 itemized deductions (IRS Form 1040, Schedule A, line 28. Write in "0" if deductions were not itemized.)   **52.** $_____.00

53. 1996 income earned from work by father   **53.** $_____.00

54. 1996 income earned from work by mother   **54.** $_____.00

55. 1996 untaxed income and benefits (Give total amount for the year. Do not give monthly amounts.)

   a. Social security benefits   **55. a.** $_____.00

   b. Aid to Families with Dependent Children   **b.** $_____.00

   c. Child support received for all children   **c.** $_____.00

   d. Deductible IRA and/or Keogh payments (See instructions.)   **d.** $_____.00

   e. Payments to tax-deferred pension and savings plans (See instructions.)   **e.** $_____.00

   f. Amounts withheld from wages for dependent care and medical spending accounts   **f.** $_____.00

   g. Earned Income Credit (IRS Form 1040, line 54 or 1040A, line 29c or 1040EZ, line 8)   **g.** $_____.00

   h. Housing, food and other living allowances (See instructions.)   **h.** $_____.00

   i. Tax-exempt interest income (IRS Form 1040, line 8b or 1040A, line 8b)   **i.** $_____.00

   j. Foreign income exclusion (IRS Form 2555, line 43 or Form 2555EZ, line 18)   **j.** $_____.00

   k. Other - write in the total from the worksheet in the instructions, page 7.   **k.** $_____.00

WRITE ONLY IN THE ANSWER SPACES. DO NOT WRITE ANYWHERE ELSE.

Section L - Parents' 1997 Expected Income & Benefits

If the expected total income and benefits will differ from the 1996 total income by $3,000 or more, explain in Section P.

56. 1997 income earned from work by father $_____.00

57. 1997 income earned from work by mother $_____.00

58. 1997 other taxable income $_____.00

59. 1997 untaxed income and benefits (See 55a-k.) $_____.00

These forms have been reprinted with permission. They are for information purposes only. Do not send in. This is a draft version of the form; the final version may have some changes.

Section M - Family Member Listing - Give information for all family members entered in question 1 or 28, but don't give information about yourself.
List up to seven other family members here. If there are more than seven, list first those who will be in school or college at least half-time. List the others in Section

60.

Full name of family member / You - the student applicant	Use codes from below.	Age	Claimed by parents as tax exemption in 1996? Yes?	No?	1996-1997 school year Name of school or college	Year in school	Scholarships and grants	Parents' contri-bution	1997-1998 school year Attend college at least one term full-time	half-time	School or college Type	Name
1												
2			○	○					1 ○	2 ○		
3			○	○					1 ○	2 ○		
4			○	○					1 ○	2 ○		
5			○	○					1 ○	2 ○		
6			○	○					1 ○	2 ○		
7			○	○					1 ○	2 ○		
8			○	○					1 ○	2 ○		

Write in the correct code from the right. ↑ 1 - Student's parent. 2 - Student's stepparent. 3 - Student's brother or sister, 4 - Student's husband or wife, 5 - Student's son or daughter, 6 - Student's grandparent. 7 - Other

Write in the correct code from the instructions on page 8.

Section N - Parents' Information

61. Fill in one: ○ Father ○ Stepfather ○ Legal guardian ○ Other (Explain in P.)

a. Name _____ Age [ ]

b. Fill in if: ○ Self-employed ○ Unemployed - Date: _____

c. Occupation _____

d. Employer _____ No. years _____

e. Work telephone [ ][ ][ ] – [ ][ ][ ] – [ ][ ][ ][ ]

f. Retirement plans:
○ Social security   ○ Union/employer
○ Civil service/state ○ IRA/Keogh/tax-deferred
○ Military   ○ Other

62. Fill in one: ○ Mother ○ Stepmother ○ Legal guardian ○ Other (Explain in P.)

a. Name _____ Age [ ]

b. Fill in if: ○ Self-employed ○ Unemployed - Date: _____

c. Occupation _____

d. Employer _____ No. years _____

e. Work telephone [ ][ ][ ] – [ ][ ][ ] – [ ][ ][ ][ ]

f. Retirement plans:
○ Social security   ○ Union/employer
○ Civil service/state ○ IRA/Keogh/tax-deferred
○ Military   ○ Other

Section O - Divorced, Separated, or Remarried Parents
(to be answered by the parent who completes this form if the student's natural or adoptive parents are divorced, separated, or remarried)

63. a. Year of separation [ ][ ] Year of divorce [ ][ ]

b. Other parent's name: _____
Home address _____
_____
Occupation/Employer _____

c. According to court order, when will support for the student end? [ ][ ] [ ][ ] Month Year

d. Who last claimed the student as a tax exemption? _____
_____ Year? [ ][ ]

e. How much does the other parent plan to contribute to the student's education for the 1997-1998 school year? $ _____ .00

f. Is there an agreement specifying this contribution for the student's education? Yes ○ No ○

Section P - Explanations/Special Circumstances
Use this space to explain any unusual expenses such as high medical or dental expenses, educational and other debts, child care, elder care, or special circumstances. Also, give information for any outside scholarships you have been awarded. If more space is needed, use sheets of paper and send them directly to your schools and programs.

Certification:
All the information on this form is true and complete to the best of my knowledge. If asked, I agree to give proof of the information that I have given on this form. I realize that this proof may include a copy of my U.S., state, or local income tax returns. I certify that all information is correct at this time, and that I will send timely notice to my schools/programs of any significant change in family income or assets, financial situation, college plans of other children, or the receipt of other scholarships or grants.

1. Student's signature _____

2. Student's spouse's signature _____

3. Father's (stepfather's) signature _____

4. Mother's (stepmother's) signature _____

Date completed: 1 ○ 1996 2 ○ 1997 3 ○ 1998
[ ][ ] [ ][ ]
Month Day

CSS Use Only
[   ]

CSSAPA

These forms have been reprinted with permission. They are for information purposes only. Do not send in. This is a draft version of the form; the final version may have some changes.

Application and Promissory Note for
Federal Stafford Loans *(subsidized and unsubsidized)*

WARNING: Any person who knowingly makes a false statement or misrepresentation on this form is subject to penalties which may include fines or imprisonment under the United States Criminal Code and 20 U.S.C. 1097.

Guarantor or Program Identification

UNITED STUDENT AID FUNDS, INC.

US

PROC CODE: MKTXX

Borrower Section

Please print neatly or type. Read the instructions carefully.

1. Last Name	First Name	MI	2. Social Security Number

3. Permanent Street Address (If P.O. Box, see instructions.)		4. Telephone Number ( )	5. Loan Period (Month/Year) From: To:
City	State	Zip Code	6. Driver's License Number (List state abbreviation first.)	

7. Lender Name	City	State	Zip Code	8. Lender Code, if known	9. Date of Birth (Month/Day/Year)

10. References: You must provide two separate references with different U.S. addresses. The first reference should be a parent or legal guardian (if living). Both references must be completed fully.

Name 1.   2.

Permanent Address

City, State, Zip Code

Area Code/Telephone ( ) ( )

Relationship to Borrower

Loan Assistance Requested

11. I request the following loan type(s), to the extent I am eligible (see instructions):
☐ a. Subsidized Federal Stafford   ☐ b. Unsubsidized Federal Stafford

12. I request a total amount under these loan types not to exceed (see instructions for loan maximums): My school will certify my eligibility for each loan type for which I am applying. The amount and other details of my loan(s) will be described to me in a disclosure statement.
$ **.00**

13. If I check yes, I am requesting postponement (deferment) of repayment for my Stafford and prior SLS loan(s) during the in-school and grace periods. If I check no, I do not want to defer repayment.
☐ a. Yes, I want a deferment   ☐ b. No, I do not want a deferment

14. If I check yes, I am requesting that the lender add the interest on my unsubsidized Stafford and prior SLS loan(s) which accrues during the in-school and deferment periods, to my loan principal (capitalization). If I check no, I prefer to pay the interest.
☐ a. Yes, I want my interest capitalized   ☐ b. No, I prefer to pay the interest

15. If my school participates in electronic funds transfer (EFT), I authorize the school to transfer the loan proceeds received by EFT to my student account.
☐ a. Yes, transfer funds   ☐ b. No, do not transfer funds

Promissory Note

Continued on the reverse side.

Promise to Pay: I promise to pay to the lender, or a subsequent holder of this Promissory Note, all sums disbursed (hereafter "loan" or "loans") under the terms of this Note, plus interest and other fees which may become due as provided in this Note. If I fail to make payments on this Note when due, I will also pay reasonable collection costs, including attorney's fees, court costs, and collection fees. I understand I may cancel or reduce the size of any loan by refusing to accept any disbursement that is issued. I understand that this is a Promissory Note. I will not sign this Note before reading it, including the writing on the reverse side, even if otherwise advised. I am entitled to an exact copy of this Promissory Note and the Borrower's Rights and Responsibilities. My signature certifies I have read, understand, and agree to the terms and conditions of this Application and Promissory Note, including the Borrower Certification and Authorization printed on the reverse side and the accompanying Borrower's Rights and Responsibilities statement.

THIS IS A LOAN(S) THAT MUST BE REPAID.

16. Borrower's Signature _____ Today's Date *(Month/Day/Year)* _____

School Section

To be completed by an authorized school official.

17. School Name	23. School Code/Branch	28. Telephone Number ( )
18. Street Address	24. Cost of Attendance $ .00	29. Recommended Disbursement Date(s) (Month/Day/Year) 1st 2nd
City State Zip Code	25. Federal Expected Family Contribution $ .00	3rd 4th
19. Loan Period (Month/Day/Year) From: To:	26. Estimated Financial Aid $ .00	30. School Certification (See box on the reverse side.)
20. Grade Level	27. Certified Loan Amounts a. Subsidized $ .00	Signature of Authorized School Official
21. Enrollment Status (Check one.) ☐ Full Time ☐ At Least Half Time	b. Unsubsidized $ .00	Print or Type Name and Title
22. Anticipated Completion (Graduation) Date (Month/Day/Year)		Date Check box if electronically transmitted to guarantor: ☐

Lender Section

To be completed by an authorized lending official.

31. Lender Name	32. Lender Code/Branch	33. Telephone Number (800 824-7044	34. Lender Use Only
Street Address	35. Amount(s) Approved a. Subsidized $ .00	b. Unsubsidized $ .00	
City State Zip Code	36. Signature of Authorized Lending Official	Print or Type Name, Title, and Date	

1/31/94

LENDER COPY

The above form is a draft version. It is for information purposes only. Do not send in.

Application and Promissory Note for Federal PLUS Loan

WARNING: Any person who knowingly makes a false statement or misrepresentation on this form is subject to penalties which may include fines or imprisonment under the United States Criminal Code and 20 U.S.C. 1097.

Guarantor or Program Identification

UNITED STUDENT AID FUNDS, INC.

US

PROC CODE: MKTXX

Borrower Section (To be completed by the parent.)

Please print neatly or type. Read the instructions carefully.

1. Last Name	First Name	MI	2. Social Security Number

3. Permanent Street Address (If P.O. Box, see instructions.)	4. Telephone Number ( )	5. Loan Period (Month/Year) From: To:

City	State	Zip Code	6. Driver's License Number (List state first.)	7. Date of Birth (Month/Day/Year)

8. Lender Name	City	State	Zip Code	9. Lender Code, if known	10. Requested Loan Amount $

11. U.S. Citizenship Status (Check one and list ID number if applicable.) ☐ a. Citizen/National ☐ b. Eligible Non-Citizen Alien ID #

12. a. State of Legal Residence	b. Since (Month/Year)	13. Employer (Name, City, State)	Telephone Number ( )

14. Are you currently in default on a federal education loan, or do you owe a refund on a federal student grant? If yes, carefully read instructions and attach required documentation. ☐ a. Yes ☐ b. No

15. If the school your dependent is attending participates in electronic funds transfer (EFT), do you authorize the school to transfer the loan proceeds received by EFT to your dependent's student account? ☐ a. Yes ☐ b. No

16. Do you have an outstanding Federal Stafford, Supplemental Loan for Students, Parent PLUS, or Consolidation Loan which was disbursed before July 1, 1993? ☐ a. Yes ☐ b. No

If you checked "yes", do you want to postpone (defer) payment of the principal of this loan based on the student's in-school status? (See instructions—additional documentation may be required if the student is not enrolled full time.) ☐ c. Yes ☐ d. No

If you checked "yes" to Box (a) and (c), do you want the interest that accrues on this loan deferred and capitalized? If no, you will be required to pay the interest. ☐ e. Yes ☐ f. No

17. **References:** You must provide two separate references with different U.S. addresses. Both references must be completed fully.

	1.	2.
Name		
Permanent Address		
City, State, Zip Code		
Area Code/Telephone	( )	( )

Promissory Note

Continued on the reverse side.

Promise to Pay: I promise to pay to the lender, or a subsequent holder of this Promissory Note, all sums disbursed (hereafter "loan" or "loans") under the terms of this Note, plus interest and other fees which may become due as provided in this Note. If I fail to make payments on this Note when due, I will also pay reasonable collection costs, including attorney's fees, court costs and collection fees. I understand I may cancel or reduce the size of any loan by refusing to accept any disbursement that is issued. I understand that this is a Promissory Note. I will not sign this Note before reading it, including the writing on the reverse side, even if otherwise advised. I am entitled to an exact copy of this Promissory Note and the Borrower's Rights and Responsibilities. My signature certifies I have read, understand, and agree to the terms and conditions of this Application and Promissory Note, including the Borrower Certification and Authorization printed on the reverse side, and the accompanying Borrower's Rights and Responsibilities statement.

THIS IS A LOAN THAT MUST BE REPAID.

18. Borrower's Signature	Today's Date (Month/Day/Year)

Student Section (To be completed by the student.)

Please print neatly or type. Read the instructions carefully.

19. Last Name	First Name	MI	20. Social Security Number / /	21. Date of Birth (Month/Day/Year)

22. U.S. Citizenship Status (Check one and list ID number if applicable.) ☐ a. Citizen/National ☐ b. Eligible Non-Citizen Alien ID #

23. Are you currently in default on a federal education loan, or do you owe a refund on a federal student grant? If yes, carefully read instructions and attach required documentation. ☐ a. Yes ☐ b. No

24. My signature certifies that I have read, understand and agree to the conditions in the Student Certification and Authorization printed on the reverse of this Application and Promissory Note.

Student's Signature	Today's Date (Month/Day/Year)

School Section (To be completed by an authorized school official.)

25. School Name	31. School Code/Branch	36. Telephone Number ( )

26. Street Address	32. Cost of Attendance $ .00	37. Recommended Disbursement Date(s) (Month/Day/Year)

City	State	Zip Code	33. Estimated Financial Aid $ .00	1st	2nd

27. Loan Period (Month/Day/Year) From: To:	28. Grade Level	34. Certified Loan Amount $ .00	3rd	4th

29. Enrollment Status (Check one.) ☐ Full Time ☐ At Least Half Time

35. Signature of Authorized School Official/Date (See School Certification box on the reverse side.)

Print or Type Name and Title

Check box if electronically transmitted to guarantor. ☐

30. Anticipated Completion (Graduation) Date (Month/Day/Year)

Lender Section (To be completed by an authorized lending official.)

38. Lender Name	39. Lender Code/Branch	40. Telephone Number (800) 824-7044	41. Amount Approved

Street Address	42. Signature of Authorized Lending Official	43. Lender Use Only

City	State	Zip Code	Print or Type Name and Title	Date

4/25/94

LENDER COPY

The above form is a draft version. It is for information purposes only. Do not send in.

Form 1040

Department of the Treasury—Internal Revenue Service

U.S. Individual Income Tax Return 1996

IRS Use Only—Do not write or staple in this space.

For the year Jan. 1–Dec. 31, 1996, or other tax year beginning , 1996, ending , 19 | OMB No. 1545-0074

Label (See instructions.)

Use the IRS label. Otherwise, please print or type.

LABEL HERE

Your first name and initial | Last name | Your social security number

If a joint return, spouse's first name and initial | Last name | Spouse's social security number

Home address (number and street). If you have a P.O. box, see page 11. | Apt. no.

City, town or post office, state, and ZIP code. If you have a foreign address, see page 11.

For help finding line instructions, see pages 2 and 3 in the booklet.

Presidential Election Campaign (See page 11.) ▶

Do you want $3 to go to this fund? . . . .
If a joint return, does your spouse want $3 to go to this fund? . . . .

Yes | No | Note: Checking "Yes" will not change your tax or reduce your refund.

Filing Status

Check only one box.

1 ☐ Single
2 ☐ Married filing joint return (even if only one had income)
3 ☐ Married filing separate return. Enter spouse's social security no. above and full name here. ▶ _____
4 ☐ Head of household (with qualifying person). (See instructions.) If the qualifying person is a child but not your dependent, enter this child's name here. ▶ _____
5 ☐ Qualifying widow(er) with dependent child (year spouse died ▶ 19). (See instructions.)

Exemptions

If more than six dependents, see the line 6c instructions.

6a ☐ **Yourself.** If your parent (or someone else) can claim you as a dependent on his or her tax return, **do not** check box 6a . . . .
b ☐ **Spouse** . . . .

No. of boxes checked on lines 6a and 6b

No. of your children on line 6c who:
• lived with you
• didn't live with you due to divorce or separation (see instructions)

Dependents on 6c not entered above

Add numbers entered on lines above ▶ ☐

c Dependents:

(1) First name Last name	(2) Dependent's social security number. If born in Dec. 1996, see inst.	(3) Dependent's relationship to you	(4) No. of months lived in your home in 1995

d Total number of exemptions claimed . . . .

Income

Attach Copy B of your Forms W-2, W-2G, and 1099-R here.

If you did not get a W-2, see the line 7 instructions.

Please send any payment separately with Form 1040-V. See the line 62a instructions.

7 Wages, salaries, tips, etc. Attach Form(s) W-2 | 7
8a **Taxable interest.** Attach Schedule B if over $400 . . . . | 8a
b **Tax-exempt** interest. DON'T include on line 8a . . . | 8b |
9 Dividend income. Attach Schedule B if over $400 . . . | 9
10 Taxable refunds, credits, or offsets of state and local income taxes (see instructions) . | 10
11 Alimony received . . . . | 11
12 Business income or (loss). Attach Schedule C or C-EZ . . . | 12
13 Capital gain or (loss). If required, attach Schedule D . . . | 13
14 Other gains or (losses). Attach Form 4797 . . . . | 14
15a Total IRA distributions . . | 15a | b Taxable amount (see inst.) | 15b
16a Total pensions and annuities | 16a | b Taxable amount (see inst.) | 16b
17 Rental real estate, royalties, partnerships, S corporations, trusts, etc. Attach Schedule E | 17
18 Farm income or (loss). Attach Schedule F . . . . | 18
19 Unemployment compensation . . . . | 19
20a Social security benefits . | 20a | b Taxable amount (see inst.) | 20b
21 Other income. List type and amount—see instructions _____
| 21
22 Add the amounts in the far right column for lines 7 through 21. This is your **total income** ▶ | 22

Adjusted Gross Income

If line 31 is under $28,495 (under $9,500 if a child didn't live with you), see the line 54 instructions.

23a Your IRA deduction (see instructions) . . . . . . | 23a
b Spouse's IRA deduction (see instructions) . . . . . | 23b
24 Moving expenses. Attach Form 3903 or 3903-F . . . | 24
25 One-half of self-employment tax. Attach Schedule SE . | 25
26 Self-employed health insurance deduction (see inst.) . | 26
27 Keogh & self-employed SEP plans. If SEP, check ▶ ☐ | 27
28 Penalty on early withdrawal of savings . . . . . | 28
29 Alimony paid. Recipient's SSN ▶ _____ | 29
30 Add lines 23a through 29 . . . . | 30
31 Subtract line 30 from line 22. This is your **adjusted gross income** . . . . . ▶ | 31

The above form is a draft version of the 1996 form. It is for information purposes only. Do not send in.

Form 1040 (1996)   Page **2**

Tax Compu- tation	32	Amount from line 31 (adjusted gross income)	32	
	33a	Check if: ☐ **You** were 65 or older, ☐ Blind; ☐ **Spouse** was 65 or older, ☐ Blind. Add the number of boxes checked above and enter the total here . . . . ▶ 33a		
	b	If you are married filing separately and your spouse itemizes deductions or you are a dual-status alien, see instructions and check here . . . . . . ▶ 33b ☐		
	34	Enter the larger of your: **Itemized deductions** from Schedule A, line 28, **OR** **Standard deduction** shown below for your filing status. **But** see the instructions if you checked any box on line 33a or b **or** someone can claim you as a dependent. • Single—$4,000 • Married filing jointly or Qualifying widow(er)—$6,700 • Head of household—$5,900 • Married filing separately—$3,350	34	
	35	Subtract line 34 from line 32	35	
If you want the IRS to figure your tax, see the line 37 instructions.	36	If line 32 is $88,475 or less, multiply $2,550 by the total number of exemptions claimed on line 6d. If line 32 is over $88,475, see the worksheet in the inst. for the amount to enter	36	
	37	**Taxable income.** Subtract line 36 from line 35. If line 36 is more than line 35, enter -0-	37	
	38	**Tax.** See instructions. Check if total includes any tax from a ☐ Form(s) 8814 b ☐ Form 4970 c ☐ Form 4972 . . . . ▶	38	

Credits	39	Credit for child and dependent care expenses. Attach Form 2441	39		
	40	Credit for the elderly or the disabled. Attach Schedule R .	40		
	41	Foreign tax credit. Attach Form 1116	41		
	42	Other. Check if from a ☐ Form 3800 b ☐ Form 8396 c ☐ Form 8801 d ☐ Form (specify)	42		
	43	Add lines 39 through 42		43	
	44	Subtract line 43 from line 38. If line 43 is more than line 38, enter -0- . . . . . ▶		44	

Other Taxes	45	Self-employment tax. Attach Schedule SE	45	
	46	Alternative minimum tax. Attach Form 6251	46	
	47	Social security and Medicare tax on tip income not reported to employer. Attach Form 4137	47	
	48	Tax on qualified retirement plans, including IRAs. If required, attach Form 5329 . .	48	
	49	Advance earned income credit payments from Form W-2	49	
	50	Household employment taxes. Attach Schedule H	50	
	51	Add lines 44 through 50. This is your **total tax** . . . . ▶	51	

Payments	52	Federal income tax withheld from Form(s) W-2 and 1099 .	52		
	53	1996 estimated tax payments and amount applied from 1995 return .	53		
Attach Forms W-2, W-2G, and 1099-R on the front.	54	**Earned income credit.** Attach Schedule EIC if you have a qualifying child. Nontaxable earned income: amount ▶ [ ] and type ▶	54		
	55	Amount paid with Form 4868 (extension request) . . .	55		
	56	Excess social security and RRTA tax withheld (see inst.) .	56		
	57	Other payments. Check if from a ☐ Form 2439 b ☐ Form 4136	57		
	58	Add lines 52 through 57. These are your **total payments** . . . . ▶		58	

Refund	59	If line 58 is more than line 51, subtract line 51 from line 58. This is the amount you **OVERPAID**	59	
Send it right to your bank! See inst. and fill in 60b, c, and d.	60a	Amount of line 59 you want **REFUNDED TO YOU** . . . . ▶	60a	
	b	Routing number [ ] c Type: ☐ Checking ☐ Savings		
	d	Account number [ ]		
	61	Amount of line 59 you want **APPLIED TO YOUR 1997 ESTIMATED TAX** ▶	61	

Amount You Owe	62a	If line 51 is more than line 58, subtract line 58 from line 51. This is the **AMOUNT YOU OWE.** For details on how to pay and use **Form 1040-V**, see instructions . . . . ▶	62a	
	b	Are you paying the amount on line 62a **in full with Form 1040-V**? ▶ ☐ Yes ☐ No		
	63	Estimated tax penalty. Also include on line 62a . . .	63	

Sign Here Keep a copy of this return for your records.	Under penalties of perjury, I declare that I have examined this return and accompanying schedules and statements, and to the best of my knowledge and belief, they are true, correct, and complete. Declaration of preparer (other than taxpayer) is based on all information of which preparer has any knowledge.

Your signature	Date	Your occupation
Spouse's signature. If a joint return, BOTH must sign.	Date	Spouse's occupation

Paid Preparer's Use Only	Preparer's signature ▶	Date	Check if self-employed ☐	Preparer's social security no.
	Firm's name (or yours if self-employed) and address		EIN	
			ZIP code	

✱ *Printed on recycled paper*

The above form is a draft version of the 1996 form. It is for information purposes only. Do not send in.

Form

1040A | U.S. Individual Income Tax Return | 1996

Department of the Treasury—Internal Revenue Service

IRS Use Only—Do not write or staple in this space.

Label (See page 15.) Use the IRS label. Otherwise, please print in **ALL CAPITAL LETTERS.**

OMB No. 1545-0085

L A B E L H E R E	Your first name	Init.	Last name		Your social security number
	If a joint return, spouse's first name	Init.	Last name		Spouse's social security number
	Home address (number and street). If you have a P.O. box, see page 15.			Apt. no.	
	City, town or post office. If you have a foreign address, see page 15.	State	ZIP code		

For Privacy Act and Paperwork Reduction Act Notice, see page 9.

Presidential Election Campaign Fund (See page 15.)
Do you want $3 to go to this fund? .... Yes No
If a joint return, does your spouse want $3 to go to this fund? .....

Note: *Checking "Yes" will not change your tax or reduce your refund.*

1 ☐ Single

2 ☐ Married filing joint return (even if only one had income)

3 ☐ Married filing separate return. Enter spouse's social security number above and full name here. ▶ _____

4 ☐ Head of household (with qualifying person). (See page 16.) If the qualifying person is a child but not your dependent, enter this child's name here. ▶ _____

5 ☐ Qualifying widow(er) with dependent child (year spouse died ▶ 19___). (See page 16.)

6a ☐ **Yourself.** If your parent (or someone else) can claim you as a dependent on his or her tax return, **do not** check box 6a.

b ☐ **Spouse**

c **Dependents.** If more than six dependents, see page 17.

(1) First name	Last name	(2) Dependent's social security number. If born in Dec. 1996, see page 18.	(3) Dependent's relationship to you	(4) No. of months lived in your home in 1996

No. of boxes checked on lines 6a and 6b ☐

No. of your children on line 6c who:
• lived with you ☐
• didn't live with you due to divorce or separation (see page 18) ☐

Dependents on 6c not entered above ☐

d Total number of exemptions claimed.

Add numbers entered in boxes above ☐

7 Wages, salaries, tips, etc. This should be shown in box 1 of your W-2 form(s). Attach Form(s) W-2. ... **7** $

8a **Taxable** interest income. If over $400, attach Schedule 1. ... **8a** $

b **Tax-exempt** interest. DO NOT include on line 8a. | **8b** $

9 Dividends. If over $400, attach Schedule 1. ... **9** $

10a Total IRA distributions. **10a** $ | 10b Taxable amount (see page 20). **10b** $

11a Total pensions and annuities. **11a** $ | 11b Taxable amount (see page 20). **11b** $

12 Unemployment compensation. **12** $

13a Social security benefits. **13a** $ | 13b Taxable amount (see page 22). **13b** $

14 Add lines 7 through 13b (far right column). This is your **total income.** ▶ **14** $

15a Your IRA deduction (see page 22). **15a** $

b Spouse's IRA deduction (see page 22). **15b** $

c Add lines 15a and 15b. These are your **total adjustments.** **15c** $

16 Subtract line 15c from line 14. This is your **adjusted gross income.**
If under $28,495 (under $9,500 if a child didn't live with you), see the instructions for line 29c on page 29. ▶ **16** $

Cat. No. 11327A

1996 Form 1040A page 1

The above form is a draft version of the 1996 form. It is for information purposes only. Do not send in.

1996 Form 1040A page 2

17	Enter the amount from line 16.	17	$

18a Check if: ☐ **You** were 65 or older ☐ Blind ☐ **Spouse** was 65 or older ☐ Blind **Enter number of boxes checked ▶ 18a** ☐

b If you are married filing separately and your spouse itemizes deductions, see page 25 and check here . . . . **▶ 18b** ☐

19	Enter the **standard deduction** for your filing status. **But see page 25** if you checked any box on line 18a or b **OR** someone can claim you as a dependent. • Single—$4,000 • Married filing jointly or Qualifying widow(er)—$6,700 • Head of household—$5,900 • Married filing separately—$3,350	19	$
20	Subtract line 19 from line 17. If line 19 is more than line 17, enter -0-.	20	$
21	Multiply $2,550 by the total number of exemptions claimed on line 6d.	21	$
22	Subtract line 21 from line 20. If line 21 is more than line 20, enter -0-. This is your **taxable income.** If you want the IRS to figure your tax, see page 26. ▶	22	$
23	Find the tax on the amount on line 22 (see page 26).	23	$

24a Credit for child and dependent care expenses. Attach Schedule 2. 24a $

b Credit for the elderly or the disabled. Attach Schedule 3. 24b $

c	Add lines 24a and 24b. These are your **total credits.**	24c	$
25	Subtract line 24c from line 23. If line 24c is more than line 23, enter -0-.	25	$
26	Advance earned income credit payments from Form W-2.	26	$
27	Household employment taxes. Attach Schedule H.	27	$
28	Add lines 25, 26, and 27. This is your **total tax.** ▶	28	$

29a Total Federal income tax withheld from Forms W-2 and 1099. 29a $

b 1996 estimated tax payments and amount applied from 1995 return. 29b $

c **Earned income credit.** Attach Schedule EIC if you have a qualifying child. 29c $

Nontaxable earned income: amount ▶ $ _____ and type ▶

d	Add lines 29a, 29b, and 29c (don't include nontaxable earned income). These are your **total payments.** ▶	29d	$
30	If line 29d is more than line 28, subtract line 28 from line 29d. This is the amount you **overpaid.**	30	$

31a Amount of line 30 you want **refunded to you.** If you want it sent right to your bank, see page 35 and fill in 31b, c, and d. 31a $

b Routing number _____ **c** Type: ☐ Checking ☐ Savings

d Account number _____

32	Amount of line 30 you want **applied to your 1997 estimated tax.**	32	$
33	If line 28 is more than line 29d, subtract line 29d from line 28. This is the **amount you owe.** For details on how to pay, including what to write on your payment, see page 35.	33	$
34	Estimated tax penalty (see page 35).	34	$

Sign here

Keep a copy of this return for your records.

Under penalties of perjury, I declare that I have examined this return and accompanying schedules and statements, and to the best of my knowledge and belief, they are true, correct, and accurately list all amounts and sources of income I received during the tax year. Declaration of preparer (other than the taxpayer) is based on all information of which the preparer has any knowledge.

Your signature	Date	Your occupation
Spouse's signature. If joint return, BOTH must sign.	Date	Spouse's occupation

Paid preparer's use only

Preparer's signature	Date	Check if self-employed ☐	Preparer's SSN
Firm's name (or yours if self-employed) and address		EIN	
		ZIP code	

⊛ Printed on recycled paper

1996 Form 1040A page 2

The above form is a draft version of the 1996 form. It is for information purposes only. Do not send in.

Form **1040EZ**

Department of the Treasury—Internal Revenue Service

Income Tax Return for Single and Joint Filers With No Dependents **1996**

OMB No. 1545-0675

Use the IRS label here

Your first name and initial | Last name

If a joint return, spouse's first name and initial | Last name

Home address (number and street). If you have a P.O. box, see page 7. | Apt. no.

City, town or post office, state, and ZIP code. If you have a foreign address, see page 7.

Your social security number

Spouse's social security number

Presidential Election Campaign
(See page 7.)

Note: *Checking "Yes" will not change your tax or reduce your refund.*

Do you want $3 to go to this fund? ▶ Yes ☐ No ☐

If a joint return, does your spouse want $3 to go to this fund? ▶ Yes ☐ No ☐

Dollars | Cents

Income

Attach Copy B of Form(s) W-2 here. Enclose, but do not attach, any payment with your return.

1 Total wages, salaries, and tips. This should be shown in box 1 of your W-2 form(s). Attach your W-2 form(s). **1**

2 Taxable interest income of $400 or less. If the total is over $400, you cannot use Form 1040EZ. **2**

3 Unemployment compensation (see page 9). **3**

4 Add lines 1, 2, and 3. This is your **adjusted gross income.** If under $9,500, see page 9 to find out if you can claim the earned income credit on line 8. **4**

Note: *You must check Yes or No.*

5 Can your parents (or someone else) claim you on their return?

Yes. Enter amount from worksheet on back. ☐

No. If **single**, enter 6,550.00. If **married**, enter 11,800.00. See back for explanation. **5**

6 Subtract line 5 from line 4. If line 5 is larger than line 4, enter 0. This is your **taxable income.** ▶ **6**

Payments and tax

7 Enter your Federal income tax withheld from box 2 of your W-2 form(s). **7**

8 **Earned income credit** (see page 9). Enter type and amount of nontaxable earned income below.

Type | $ **8**

9 Add lines 7 and 8 (don't include nontaxable earned income). These are your **total payments.** **9**

10 **Tax.** Use the amount on **line 6** to find your tax in the tax table on pages 20–24 of the booklet. Then, enter the tax from the table on this line. **10**

Refund

Send it right to your bank! See page xx and fill in 11b, 11c, and 11d.

11a If line 9 is larger than line 10, subtract line 10 from line 9. This is your **refund.** **11a**

b Routing number

c Type of account
Checking ☐ Savings ☐

d Account number

Amount you owe

12 If line 10 is larger than line 9, subtract line 9 from line 10. This is the **amount you owe.** See page 14 for details on how to pay and what to write on your payment. **12**

I have read this return. Under penalties of perjury, I declare that to the best of my knowledge and belief, the return is true, correct, and accurately lists all amounts and sources of income I received during the tax year.

Sign here

Keep copy for your records.

Your signature | Spouse's signature if joint return

Date | Your occupation | Date | Spouse's occupation

For Official Use Only

| 1 | 2 | 3 | 4 | 5 |
| 6 | 7 | 8 | 9 | 10 |

For Privacy Act and Paperwork Reduction Act Notice, see page 5.

Cat. No. 11329W

Form 1040EZ (1996)

The above form is a draft version of the 1996 form. It is for information purposes only. Do not send in.

Glossary

GLOSSARY

ACADEMIC YEAR: A measure of academic work to be performed by the student, subject to definition by the school.

ACCESS GROUP: An educational and financing organization that distributes and processes the Needs Access computer diskette.

AGI: Adjusted gross income. In 1995 and 1996, this is Line 31 on the IRS 1040; line 16 on the IRS 1040A; line 4 on the IRS 1040EZ.

AMERICAN COLLEGE TESTING PROGRAM (ACT): A federally approved need analysis service that processes the Free Application for Federal Student Aid (FAFSA). Also the administrator of a group of standardized tests in English, mathematics, reading, and science reasoning.

BASE INCOME YEAR (also known as the BASE YEAR): The calendar year preceding the academic year for which aid is being sought.

BUSINESS/FARM SUPPLEMENT: A supplemental aid application required by a few colleges for aid applicants whose parents own businesses or farms or who are self-employed. The individual school's aid policy will determine if this form must be completed.

CAMPUS-BASED PROGRAMS: Three federal student aid programs that are administered directly by the school's financial aid office (the Perkins loan, the Supplemental Educational Opportunity Grant, and the Federal Work-Study program).

COLLEGE SCHOLARSHIP SERVICE (CSS): The financial aid division of the College Board. CSS writes and processes the Financial Aid PROFILE form.

COOPERATIVE EDUCATION: A college program offered at many schools that combines periods of academic study with periods of paid employment related to the student's field of study. In most cases, participation will extend the time required to obtain a bachelor's degree to five years.

COST OF ATTENDANCE: A figure, estimated by the school, that includes the cost of tuition, fees, room, board, books, and supplies as well as an allowance for transportation and personal expenses. This figure is compared to the Expected Family Contribution to determine a student's aid eligibility. Also known as the *student budget*.

DEFAULT: Failure to repay a loan according to the terms of the promissory note.

DEPENDENT STUDENT: A classification for aid purposes for a student who is considered to be dependent upon his or her parent(s) for financial support.

DIVORCED/SEPARATED PARENT'S STATEMENT: A supplemental aid application required by a few colleges for aid applicants whose parents are separated or divorced. The individual school's aid policy will determine if this form must be completed. If required, this form will be completed by the noncustodial parent. This is generally the parent with whom the child spent the least amount of time in the preceding 12 months prior to completion of the form.

EDUCATIONAL TESTING SERVICE: The organization that writes the Scholastic Assessment Test (SAT).

EMPLOYMENT ALLOWANCE: A deduction against income in the federal and institutional methodologies for two-parent families in which both parents work or a single-parent family in which that parent works.

EXPECTED FAMILY CONTRIBUTION (EFC): The amount of money the family is expected to contribute for the year toward the student's cost of attendance. This figure is compared to the cost of attendance to determine a student's aid eligibility.

FAF: See Financial Aid Form.

FAFSA: See Free Application for Federal Student Aid.

FAMILY CONTRIBUTION: Another name used to refer to the Expected Family Contribution.

FAO: See Financial Aid Officer.

FEDERAL METHODOLOGY: The generally accepted method used to calculate the family's expected contribution to college costs for federal aid purposes. Depending on the individual college's policy, the federal methodology may also be used to determine eligibility for money under the school's control.

FEDERAL WORK-STUDY (FWS): A federally funded aid program that provides jobs for students. Eligibility is based on need.

FINANCIAL AID: A general term used to refer to a variety of programs funded by the federal and state governments as well as the individual schools to assist students with their educational costs. While the names may vary, financial aid comes in three basic forms: (1) gift aid (grants and scholarships) which do not have to be paid back (2) student loans, and (3) work-study jobs.

FINANCIAL AID FORM (FAF): A need analysis document that was written and processed by the College Scholarship Service (CSS) in Princeton, New Jersey. The 1995–96 version of the FAF was the last one written.

FINANCIAL AID PROFILE FORM: See PROFILE form.

FINANCIAL AID OFFICER: An administrator at each school who determines whether a student is eligible for aid and if so, the types of aid to be awarded.

FREE APPLICATION FOR FEDERAL STUDENT AID (FAFSA): The need analysis document written by the U.S. Department of Education. This form is required for virtually all students seeking financial aid including the unsubsidized Stafford loan.

401(k), 403(b): The names of two of the more popular deferred compensation plans in which employees elect to defer part of their earnings until a later date.

GIFT AID: Financial aid, usually a grant or scholarship, that does not have to be paid back and that does not involve employment.

GRANTS: Gift aid that is generally based on need. The programs can be funded by the federal and state governments as well as the individual schools.

GUARANTEED STUDENT LOANS (GSL): See Stafford Student Loan program.

HALF-TIME STATUS: Refers to students taking at least 6 credits per semester, or the equivalent.

INDEPENDENT STUDENT: A student who, for financial aid purposes, is not considered dependent on his or her parent(s) for support. Also known as a self-supporting student.

INCOME PROTECTION ALLOWANCE: A deduction against income in both the federal and the institutional methodologies.

INET: A federally approved need analysis service that processes the Free Application for Federal Student Aid (FAFSA).

INSTITUTIONAL FORMS: Supplemental forms required by the individual schools to determine aid eligibility.

INSTITUTIONAL METHODOLOGY: An alternative method used to calculate the family's expected contribution to college costs. This methodology is generally used by private and a few state schools to determine eligibility for aid funds under the school's direct control. Colleges that use the institutional methodology usually require completion of the PROFILE form.

LONG FORM: This generally refers to the IRS 1040 form.

NATIONAL DIRECT STUDENT LOANS (NDSL): See Perkins Loan program.

NEED: The amount of aid a student is eligible to receive. This figure is calculated by subtracting the Expected Family Contribution from the cost of attendance.

NEED ACCESS APPLICATION DISKETTE: A need analysis computer program distributed and processed by the Access Group. It is required by many graduate and professional schools to determine eligibility for institutional aid.

NEED ANALYSIS: The process of analyzing the information on the aid form to calculate the amount of money the student and parent(s) can be expected to contribute toward educational costs.

NEED ANALYSIS FORMS: Aid applications used to calculate the expected family contribution. The most common need analysis forms are: the Free Application for Federal Student Aid (FAFSA) and the Financial Aid PROFILE form. Consult the individual school's financial aid filing requirements to determine which form(s) are required for that particular school.

PARENTS' CONTRIBUTION: The amount of money the parent(s) are expected to contribute for the year toward the student's cost of attendance.

PARENT LOANS FOR UNDERGRADUATE STUDENTS (PLUS): A federally subsidized educational loan program in which parents can borrow up to the total cost

of attendance minus any financial aid received for each child in an undergraduate program. Eligibility is not based on need. The interest rate is variable, currently with a 9% cap.

PELL GRANT: The largest federally funded need-based aid program for first-time undergraduate students (i.e., the student has not as yet earned a bachelor's or first professional degree). Funds from this program are generally awarded to lower- and lower-middle-income families. Years ago, this program was called the Basic Educational Opportunity Grant (BEOG).

PERKINS LOAN PROGRAM: Formerly known as National Direct Student Loans (NDSL), this federally funded need-based program provides low interest loans to undergraduate and graduate students and is administered by the school's financial aid office. In most cases, repayment does not begin until nine months after the student graduates or leaves school and there are no interest charges while the student is in school. The interest rate is currently 5%.

PHEAA: The Pennsylvania Higher Education Assistance Agency.

PLUS LOANS: See Parent Loans for Undergraduate Students.

PREFERENTIAL PACKAGING: The situation in which the more desired aid applicants get better aid packages, which are larger in total dollar amount and/or contain a higher percentage of grants versus loans.

PROFILE FORM: A need analysis document written and processed by the College Scholarship Service (CSS) in Princeton, New Jersey. The 1996–97 version was the first one written.

PROMISSORY NOTE: The legal document which the borrower signs to obtain the loan proceeds and which specifies the terms of the loan, the interest rate, and the repayment provisions.

ROTC: The Reserve Officer Training Corps programs that are coordinated at many college campuses by the U.S. Army, Navy, and Air Force.

SAT: The Scholastic Assessment Test, administered by the College Board, which has a verbal section and a mathematical reasoning section.

SAR: See Student Aid Report.

SCHOLARSHIPS: Gift aid that is usually based on merit or a combination of need and merit.

SELF-HELP: The portion of the aid package relating to student loans and/or work-study.

SEOG: See Supplemental Educational Opportunity Grant.

SHORT FORM: This generally refers to the IRS 1040A or the 1040EZ forms.

SIMPLIFIED NEEDS TEST: An alternative method used to calculate the family's expected contribution to college costs for federal aid purposes, in which all assets are

excluded from the federal aid formula. The Simplified Needs Test is of use to families who have adjusted gross incomes below $50,000 and who do not need to file the 1040 long form.

SLS: See Supplemental Loans for Students.

STAFFORD STUDENT LOAN (SSL) PROGRAM: Formerly known as the Guaranteed Student Loan (GSL) program, this federally funded program provides low-interest loans to undergraduate and graduate students and is administered by a bank or other lending institution, which can sometimes be the college itself. In most cases, repayment does not begin until six months after the student graduates or leaves school and there are no interest charges while the student is in school. For new borrowers, the interest rate is variable, currently with a 8.25% cap. There are two types of Stafford loans: subsidized and unsubsidized. The **subsidized Stafford loan** is need-based and the government pays the interest while the student is in school. The **unsubsidized Stafford loan** is non-need-based and can be taken out by virtually all students. In many cases, students can elect to let the interest accumulate until after they graduate.

STANDARDIZED FORMS: The generic term used in this book when referring to any of the need analysis forms that must be sent to a processing service. The two most commonly used standardized forms are the U.S. Department of Education's Free Application for Federal Student Aid (FAFSA) and the College Scholarship Service's (CSS) Financial Aid PROFILE form.

STUDENT AID REPORT (SAR): The multipage report that is issued to students who have sent a completed FAFSA to one of the processing services.

STUDENT BUDGET: See Cost of Attendance.

STUDENT'S CONTRIBUTION: The amount of money the student is expected to contribute for the year toward his or her cost of attendance.

SUBSIDIZED STAFFORD LOAN: See Stafford Student Loan (SSL) program.

SUPPLEMENTAL EDUCATIONAL OPPORTUNITY GRANT: A federally funded need-based aid program that is awarded by the school's financial aid office.

SUPPLEMENTAL LOANS FOR STUDENTS (SLS): A federally subsidized educational loan program for independent undergraduate and graduate students. Eligibility is not based on need. This loan program has been phased into the Stafford Loan Program. Previous borrowing limits under this program are now represented by the mandatory unsubsidized portion of the Stafford Loan.

UNIFORM AID SUPPLEMENT: A standardized set of supplemental aid questions developed and utilized by a number of highly selective private colleges.

UNSUBSIDIZED STAFFORD LOAN: See Stafford Student Loan (SSL) program.

VERIFICATION: A process in which the financial aid office requires additional documentation to verify the accuracy of the information reported on the aid applications.

WORK-STUDY: See Federal Work-Study.

ABOUT THE AUTHORS

KALMAN A. CHANY is the founder and president of Campus Consultants Inc., a New York City–based firm that guides parents and students through the financial aid process. In addition to counseling thousands of families on the aid process, he has conducted workshops for corporations, schools, and other organizations. He is a frequent guest on television and radio shows across the country.

GEOFF MARTZ is a writer living in New York City.

THE PRINCETON REVIEW WORLDWIDE

Each year, thousands of students from countries throughout the world prepare for the TOEFL and for U.S. college and graduate school admissions exams. Whether you plan to prepare for your exams in your home country or the United States, The Princeton Review is committed to your success.

INTERNATIONAL LOCATIONS: If you are using our books outside of the United States and have questions or comments, or want to know if our courses are being offered in your area, be sure to contact The Princeton Review office nearest you:

- ◆ CANADA (Montreal)   514-499-0870
- ◆ CANADA (Toronto)   800-495-7737
- ◆ HONG KONG   852-2517-3016
- ◆ JAPAN (Tokyo)   8133-463-1343
- ◆ KOREA (Seoul)   822-508-0081
- ◆ MEXICO (Mexico City)   525-564-9468
- ◆ PAKISTAN (Lahore)   92-42-571-2315
- ◆ SAUDI ARABIA   413-584-6849 (a U.S. based number)
- ◆ SPAIN (Madrid)   341-323-4212
- ◆ TAIWAN (Taipei)   886-27511293

U.S. STUDY ABROAD: *Review USA* offers international students many advantages and opportunities. In addition to helping you gain acceptance to the U.S. college or university of your choice, *Review USA* will help you acquire the knowledge and orientation you need to succeed once you get there.

Review USA is unique. It includes supplements to your test-preparation courses and a special series of *AmeriCulture* workshops to prepare you for the academic rigors and student life in the United States. Our workshops are designed to familiarize you with the different U.S. expressions, real-life vocabulary, and cultural challenges you will encounter as a study-abroad student. While studying with us, you'll make new friends and have the opportunity to personally visit college and university campuses to determine which school is right for you.

Whether you are planning to take the TOEFL, SAT, GRE, GMAT, LSAT, MCAT, or USMLE exam, The Princeton Review's test preparation courses, expert instructors, and dedicated International Student Advisors can help you achieve your goals.

For additional information about *Review USA*, admissions requirements, class schedules, F-1 visas, I-20 documentation, and course locations, write to:

The Princeton Review • Review USA
2315 Broadway, New York, NY 10024
Fax: 212/874-0775